RADICAL SPIRITUAL
MOTHERHOOD

RADICAL SPIRITUAL
MOTHERHOOD

Autobiography and Empowerment
in Nineteenth-Century African American Women

ROSETTA R. HAYNES

Luann and Kurt,
    Thanks so much for your support.
I really hope you enjoy my book!

                  Warm Regards,
                  Rosetta Haynes

1/9/11

Louisiana State University Press)|(*Baton Rouge*

Published by Louisiana State University Press
Copyright © 2011 by Louisiana State University Press
All rights reserved
Manufactured in the United States of America
First printing

Designer: Michelle A. Neustrom
Typeface: Berthold Baskerville Book
Printer: McNaughton & Gunn, Inc.
Binder: John H. Dekker & Sons

Library of Congress Cataloging-in-Publication Data
Haynes, Rosetta Renae.
Radical spiritual motherhood : autobiography and empowerment in
nineteenth-century African American women / Rosetta R. Haynes.
    p. cm.
Includes bibliographical references and index.
ISBN 978-0-8071-3694-2 (cloth : alk. paper)
1. African American women evangelists—Biography. 2. African American women
evangelists—Biography—History and criticism. 3. African American women—
Biography—History and criticism. 4. African American women—Intellectual life—
19th century. 5. African American women—Race identity. 6. Identity (Psychology)
in literature. 7. Autobiography—Social aspects. I. Title.
BV3780.H39 2010
269'.2092396073—dc22

2010021240

For Roosevelt and LaPearl Haynes, with love

CONTENTS

ACKNOWLEDGMENTS

I first want to give thanks and praise to God, whose love, strength, and guidance have inspired and sustained me throughout the long process of completing this project. I also want to thank my parents, Roosevelt and La-Pearl Haynes, for their constant love and support. And many thanks go to my brother, Terrence Haynes, for his steady support. Thanks also to my aunt Lester Hill for her kind words of assurance. Also meaningful was the encouragement I received over the years from longtime friend and "grandmother" Helen McKee. And I certainly appreciate the encouragement and spiritual support of my church family at Unity Presbyterian Church in Terre Haute, Indiana, pastored by Rev. Linda Peters.

Since this book grew out of my doctoral dissertation, I would also like to acknowledge those who generously and patiently served on my graduate committee: Shirley Samuels (committee chair), Hortense Spillers, Harryette Mullen, Mary Jacobus, and Lois Brown. Thanks also to my wonderful dissertation writing group for helping to keep me motivated through their friendship and their useful critiques of my writing: Margo Perkins, Elizabeth Davey, Shuchi Kapila, and Henri Boyi.

As this project evolved from dissertation to book manuscript, I received thoughtful feedback on my writing from several colleagues: Keith Byerman, Nancy McEntire, Laurel Cummins, Alden Cavanaugh, and Jennifer Drake. I am especially grateful for the assistance of Jean Humez, whose thorough reader's reports were invaluable for enhancing the quality of this book. And I also want to thank Joycelyn Moody for her reader's report, which provided insightful feedback on earlier portions of the book.

Earlier versions of parts of this book appeared in *Gender, Genre, and Identity in Women's Travel Writing*, edited by Kristi Siegel and published in New York by Peter Lang in 2004 (181–91); *The Literary Griot* 11.1 (1999): 18–32; and *Women of Color: Defining the Issues, Hearing the Voices*, edited by Diane Long Hoeveler and Janet K. Boles and published in Westport, Connecticut, by Greenwood in 2001 (133–45).

RADICAL SPIRITUAL
MOTHERHOOD

INTRODUCTION

It never occurred to me that they were thinking other thoughts, feeling other feelings, putting their lives together in ways I never dreamed of.
—Toni Morrison, *Jazz*

In her sixth novel, *Jazz,* Toni Morrison foregrounds the creative act of improvisation, not only as a practice that lies at the heart of the African American musical form jazz, which informs the structure and rhythms of her text, but also as a fundamentally human practice in which each person is called upon to engage as he or she goes about fashioning a life from a variety of experiences. In the quotation above, the narrator reveals her failure to understand the subtlety and complexity of the process by which people go about "putting their lives together," or engaging in the process of self-improvisation. The character Joe Trace speaks of becoming a new person seven times throughout his life; he is repeatedly reborn as significant events fundamentally alter his consciousness and call upon him to change his ways of thinking and being in the world. Joe Trace, like each of us, is ultimately the author of his own life. And it is this realization that can empower us to creatively shape, to fashion, to improvise a self.

Understanding the ways in which five nineteenth-century African American women itinerant preachers responded to and textually represented the call to self-improvisation is the main focus of this book. Specifically, it is a study of the ways in which Jarena Lee, Zilpha Elaw, Julia Foote, Amanda Smith, and Rebecca Jackson employed the trope of motherhood to represent the process by which they drew upon religion and the material conditions of their lives to fashion empowered subjectivities that enabled them to pursue their missions as divinely appointed religious leaders.[1] Using feminist literary theory, historical methods, and liberation theology, I have developed a conceptual framework for interpreting the spiritual autobiographies of these nineteenth-century Methodist and Shaker leaders. This framework, which I call radical spiritual motherhood, offers a new way of understanding their writings, one that foregrounds the central paradox distinguishing each of their texts: these authors at once

1

draw upon familiar models of womanhood and motherhood to construct new identities as public figures and repudiate these same forms in their personal lives. Participating in a kind of serial domesticity, they travel from house to house and church to church in their roles as itinerant preachers. In so doing, they disrupt and transform the dominant domestic ideology that sought to confine them to their own homes and to restrictive roles.

The radical spiritual mothers' pursuits of spiritual and physical freedom are largely defined by an awareness of their connectedness to the plight of enslaved black women. Not only do the spiritual autobiographies and the narratives of enslaved women reveal similar concerns, such as desires for freedom and literacy, but the degraded status of enslaved women bore directly upon the ways in which radical spiritual mothers were perceived and treated. For this reason, I also examine the spiritual autobiographies within the context of the emancipatory narratives of Harriet Jacobs, Mary Prince, and Sojourner Truth in order to explore the links between the treatment of sexuality and the body in the texts of enslaved and free black women.[2] In doing so, I place radical spiritual motherhood alongside Joanne Braxton's archetype of "outraged motherhood," the counterpart she proposes to the paradigm of the heroic male slave.[3] In efforts to establish a more expansive and balanced understanding of the emancipatory narrative genre, she offers this archetype, which helps to reveal the ways in which enslaved women shaped their experiences into a different kind of literary language. Sexual abuse is a primary factor in determining the behavior of the outraged mother; the ways that she negotiates the sexual aggression of white masters is central to her creation of an empowered subjectivity that challenges the object status that her owners attempt to force upon her. This status has, I believe, a profound impact upon the psyche and behavior of radical spiritual mothers, the narratives of whom suggest a conscious awareness and refiguration of the physical degradation of enslaved women, as well as parallels of enslaved women's acts of resistance to this degradation.

The interconnectedness of the radical spiritual mothers and outraged mothers is also revealed in the hybridity of their texts as they sometimes reflect characteristics of both the emancipatory narrative and spiritual autobiography genres. For example, Jean Humez observes the presence of a skeletal spiritual autobiography in the emancipatory narratives of Harriet Tubman and Sojourner Truth; in particular, these narratives link physical emancipation with spiritual liberation.[4]

In order to show the continued relevance of the lives and writing of the radical spiritual mothers, I also include a chapter on Pauli Murray, the first African American woman and the second African American to be ordained an Episcopal priest. By tracing Murray's personal evolution into a spiritual leader, I argue that she in fact is a modern-day radical spiritual mother who embodies and celebrates the spiritual and cultural tradition of her nineteenth-century foremothers.

My book complements other important studies of nineteenth-century African American women's spiritual autobiographies, offering a new perspective on these texts. For example, in *Sentimental Confessions: Spiritual Narratives of Nineteenth-Century African American Women,* Joycelyn Moody examines how six women use "Christian evangelicalism, literary sentimentalism, and African American nationalism for the articulation of their experiences as black holy women."[5] Moody argues that these narratives should be valued not only as literary texts, but also as *holy* texts that express a unique theology: "For their life stories not only investigate black women's interior spiritual lives and the centrality of Christianity to their individual identities, but each holy woman also theorizes on who and how God is."[6] Recognizing the important work done by the African American feminist historian Darlene Clark Hine in recovering the writing and history of early African American women, Moody points out that Hine encourages "the development of an array of analytical frameworks that allow us to understand why black women of all classes behave in certain ways and how they acquired agency."[7] My study provides another such analytical framework, that of radical spiritual motherhood.

In *Preacher Woman Sings the Blues: The Autobiographies of Nineteenth-Century African American Evangelists,* Richard J. Douglass-Chin draws upon the trope of the blues "bad" woman to investigate the formal and rhetorical evolution of black women's spiritual autobiographies during the nineteenth century, linking this genre with the petition of an eighteenth-century predecessor, Belinda, and with the writing of contemporary African American women authors such as Zora Neale Hurston, Alice Walker, Toni Cade Bambara, and Toni Morrison.[8] Moreover, Douglass-Chin "examine[s] the ways in which the evangelists employ discourses produced by socioeconomic determinants such as race, gender, and class to create a complex black female narrative economy with its own unique figurations and forms."[9]

My approach acknowledges the historical process by which Africans within the American context have set about adapting, improvising, and creating spaces for self-expression. Yet it also acknowledges the peculiar circumstances of black women within this process, who have been faced with the challenge of nego-tiating identities in a nexus of racial and sexual oppression. From a literary standpoint, these narratives provide valuable insights into the ways that one group of nineteenth-century free black women creates authentic selves in and through the genre of autobiography. By shaping remembered experience into a language of liberation, these authors not only assert the validity of their in-dividual acts of self-empowerment but also gesture toward a broader cultural transformation that becomes possible as readers seriously engage the social and political implications of these acts.

Radical spiritual motherhood derives from the authors' experiences of sanctification, which, within the Wesleyan tradition of Methodism, is a second blessing following conversion, a kind of spiritual perfection experienced by a believer when she is wholly attuned to and governed by God's will.[10] The transformed consciousness resulting from sanctification and the divine calling that each woman receives to travel widely to preach the gospel authorizes her to step out of traditional roles to minister to the spiritual and material needs of those she serves. Drawing on biological motherhood for patterns of maternal nurturance, yet rejecting the notion that they should stay at home to care for their children, these women felt justified in leaving their families to fulfill their ministerial obligations. Contrary to social mandates, they became leaders and intellectuals who actively participated in the public sphere. Moreover, these women asserted their physical and sexual autonomy by remaining celibate after the deaths of their husbands, and in so doing implicitly critiqued racist assump-tions about black female sexuality by insisting upon their unavailability for exploitation by white men (and black men).[11] Radical spiritual motherhood is a self-styled identity that draws upon and validates their unique experiences as black women called to do God's work. But perhaps the most radical aspect of their identities was the bold approach they took to critiquing the sexism exhib-ited by male church authorities who opposed women's leadership roles within the church.

Because these writers were excluded from positions of power and authority within their families, churches, and the larger society, they sought alternative communities in which to exercise leadership. Their engagement in the activ-ity of itinerancy is central to their pursuits of communities that valued their authority as spiritual leaders and that shared their visions of a more just world characterized by equality, inclusivity, and spiritual integrity. Not only was phys-ical circulation central to the process of community building, but it also played an integral role in the authors' identity development as radical spiritual mothers. Drawing on Carole Boyce Davies's conception of "migratory subjectivity," I discuss the process by which identity is shaped within the many contexts in which they find themselves during their travels.[12]

The narratives of the radical spiritual mothers may be placed within the tradition of American spiritual autobiography—the roots of which may be traced to the writings of St. Augustine—that includes works written by seventeenth- and eighteenth-century Puritans, Quakers, and Wesleyan Methodists. Each group encouraged its members to keep journals and diaries in which individuals closely examined their lives and recorded their personal journeys of spiritual development; in so doing, they came to a new understanding of their place and fate within God's plan. These narratives were not meant only for personal enlightenment but were also produced for the moral instruction of others in their religious communities.[13]

Angelo Constanzo further elaborates on the characteristics of spiritual autobiography: "Spiritual autobiography is a study in the ascending levels of awareness that the narrator has experienced and continues to experience in the mind's expansion of consciousness. In spiritual autobiography, the awareness of self is coupled with the writer's awareness of others to form a larger awareness that is gradually and constantly varying, growing, and changing."[14] This dynamic process of expanding consciousness is conventionally represented as a series of stages of grace that include the narrator's initial conviction of sin, his or her descent into a phase of depression stemming from this conviction, the elation of conversion and the assurance of achieving this experience, and periodic episodes of spiritual deadness.[15] The narrator thus engages in a spiritual journey through the trials of life, growing in strength and wisdom as he or she grapples with these trials, gradually becoming worthy of his or her ultimate destination of everlasting life with God.[16]

Spiritual autobiographers characteristically describe the central role that Providence has played in their lives in bestowing divine favor and mercy. In examining their lives, these writers look for the ways that God's intervening and managing presence has been evident in both positive and negative experiences. Even tragedies are analyzed in the light of divine intervention in order to recognize the benefits that resulted from them. In this way, the narrator is able to discern the patterns by which God has orchestrated the circumstances of their lives.[17] A related thematic concern in this genre is the frequent tension that occurs within the individual as he or she struggles to subordinate his or her will to that of God, who demands this submission in order to bless the individual. The writer must learn that he or she will experience divine love and peace more acutely as he or she subjugates self to God.[18]

The seventeenth-century English preacher and writer John Bunyan was influential in establishing a pattern of biblical hermeneutic within spiritual autobiography that was appropriated by subsequent writers of this genre. In his *Grace Abounding* and *Pilgrim's Progress,* Bunyan drew upon biblical typology, or prominent characters and events in the Bible such as Moses, Christ, and the Exodus of the Israelites from Egypt, to interpret himself and his experiences.[19] Following in this tradition, black spiritual autobiographers, particularly ex-slaves, took satisfaction in envisioning themselves in the dramatic roles of figures like Job, David, Paul, and Moses as they imagined the world of possibilities that freedom opened up for them. Moreover, biblical typology and its hermeneutic value helped black writers to make sense of themselves and their lives within the context of a world that was often strange and hostile. Treatment that seemed incomprehensible could be scrutinized in relation to biblical analogues to reveal its true meaning.[20]

In addition to biblical typology, the incorporation of dreams and visions was a common facet of the spiritual journals of Quakers, who regarded such mediums as potential sources of divine revelation. Dreams, which came involuntarily, were often puzzling to the author, but they usually represented his or her preoccupations in allegorical form. Such a manner of representation enabled the author to transform a personal concern into an externally derived affirmation of truth.[21]

In her study of nineteenth-century American conversion narratives, Virginia Brereton has noticed some differences in the experiences revealed in men's and women's narratives. Women's narratives generally "reveal more struggle, more painful self-examination, more intensity, more agonizing about 'sins' that a later age would consider harmless." By contrast, "[m]en's conversions appear to have been more matter-of-fact; some even seem pro forma."[22] Brereton reasons that this may be because some men may have converted partly to appease an insistent wife or other female family member. Men also frequently converted in an effort to reform their behavior, eliminating such habits as womanizing, gambling, drinking, or swearing. In resisting conversion, women often struggled to subdue "a rebellious heart, an unwillingness to surrender"; men, however, were more likely to show "resistance to the whole idea of religion, to the social and cultural pressure to convert."[23] It was also hard for men to admit to being sinful when they felt they had lived virtuous lives. In terms of actually undergoing conversion, women normally expressed an initial willingness to be converted, but they frequently had trouble following through; men, on the other hand, often opposed the idea at first but usually achieved it more easily than women once they began the process.[24]

In participating in the genre of American spiritual autobiography, the radical spiritual mothers, like other African Americans writing spiritual autobiographies, asserted their rights to be regarded as subjects worthy of divine selection for salvation and, in so doing, fundamentally affirmed their humanity.[25] Nellie McKay explains that black women's spiritual autobiographies are particularly significant for the ways that they extended the range of the genre beyond that established by black men:

> [A]s male slave and spiritual narrators sought autonomy in a world dominated by racist white male views, black women writers demonstrated that sexism, inside and outside of the black community, was an equal threat to their quest for a positive identity. Black women use the personal narrative to document their differences in self-perception as well as their concerns for themselves and others, their sense of themselves as part of a distinct women's and racial community, and the complexities of the combined forces of race and gender for the only group beleaguered by both.[26]

Black women thus placed their own individual stamp upon the genre of spiritual autobiography, using it "to express female identity through the religious faith that gave them direct access to God in the Self—the highest authority; this knowledge imbued them with pride, self-respect, and control over their intellectual lives."[27]

The black women preachers, in drawing upon religion to achieve greater personal freedom and to advocate for societal transformation, engaged in a praxis that today might be labeled a theology of liberation. As Christian Smith explains: "[L]iberation theology essentially is an attempt to reconceptualize the Christian faith from the perspective of the poor and oppressed. At heart, it contends that the Christian gospel, the 'good news,' is that God is working—and that God's people should therefore be working—in history to combat and eradicate all forms of oppression and domination, whether social, cultural, political, economic, or spiritual."[28] Since the 1960s, numerous liberation theologies have arisen throughout the world as Christian theologians have responded to movements of oppressed people. In Latin America, Europe, Asia, Africa, and the United States, movements have emerged that link Christian theology with social action. Each theology is contextual, deriving from the concrete experiences of specific groups. Within the American context, for example, black theology is concerned with African Americans' experiences with white racism, and feminist theology focuses on women's struggles against sexist oppression. All of these theologies regard Jesus Christ as a liberator who offers humans spiritual, social, and political salvation. As savior, Christ frees humans from sin, which is believed to be the source of all forms of injustice.[29]

Letty Russell identifies some important themes that run through liberation theologies, two of which are particularly relevant to the experiences of the black women preachers. One theme is that of "humanization," or the search for a sense of wholeness in the face of forces that negate one's humanity. Finding such wholeness and dignity includes being part of a supportive community that helps the individual to define who he or she is. Humanization means possessing the power and opportunity to help shape the world in which we live.[30] In challenging racial and gender oppression and asserting their rights to exercise their God-given gifts, the nineteenth-century authors worked toward their own humanization as well as that of the many people to whom they ministered.

Another important theme of liberation theology is that of "conscientization," or a coming to critical consciousness of one's ability to participate in shaping the world. Conscientization is a "continuing process of new actions (however small) and new reflections and learning."[31] It is the black women's experiences of sanctification in particular that provide the most significant impetus toward conscientization. It is this spiritual event that enables these women to perceive injustice more sharply and to struggle more determinedly against it.

The race, gender, and class oppression that marked the material conditions of the lives of the radical spiritual mothers engendered a consciousness out of which they created a kind of womanist theology. Womanist theology, Jacquelyn Grant explains, "begins with the experiences of Black women as its point of departure. . . . Those experiences had been and continue to be defined by racism, sexism and classism and therefore offers [*sic*] a unique opportunity and a new challenge for developing a relevant perspective in the theological enterprise."[32] Womanist theology asserts the validity of black women's experiences as a basis for formulating ideas about the nature of God and the nature of the relationship of humans to the divine. Rebecca Jackson's conceptualization of a Mother-Father God, for example, and her adaptation of Shaker doctrines to enhance their relevancy to the experiences of her predominantly black female Shaker community in Philadelphia are strong expressions of theological womanism.

Though women make up the majority of members in black churches and play an integral role within the larger black community, they have been systematically excluded from participating in the important task of shaping black theology. Womanist theologians challenge black theology by asking such questions as: "How . . . can an authentic theology of liberation arise out of these communities [the black community and church] without specifically addressing the liberation of the women in both places? Does the fact that certain questions are raised by Black women make them any less Black concerns?"[33] These are the kinds of questions that the radical spiritual mothers implicitly posed when asserting their rights to preach against the objections of black male church leaders.

Grant argues that the tridimensional reality of black women's experience (that is, race, class, and gender) provides a context for a theology that is potentially holistic and liberating: "The theology is potentially wholistic [*sic*] because the experience out of which it emerges it [*sic*] totally interconnected with other experiences. It is potentially liberating because it rests not on one single issue . . . but it is multi-faceted."[34] The way in which the radical spiritual mothers emphasize their ability to communicate their liberating messages to men and women of all races and classes, and their ability to draw upon their own experiences to envision alternative, inclusive, more egalitarian models of human relationships, reflects the holistic and liberating qualities of their theology at work.

The missions in which the radical spiritual mothers engaged seem to be as much an expression of their own creativity as they were the fulfillment of divine mandates. Their spiritual callings were the means through which they authorized their participation in the act of self-creation, of self-improvisation. Alice Walker reminds us that it is, after all, spirituality that is the foundation of all artistic expression. In *In Search of Our Mothers' Gardens,* Walker writes of the ways in which black women who have been denied conventional outlets for their talents throughout history have nevertheless found alternative ways of employing their gifts. She also describes the tragedy of women, such as those in slavery, who were never able to engage their creativity.[35] Lee, Elaw, Foote, Smith, and Jackson, though faced with seemingly insurmountable odds, refused to stifle the gifts they knew must be cultivated at all costs. It was their creative spirit that sustained and transformed them into radical spiritual mothers.

1

THE WORLD OF THE
RADICAL SPIRITUAL MOTHERS
Socioeconomic, Political, and Religious Milieu

To contextualize the lives and experiences of the radical spiritual mothers, I begin with a brief biographical sketch of the five nineteenth-century spiritual autobiographers Jarena Lee, Zilpha Elaw, Julia Foote, Amanda Berry Smith, and Rebecca Cox Jackson. I then discuss the socioeconomic and political conditions of nineteenth-century American life as they pertained to African Americans, especially women. I focus in particular on the lives of northern free blacks in urban areas since they most closely reflect the socioeconomic and political reality of the radical spiritual mothers. Specifically, I examine working and living patterns, organized participation in benevolent and reform work such as abolitionism, and women's rights activism.

Moreover, in order to show the kinds of thinking and practices the radical spiritual mothers were working against and attempting to modify, I also explore ecclesiastical practices and institutions as well as mainstream theological issues that were prevalent during the nineteenth century in the United States. Specifically, I examine church polity and social attitudes as they pertained to women's preaching and ordination in the Methodist Episcopal, African Methodist Episcopal (AME), African Methodist Episcopal Zion (AMEZ), and Shaker sect, since it was with these churches that the radical spiritual mothers were affiliated. I also examine the presence and impact of Catholic nuns in the nineteenth-century United States as a parallel model of spiritual maternity for radical spiritual motherhood and as an example of women's spiritual empowerment. And since the radical spiritual mothers actively participated in the Holiness and social gospel movements, I discuss these movements, particularly as they pertain to women's involvement. Lastly, I provide a brief discussion of Spiritualism since Rebecca Jackson's religious beliefs combined Shakerism, African Methodism, and Spiritualism.

* * *

Jarena Lee was born to free parents on February 11, 1783, at Cape May, New Jersey. Due to her family's poverty, she was sent sixty miles from home to work as a servant maid when she was only seven years old. Lee underwent a conversion to Christianity in 1804 after joining Bethel African Methodist Episcopal Church in Philadelphia, which was founded by Rev. Richard Allen. During this conversion inspired by a sermon by Allen, Lee demonstrated the ability to exhort sinners as she stood up to extemporaneously address a congregation of hundreds of listeners. Her conversion did not, however, shield her from periods of inner turmoil regarding her spiritual condition; in fact, so convinced was she about her own sinfulness that she contemplated suicide on three occasions. These periods of intense distress would be alleviated only after she experienced a more advanced stage of spiritual grace called sanctification or holiness, which she achieved four years following her conversion after learning about this second blessing from an African American man named William Scott.

Four or five years following her sanctification, Lee became convinced that she had been divinely called to preach the gospel. Confident of her calling, Lee approached Rev. Richard Allen in 1809 for permission to preach. Allen discouraged her from pursuing her intended path since women's preaching was not supported by Methodist Church Discipline. Thus temporarily dissuaded from her mission, Lee went on with her life, marrying Joseph Lee in 1811 and moving from Philadelphia to Snow Hill, New Jersey, to be with her husband, who pastored a church there.

The move to Snow Hill proved to be a time of trial for Lee for several reasons, one being that she was separated from the religious community she had cultivated in Philadelphia. She also suffered physically, succumbing to a protracted illness; and she suffered emotionally when five family members, including her husband, died over a six-year period. She thus found herself facing the task of raising her two small children alone. Eight years after approaching Rev. Allen about her desire to preach, Lee again felt a renewed sense of calling. Thus, in 1817, she asked Allen, who had since become bishop of the African Methodist Episcopal Church, for the privilege of holding prayer meetings in her home and exhorting as she felt led, which she was granted. Lee demonstrated the authenticity of her calling when Rev. Richard Williams was scheduled to preach one day at Bethel Church. When Williams lost the spirit in the midst of his sermon, Lee jumped to her feet and took over, exhorting the congregation on the very scripture on which Williams had intended to preach. This successful performance convinced Rev. Allen, who was present that day, that Lee had indeed been called to preach the gospel. Before beginning her career as a public preacher, Lee honed her preaching skills by addressing smaller audiences in private homes and prayer meetings. She then expanded her venue beyond Philadelphia, going on to preach in the Middle Atlantic and northeastern states and Canada, and addressed audiences across racial, gender, and denominational lines.

Lee had long felt a desire to make her religious experiences and activities known by publishing her autobiography so that her personal example might inspire others to lead Christian lives. With editorial help, she therefore prepared a part of her religious journal for this purpose; it was published in 1836. This publication made her the first African American woman in the United States to publish a prose narrative. Lee published an expanded edition of the narrative in 1849, which detailed her experiences up to age fifty. Approximately three thousand copies of her narrative were in print by the time the second edition appeared.[1]

Zilpha Elaw was born about 1790 near Philadelphia, one of three surviving children of free parents. When Zilpha was twelve years old, her mother died while giving birth to her twenty-second child. After this tragedy, Zilpha and her siblings were separated, with Zilpha being placed in service to a Quaker couple until she was eighteen years old. Her father died after she had lived with the couple for a year and a half.

Though Zilpha did not readily connect with the subdued style of worship of her Quaker guardians, she was receptive to the Methodists who held meetings in her area. Her spiritual development was also periodically punctuated by dreams and visions, some of which she believed convicted her of her sinfulness; one dream, however, precipitated a conversion experience: while milking a cow one day, she saw Jesus approach her in a long white robe with his arms open to her. Of this vision and the profound impact it had upon her, she exclaims: "After this wonderful manifestation of my condescending Saviour, the peace of God which passeth understanding was communicated to my heart . . . from that happy hour, my soul was set at glorious liberty" (Elaw 57). Zilpha formally joined a Methodist Episcopal Society near Philadelphia in 1808.

Zilpha married Joseph Elaw in 1810. Her husband was a nominal Christian, however, which caused tension in their marriage. They moved to Burlington, New Jersey, to take advantage of employment opportunities for her husband, who was a fuller. The couple had a daughter in 1812.

Among the significant experiences described by Elaw in her narrative is her participation at camp meetings, the first of which she attended in 1817. It was at this meeting that she became sanctified and initiated her career of public speaking by praying for the people in attendance. At another camp meeting two years later, Elaw not only felt strongly moved to exhort the people in the presence of a large number of ministers but also believed herself to be divinely commissioned to preach the gospel. After finishing her exhortation, she saw a resplendent light both within and around her, and she heard a voice say, "Now thou knowest the will of God concerning thee; thou must preach the gospel; and thou must travel far and wide" (Elaw 82).

Although Elaw received support for her calling from the ministers of the Methodist Society in Burlington, New Jersey, when she approached them regarding her mission, her husband opposed her preaching, fearing that she would be derided for her work. Elaw, however, insisted on privileging divine authority over that of her husband. Joseph Elaw died in 1823 of consumption.

Following her husband's death, Elaw procured service jobs for her daughter and herself. She also opened a school for black children for two years since they were not permitted to attend the public schools in Burlington. Having a renewed sense of calling to preach, Elaw closed the school, entrusted her daughter to a relative, and began her preaching career in Philadelphia in 1827. Following the guidance of the divine spirit within rather than the external direction of any particular denomination, Elaw traveled and preached in the northeastern and Middle Atlantic states; in 1828 and 1839, she risked preaching in the southern slave states, though she could have been captured and enslaved herself. In 1839, she preached with Jarena Lee in western Pennsylvania, where the two met. Traveling beyond the borders of the United States, Elaw went to London in 1840 to spread the word of God; she traveled throughout central England, preaching over one thousand sermons, according to her estimation. Elaw's narrative ends in 1845; it is not known whether or not she returned to the United States from England.[2]

The fourth child of ex-slaves, Julia A. J. Foote was born in 1823 in Schenectady, New York. Raised in a religious home, Foote delighted in the weekly worship sessions held by her family. Her father was the only member of the family who could read; his reading prompted an early desire in her to learn to read the Bible. By age nine, she had learned the alphabet from him, but racial prejudice excluded black children from attending the local schools. Opportunity for a limited education came when Foote was placed for two years in service to a white family who sent her to a country school where she was instructed from age ten to twelve.

Foote's family moved to Albany, where her parents joined an African Methodist church. She also joined this church when she was converted at age fifteen. Her strong desire to better understand the Bible created a longing for further education, but this hope was thwarted by the closing of a school she had begun to attend and by the need to work. Besides her own diligent efforts at self-education, Foote also credits the Holy Spirit with facilitating her understanding of the Bible.

As was the case with Lee and Elaw, Foote describes sanctification as a significant transforming experience in her life. She began to seek holiness after hearing it described by an elderly couple who had themselves greatly benefited from attaining it. Though her efforts were opposed by her parents and minister, who believed that sanctification was strictly for the elderly or those near death, Foote was sanctified about one and a half years following her conversion.

Julia married George Foote at age eighteen and moved with him to Boston; there she joined an African Methodist church. She regarded her move to Boston as providential; it was a divinely orchestrated opportunity to spread her knowledge of sanctification to those in her new community. Foote's husband, however, disapproved of her religious zeal, believing her to be "getting more crazy every day, and getting others in the same way" (Foote 196). George Foote's long absences at sea as a sailor granted his wife the freedom to pursue her course of visiting people house to house, exhorting and praying with them. While involved in this activity, Foote became convinced that she was being called by God to preach. This feeling was confirmed by a vision she had of an angel, who announced to her, "Thee have I chosen to preach my Gospel without delay" (Foote 200). It would be more than two months after seeing this vision that Foote would overcome her reluctance to obey God's calling.

Foote faced fierce opposition to her efforts to preach by her minister, Jehiel C. Beman, who headed Boston's African Methodist Episcopal Zion Church. Not to be dissuaded from her calling, she preached at meetings held in a church member's home and in her own home. For her tenacity in exercising her spiritual gifts, she was excommunicated from her church by Rev. Beman. When Foote appealed for justice to the Methodist Conference, her complaint was treated with contempt.

Though Foote had her share of detractors, she also found much support for her ministry, including that from a group of women in Philadelphia with whom she held a series of religious meetings. Foote went on to travel and preach throughout New York, New Jersey, Ohio, Connecticut, Pennsylvania, Rhode Island, and Maryland; she also preached in Canada. A throat ailment compelled her to stop preaching for seven years; she was able to resume her preaching in the 1870s. It is not known what activities she engaged in for the following twenty-five years; however, on May 13, 1895, she became the first woman to be ordained a deacon in the AME Zion Church. She gained further recognition by becoming the second woman to be ordained an elder in her denomination. Foote died on November 22, 1900.[3]

Amanda Berry Smith was born in slavery on January 23, 1837, in Long Green, Maryland. Her father, Samuel Berry, was able to diligently earn enough money to buy the freedom of his wife, Miriam Berry, and the five children who were born in slavery. The couple would eventually have thirteen children, with Amanda being their second child and her father's favorite.

Both of Amanda's parents were literate, with her father regularly gathering his family around him on Sundays to read the Bible. Amanda received only a limited formal education of about three months. She learned how to read with the help of her mother by cutting out letters from the newspapers brought home by her father.

When Amanda was thirteen years old, she lived in Shrewsbury, Pennsylvania, where she worked as a domestic servant and joined a Methodist church. In 1854, when she was seventeen years old, Amanda became the wife of Calvin Devine, the first of two husbands, and moved with him to Lancaster, Pennsylvania. She regretted her decision, though, when she learned that her husband drank heavily. The couple had two children, only one of whom, a daughter, survived.

Amanda became gravely ill in 1854; she was not expected to live, but during her illness she experienced "a kind of trance or vision" that seemed to foreshadow her future as a preacher (Smith 42); at the foot of her bed, she saw an angel with its wings spread, who motioned with its hand and told her to "'Go back,' three times, 'Go back, Go back, Go back'" (Smith 42). She was then transported to a large camp meeting at which thousands of people were gathered. She stood high above the people on a platform and fervently preached to them. Amanda awoke from her trance feeling "decidedly better" (Smith 43). A year after experiencing this vision, she was converted.

Following her conversion, Amanda lived in Columbia and Lancaster, Pennsylvania, working as a domestic. She and her husband separated, and he was killed during the Civil War after enlisting in the army. She then moved to Philadelphia, where she wed a second time, to James Smith, an AME preacher and deacon. Unfortunately, this marriage was also troubled, with Amanda suffering emotional abuse from her husband; the couple moved to New York, where Smith joined the Sullivan Street AME Church. It was at the predominantly white Green Street Methodist Episcopal Church, however, that she was sanctified in 1868 while listening to a sermon by the eminent holiness preacher Rev. John Inskip.

Smith's husband died in 1869, and the following year she became a traveling evangelist; beginning in Salem, New Jersey, she preached on the doctrine of sanctification and sparked several revivals around Salem. From 1870 to 1878, she carried the message of holiness to camp meetings, churches, and revivals in the northeastern region. In 1878, Smith traveled and preached abroad, going to England, Africa, and India. She continued to preach for a number of years upon her return to the United States in 1890, eventually selecting Chicago as her home, where she recorded her life story and founded a home for black orphans. Amanda Berry Smith died in 1915.[4]

Rebecca Cox Jackson was born free in 1795 in Horntown, Pennsylvania, and was brought up by both her mother, Jane Cox, and her maternal grandmother. Moving to Philadelphia, she married Samuel S. Jackson in 1830 and lived with him in the home of her brother Joseph Cox, a preacher at Bethel AME Church and a tanner. Jackson had no children of her own, but she took care of her brother's six children and worked as a seamstress.

In 1830 during a thunderstorm, Jackson experienced a dramatic conversion that led to her involvement in the Holiness movement; she led praying bands and later engaged in public preaching. The fact that she was a woman preaching and her belief in celibacy as a requirement for holiness sparked controversy within the AME church, which she criticized for its carnality. Faithfully following the guidance of a divine inner voice, she parted from her family and church in order to embark upon a career of itinerant preaching in the 1830s and 1840s.

Jackson was later drawn to the Shakers for their practice of religious celibacy, their privileging of spiritualistic experience, and their belief in a God that possessed both male and female qualities. She joined a predominantly white

Shaker community in Watervliet, New York, from 1847 to 1851; however, she became disillusioned with the community's lack of attention to the spiritual needs of the African American community. In 1851, she therefore departed with Rebecca Perot, another black member of the Watervliet community with whom she had a close relationship, and traveled to Philadelphia, where they undertook missionary work among the black community and practiced a kind of séance Spiritualism. Jackson and Perot returned to the Watervliet community for a short period in 1857; while there, Jackson received permission to return to Philadelphia in order to establish and lead a predominantly black and female Shaker community; she held her first meeting as eldress of this community in 1859. The Philadelphia "outfamily" continued to exist at least until 1901, about thirty years after Jackson's death in 1871.[5]

During a time when opportunities to improve one's economic and social status were increasing in America, free northern African Americans suffered economic exploitation and discrimination. For most black workers, racial prejudice not only involved limitations on voting privileges, public entertainment, and transportation but also created a daily struggle for survival as blacks faced the challenges of subsistence living, relegation to unskilled jobs with minimum pay, antagonism from immigrant and native-born white laborers, restrictive trade unions, and substandard housing in black ghettos. In the late eighteenth century, most black men were servants, common laborers, or seamen; most single and married black women alike made their living washing clothes.[6]

By 1860, little had changed. Though some blacks had been able to find employment at professional jobs and skilled trades, the majority still worked in menial positions. In Philadelphia, Boston, and New York, men were generally employed as laborers, servants, barbers, waiters, mariners, bootblacks, porters, coachmen, hod carriers, and dealers of secondhand clothes; women were washerwomen, cooks, seamstresses, and dressmakers. Some black women also earned income by selling flowers, cleaning hats, spinning and weaving, and hairdressing. Others pursued professions such as teaching, writing, and lecturing. In 1855, 87 percent of working blacks in New York City were employed at unskilled or menial jobs. This percentage was representative of other northern cities as well.[7]

The domestic labor that black women performed was difficult, with laundry work being the most burdensome. Tera Hunter describes the typical work rituals of the washerwoman:

Gallons of water had to be toted from wells, pumps, or hydrants for washing, boiling, and rinsing clothes. Washerwomen made their own soap from lye, starch from wheat bran, and wash tubs from beer barrels cut in half. They supplied washboards, batting blocks or sticks, work benches, fuel, and cast iron pots for boiling. Different fabrics required varying degrees of scrubbing and then soaking in separate tubs with appropriate water temperatures. When weather permitted, work was often performed outdoors under shaded trees. The saturated garments were hung on clotheslines, plum bushes, or barbed wire fences. . . . But inclement conditions moved the work inside, and clotheslines were hung across the main room. Once the clothes were dry, several heavy irons were heated on the stove and used alternately. After each use, the irons were rubbed with beeswax and wiped clean to minimize the buildup of residue. One by one items were sprayed or dampened with water or starch and pressed into crisp form.[8]

Despite the rigors of the job, washing laundry offered women flexibility since they could simultaneously work and attend to other obligations such as household chores; they could also enlist the aid of family members who could pick up and deliver laundry. Besides flexibility, washing laundry also held broader communal value: "Laundry work was critical to the process of community-building because it encouraged women to work together in communal spaces within their neighborhoods, fostering informal networks of reciprocity that sustained them through health and sickness, love and heartaches, birth and death." Specifically, this community building occurred in the context of women's work as they shared resources, assisted one another with child-care responsibilities, and passed on work skills and life lessons to their daughters, thus enhancing the relationships between mothers and daughters.[9]

Racial stereotypes fueled the belief that blacks' inability to secure professional and skilled jobs was evidence of their inferiority, as opposed to economic exploitation. Widespread beliefs that African Americans were childlike, lazy, irresponsible, untrustworthy, void of ingenuity or initiative, and incapable of managing complex machinery or operating businesses were used to both explain their economic plight and justify their exclusion from better jobs. These stereotypes together with the belief that blacks had been purposely created to perform undesirable tasks helped to confine blacks to a lowly economic state.[10]

These attitudes of black inferiority were in part informed by a complex understanding of racial identity by the white working class. David Roediger argues that during the period from 1800 to 1865, northern working-class whites developed a particular conception of whiteness: "[W]hiteness was a way in which white workers responded to a fear of dependency on wage labor and to the necessities of capitalist work discipline." He further asserts: "[T]he white working class, disciplined and made anxious by fear of dependency, began during its formation to construct an image of the Black population as 'other'— as embodying the preindustrial, erotic, careless style of life the white worker hated and longed for. This logic had particular attractions for Irish-American immigrant workers, even as the 'whiteness' of these very workers was under dispute."[11]

Immigration also threatened the economic status of African Americans. About five million immigrants came to the United States between 1830 and 1860, most of whom were German, Scandinavian, and Irish. Though many of the Germans and Scandinavians settled on farms in the Midwest, Irish immigrants primarily chose to live in the cities, expressing a willingness to accept any jobs they could find, irrespective of the working conditions or wages. This cheap labor force undermined African Americans' hold on unskilled labor. Moreover, violence often broke out between Irish and black workers as competition and hostility intensified.[12]

The Irish were often associated with African Americans for several reasons: both groups frequently lived near one another in urban slums during the 1830s; both engaged in difficult labor, particularly transportation and domestic work; both were berated and poor; and both had been oppressed and forced away from their native lands. These common experiences did not, however, engender sympathy in the Irish for African Americans; rather, they regarded their whiteness as a valuable asset that authorized them to have employment and political privileges.[13]

Economic exploitation along with segregation in northern cities resulted in the formation of black ghettos. In Cincinnati, "Little Africa" was the name given to the area of wooden shanties and shacks where African Americans thronged. "Nigger Hill" and "New Guinea" became home for many blacks in Boston. In New York, blacks settled with poor whites in the infamous "Five Points." And black-populated slums could be found in Philadelphia along narrow alleys and courts, revealing wretched houses and dismal cellars. Though these areas of squalor were quite noticeable, some well-off African Americans were able to afford lovely homes in attractive neighborhoods.[14]

Living in the slums had health consequences for African Americans; in New

York City, for example, twice as many blacks died from tuberculosis as whites. In Philadelphia, the coroner believed such factors as malnutrition, exposure, and intemperance accounted for the high mortality rate in areas where blacks were concentrated.[15]

Despite the overall low economic status of African Americans, social stratification did occur, particularly in larger northern cities, where one could observe distinct upper, middle, and lower classes of blacks, whose social status was determined by a number of factors, including family, place of birth, color, wealth, occupation, and education. Those engaged in business and who pursued professions had been able to acquire increasing amounts of capital and property by 1860. Ministers, lawyers, doctors, shopkeepers, and undertakers enjoyed high social status within the segregated communities in which they lived. Within these communities, the upper and middle classes were made up of professionals, farmers of extensive land, prosperous businessmen, carpenters, barbers, skilled mechanics, waiters at upscale establishments, coachmen, and servants. The lower class, which included the majority of African Americans, was comprised of common laborers.[16]

African American community leaders tried to address these dire economic conditions through the black press and at state and national conventions. For example, *Freedom's Journal,* the first African American newspaper, encouraged readers to value diligence and economy and to prepare young African Americans to take up useful and honorable trades. After 1831, black delegates of state and national conventions urged African Americans to pursue agricultural and mechanical jobs in lieu of menial labor and to form mutual savings banks, county associations, and joint-stock companies so that money might be pooled to buy real estate. Blacks were also asked to patronize their own businesses. By 1860, the number of African Americans who had been able to acquire the money and education they needed to pursue professional careers, skilled occupations, and small businesses had increased. However, most continued to be employed as unskilled laborers and to compete with immigrants for servile jobs.[17]

About 23 percent of married black women in the United States were wage earners in 1890, as compared to just 3 percent of married white women. The greatest factor in explaining this vast difference in the participation of black and white women in the work force is poverty due to black women's racial identity; a much larger percentage of married black women were forced to earn wages to help ensure the economic survival of their families, families that faced greater pressures because of low pay and the seasonal work in which many black men were employed.[18]

Black men exhibited a range of responses to black women's participation in the work force. While some supported the employment of black wives and mothers, others did not, with their overall response being that of reluctant acceptance. Black women historically engaged in labor in the South prior to and following the Civil War, and the black community had cultural and religious traditions that valued work. Moreover, the financial sustenance provided by black women's wages was vital to their families' survival. Despite all of these realities, black community members still did not fully endorse women's labor because it was perceived to negatively reflect upon black men's abilities to provide for their families. White middle-class norms governing the appropriate roles for men and women influenced the attitudes of blacks of all classes, particularly middle-class blacks and those who desired middle-class status; though most married and single black women had to work to support themselves and their families, they often faced private and public criticism for their employment.[19]

During the Progressive Era (1880–1930), black women began to cultivate a distinctive working-class consciousness. This consciousness was unlike that characteristic of trade unions, from which they were often excluded due to race and gender; instead, it downplayed their role as wage earners and foregrounded their roles as uplifters of the race, self-sacrificing mothers, sisters, aunts, and wives. Regarding themselves in this way enabled black women to reconcile the ideals of the prevailing middle-class domestic ideology with the reality of their need to work, thus helping them to deflect criticism of their presence in the labor force.[20]

Middle-class black women who established reformist organizations also reflected a working-class consciousness. The White Rose Industrial Association and the White Rose Working Girls' Home were established in New York City in 1897 by Victoria Earle Matthews and other notable black women in efforts to protect women in the labor force, particularly domestic workers, from exploitation by employment agencies and prospective employers. In addressing these aims, the association and home espoused goals resembling those of labor unions. Further, these organizations, along with others like them in mainly northern cities, offered working women and girls vocational training, as well as educational programs and child care. Not only did the training provided to women by these organizations approximate the apprenticeship programs of traditional trade unions, but the child-care and educational programs surpassed most conventional labor unions in their ability to provide necessary services to female members.[21]

* * *

Before the Civil War, African Americans also sought to improve their communities by participating in benevolent and reform activities through charitable organizations, temperance and moral reform societies, fraternal and maternal lodges, and literary societies. Judith Weisenfeld explains that black women cultivated skills for collective communal support in the midst of slavery by creating networks to aid one another during childbirth and while raising children; they also provided health care and supported the needs of black men. At the same time that enslaved women provided mutual support, free northern black women did the same through their benevolent and reform organizations. Gwen Athene Tarbox credits women preachers like the radical spiritual mothers for their trailblazing benevolence work: "The earliest pioneers in benevolent work were the female circuit preachers such as Jerena [*sic*] Lee, Julia Foote, Zilpha Elaw, and Antoinette Brown Blackwell." The first benevolent and mutual assistance organizations were established right after the first slaves were freed in the northeast. Besides focusing on the abolition of southern slavery, temperance, and education, these organizations sought to help orphans and widows and to control crime. The first known benevolent society of black women, the African Dorcas Society, was organized in 1828 in New York under the advisement of a committee of black male ministers. The primary charge of the organization was to aid black schoolchildren by providing them with appropriate clothing for school since the lack of such attire had been identified as a major cause of absenteeism.[22]

The number of benevolent societies rose during the 1830s as a result of black women's efforts to address the needs of a variety of black groups. Church-affiliated societies were among those being formed and were often crucial to church survival. An example is the United Sons and Daughters of Zion's Benevolent Society, which was organized by a group of black women in Troy, New York, in 1835. The purpose of the organization was to serve the needs of poor members of Troy's Black Methodist Church, which controlled the organization.[23]

Running orphanages for black children, fighting prostitution, and promoting temperance were other activities in which black women engaged in the service of benevolence and moral reform. The Colored Orphan Asylum in New York, for example, benefited from black women's involvement in its daily operations and its development of educational programs before the facility was destroyed in 1863 by an antidraft mob; it was later relocated in Riverside, New York. Hetty Reckless of Philadelphia was among those engaged in efforts aimed at fighting prostitution, opening the Moral Reform retreat in Philadelphia for the purpose of reforming prostitutes. Black women's temperance work was sometimes carried out jointly with black men as members of sexually integrated temperance organizations, and sometimes separately in all-female societies. Organizations formed in the 1830s that were open to both men and women were structured so that men held the leadership positions and women filled the supporting roles; however, in the all-female temperance societies organized in the 1840s, women had greater autonomy.[24]

Besides assisting churches and community organizations, most benevolent societies organized by black women were also designed to aid themselves and their own family members, which marked a difference from comparable societies organized by white women. Black women sought to improve and educate themselves through educational and literary societies, organizations that also supported children's education and ministerial training for young black men. For example, the Afric-American Female Intelligence Society of Boston honed its members' speaking, writing, and reading skills by making literature or their own writing the topic of discussion. The women also hosted guest lecturers to enhance their learning and contributed books to a library. The most common type of organization of free black women were the mutual aid societies, which regularly collected small sums of money from each member to ensure them of benefits for sickness and death.[25]

Black women's benevolent work frequently overlapped with self-improvement, mutual aid, community service, and social reform, thus reflecting the diverse roles they played within their families and communities. The Ladies Literary Society in New York, for example, not only strove to enrich its members' knowledge of literature and science but also provided financial support for the New York Vigilance Committee, an association of men who helped runaway slaves. This multifaceted nature of black women's work represented another way in which their organizations differed from those of white women, which tended to be organized around a single focus.[26]

Besides benevolent work, another important area of reform in which black women participated was that of abolitionism. In 1832, black women organized this country's first female abolitionist society in Salem, Massachusetts. It was called the Female Anti-Slavery Society of Salem and was formed a year after William Lloyd Garrison became well known in the abolitionist movement, and the New England Anti-Slavery Society officially became the parent organization in the region. Various black women's abolitionist societies, both secular and church-affiliated, were established in the northeast, including the Female Colored Union Society of Nantucket, Massachusetts; New York City's Female Wesleyan Anti-Slavery Society of the Methodist Episcopal Church; and the Union Anti-Slavery Society of Rochester, New York.[27]

As was the case with antislavery societies formed by white women, black women's abolitionist organizations were established as auxiliaries to local men's societies and to antislavery societies established on the state and national levels. Early in the abolitionist movement, both black and white women's organizations supported Garrison's American Anti-Slavery Society and his newspaper, the *Liberator*. They engaged in such activities as fund raising, lecturing, carrying out petition campaigns, and meeting regularly to discuss slavery.[28] To raise money for their causes, they organized annual fairs at which prominent abolitionist speakers were featured and handmade crafts, food, and antislavery publications were sold.[29]

Like black male abolitionist societies, those organized by black women expanded their focus beyond the abolition of slavery to address the pressing needs of the free black community. This broader emphasis was often expressed in their constitutions, as was the case with the Female Anti-Slavery Society of Salem: "We the undersigned, females of color, of the commonwealth of Massachusetts, being duly convinced of union and morality, have associated ourselves for our mutual improvement, and to promote the welfare of our color."[30]

Participating in the abolitionist movement inspired both black and white women to question their secondary standing as women and to demand equal treatment within the movement and in society in general. Though much attention has been given to the development of an independent movement for sexual equality by white women beginning in the 1840s, which is usually referred to as "the" women's movement, it must be recognized that a simultaneous women's rights movement was also taking place among black women, one that espoused an agenda even more extensive than that pursued by white feminists.[31]

As white women pursued their struggle for equal rights during the nineteenth century, they devoted increasingly less attention to the concerns of black women and often made efforts to exclude them from participation and membership in their suffrage organizations. Northern white women reasoned that joining with blacks might undermine their efforts to gain the support of southern white women who rejected abolitionism. In addition, white feminists were aware that many northern whites had opposed abolitionism because they worried that abolishing slavery and advocating racial equality would lead to race mixing. However, the inability of white feminists to recognize the integral role that race and class play in achieving liberation for all women not only influenced their agenda and undermined the possibility of establishing an alliance with black feminists, but this lack of perception would also impede progress in the following century.[32]

White feminists' alienation of black women led the latter to form their own black suffrage organizations. Unlike white feminists, who actively sought to distance their movement from its origins in abolitionism, black feminists recognized the importance of continuing to work toward abolitionist goals. But black women's participation in a separate movement for equal rights was not only the result of their exclusion by white feminists; they were also resuming and building upon an established tradition of protest and resistance in which sexism as well as racism must be eradicated in order to achieve true equality and liberation.[33]

Prior to the Civil War, Sojourner Truth was among the few black women who participated in meetings of predominantly white women's-rights activists; at these gatherings, Truth raised the issue of American racism, pointing out in particular the ways in which white women benefited from this racism. Truth was the only black woman present at the 1851 women's rights convention in Akron, Ohio, at which she presented her renowned "Ain't I a Woman?" speech. At the gathering, Truth faced opposition by those averse to the presence of blacks and who wanted to enforce a strict separation between abolitionist and women's-rights concerns. Despite this opposition, Truth voiced her critique of "chivalry" and expressed the ways in which racial discrimination had denied black women the respect and courtesy accorded to white women.[34]

During the Civil War, northern women were involved in a variety of activities, such as performing relief work through benevolent societies, aiding Union soldiers through nursing, taking part in politics on a national level, participating in abolitionist reform work, and teaching and providing for the needs of freed slaves.[35]

One of the most notable institutions founded to provide relief work and nursing was the Sanitation Commission, which was "the first centralized, quasi-public organization for the relief of Northern soldiers." The organization coordinated the relief efforts of about seven thousand northern and western local benevolent societies by war's end, spending $50 million. The Sanitation Commission was responsible for supplying nurses for army hospitals; providing medicine, bandages, food, and clothing; lobbying to improve army camp sanitation and to eliminate scurvy; setting up and sustaining relief camps, infirmaries, and hospital ships; aiding wounded soldiers in returning home; and helping family members to find soldiers missing in action.[36]

Along with the Civil War came an ideological shift in benevolence work. Prior to the Civil War, Protestants linked benevolence with femininity; however, the men and women who engaged in relief work for the Civil War began to view philanthropy as a masculine ideal, and they conceptualized benevolence in scientific terms instead of moral. Thus, a new brand of benevolence came into practice, one marked by centralization, discipline, nationalism, and especially efficiency.[37]

Besides providing an outlet for relief work, the Civil War also led some women to participate in politics on a national level on issues beyond women's right to vote. For example, Anna Dickinson gained fame as a northern orator. Speaking on behalf of the Republican Party, Dickinson helped her party prevail in congressional elections where seats were in fierce contention in 1862 in Connecticut and New Hampshire. She also spoke before a large assembly in 1864 in the House of Representatives chamber, which included President Lincoln as well as congressional and Supreme Court members.[38]

With the outbreak of the Civil War, many women shifted their focus away from women's rights activism. One group of women led by Susan B. Anthony and Elizabeth Cady Stanton, for example, founded the National Woman's Loyal League in 1863, with Stanton serving as president and Anthony as secretary. Specifically, the members of this organization pledged their support to the government, provided it continued to fight for freedom; further, they resolved to gather one million signatures on a petition urging congressional passage of the Thirteenth Amendment. Over a fifteen-month period, the organization's membership swelled to five thousand members, who were able to acquire almost four hundred thousand signatures on their petitions. One important accomplishment of the league was to familiarize the women with organizing as an effective tool for achieving their goals. Their work in the league, along with their other wartime activities, helped to change their negative perceptions of organization as being injurious and confining.[39]

Activism relating to abolitionism among women of the North demonstrated how the Civil War intensified currents that were already evident during the 1850s rather than breaking new ground. For example, the war strengthened the abolitionist trend away from authority grounded in religion toward that which was political and national in nature. Abolitionists regarded the war as a military and political means for bringing to fruition long-standing efforts to eliminate the evils of slavery. Thus, by the end of the war, abolitionists would no longer view themselves as engaging in benevolent work.[40]

Abolitionists and advocates for women's rights worked through established abolitionist organizations and the National Women's Loyal League to engage in large-scale petition drives, to hold conventions, and to urge President Lincoln to struggle against slavery. They increased their efforts to bolster the political rights of African Americans and women and the living conditions of African Americans after the 1863 passage of the Emancipation Proclamation.[41]

Some black and white women got involved in educating freed slaves and increasing their independence. Others built schools for former slaves through the American Missionary Association, which by 1867 had set up hundreds of schools in almost all of the southern states. These teachers of freedpeople differed most from other workers engaged in relief efforts during the Civil War in their firm antislavery stance and their belief in the continuity of their work with that of abolitionists. The unimportant status of abolitionists, the apathy of most northerners toward the welfare of former slaves, and the changed nature of benevolence work were all reflected in the exclusion by northern benevolent societies of those who worked with freedpeople.[42]

The debates over political rights in connection with the Fourteenth and Fifteenth Amendments proved particularly problematic for black women in their efforts to attain equality for they faced both racism by white feminists and sexism by black men who did not make black women a priority in their respective agendas. Though black women were aware that true equality could only be reached through the elimination of both racism and sexism, they nevertheless felt compelled to make a choice between striving for sexual or racial equality. Frances Ellen Watkins Harper, for example, though an advocate for women's rights, chose to support the Fifteenth Amendment. Although the Fifteenth Amendment extended the vote to black men only, Harper felt it was important that black women not hinder the progress of black men; for her, this meant choosing racial solidarity over women's rights.[43]

Though black women were denied the right to vote as American citizens in public elections, they nevertheless engaged in an important tradition of political activism that had its roots in the Reconstruction era. In the late 1860s and 1870s in southern black communities, particularly in Richmond, Virginia, black women actively participated in politics by voting and speaking out at mass meetings, by taking part in Republican Party conventions, and by influencing the votes of black men at the polls.[44] Elsa Barkley Brown thus explains:

> African American women and men understood the vote as a collective, not an individual possession; and furthermore, . . . African American women, unable to cast a separate vote, viewed African American men's vote as equally theirs. They believed that franchise should be cast in the best interest of both. . . . African American women assumed the political rights that came with being a member of the community even though they were denied the political rights they thought should come with being citizens of the state.[45]

During this period immediately following emancipation, black communities had an inclusive, collective conception of freedom that was informed by the experiences of slavery, war, and liberation and that gave rise to political practices encouraging mass participation by all segments of black community—men, women, and children.[46]

The 1880s and 1890s, however, brought about an increasingly narrow view of politics in African American communities, a view that downplayed the mass participation of all segments of the black community in terms of age, gender, and literacy—instead privileging middle-class black men as leaders, decision makers, and spokespersons—and restricted women's roles in the political process. These changes were fueled by increasing racial violence and the disenfranchisement of black men.[47]

Attaining racial equality and the right to vote were important goals toward which black women persisted in working following the Civil War. Heightened violence against black men and the erosion of their voting rights as well as the growing intensity of Jim Crow laws were all indicators that African Americans had yet to fight for equality. Black women who championed abolition and women's rights established an activist tradition in which the next generation of black women would take part. This younger generation, among whose ranks were included some of the daughters of the veteran feminist-abolitionists, joined the older generation in participating in black women's clubs to address the ongoing social and political needs of African Americans. Specifically, black club members worked toward improving job opportunities, advocating for voting rights, combating the lynching of black men, and advancing moral reform, temperance, and education within black communities. Among the notable members of black women's clubs were Ida B. Wells, Mary Church Terrell, Sarah Garnet, and Josephine St. Pierre Ruffin.[48]

The black church became a central arena in which activism was cultivated:[49] "African Americans, looking now to themselves to educate the masses of their people, care for the needy, facilitate economic development, and address political concerns, tapped their greatest strength from the tradition of their churches. From the early days of slavery, the black church had constituted the backbone of the black community."[50] Evelyn Brooks Higginbotham characterizes the black church at the end of the nineteenth and beginning of the twentieth century as a kind of alternative public sphere for African Americans; because blacks were legally barred from using public spaces such as meeting halls, restaurants, and libraries, they turned to the black church as an alternate venue in which they could engage in a variety of activities, such as political rallies, school graduations, and clubwomen's conferences. Black churches even provided space for such services as insurance companies, circulating libraries, and athletic clubs.[51]

In addition to being a space that provided access to needed services and communal interaction, the black church functioned, according to Higginbotham, as an interstitial space in which African Americans, severely limited by the constraints of Jim Crow segregation, could freely criticize and oppose white racism; moreover, black women valued the church as a venue in which they could discuss and formulate a public critique of sexism. Thus, "the church came to represent a deliberative arena, whose character derived from the collective nature of the church itself, namely as a body of many diverse members, and from race-conscious feelings of nationalism."[52]

The radical spiritual mothers were part of a larger tradition of evangelical women who preached in America. According to Catherine Brekus, there were over one hundred evangelical women, black and white, who preached during the eighteenth and early nineteenth centuries. The majority of these women were of the lower or lower-middle class, were uneducated, and held much in common with many nineteenth-century women in terms of their values. Brekus asserts that these women privileged their faith in biblical truths over their right to preach as women: thus, they "were 'biblical' rather than secular feminists, and they based their claims to female equality on the grounds of scriptural revelation, not natural rights."[53]

The rise of women's preaching during the early nineteenth century can be attributed to several factors, one being the broadening of civil society or the informal public, which was "a vast middle ground between the public and the private that was shared by men and women alike": "In the early nineteenth century, as American society grew increasingly complex, this informal public expanded to include antislavery and temperance organizations, orphanages, home missions, and a wide variety of other organizations that mediated between the family and the state. . . . Despite the rhetoric of separate spheres, women were active participants in shaping civil society. An ideology of domesticity may have shaped women's self-perceptions, but it did not determine their destinies."[54] With the separation of church and state that followed the American Revolution, churches became incorporated into this informal public. This transition in churches' status from state institutions to voluntary organizations changed the perceptions of many evangelicals, who now regarded both women and men as possessing the right to organize church missionary activities. A number of dissenting evangelical groups even asserted that women had the right to preach and to formally express themselves on church business through voting.[55]

Besides the enlargement of the informal public, women's preaching also increased due to a shift in the way that gender was perceived during the nineteenth century; unlike the eighteenth-century gender ideology that espoused the existence of only one sex (male), with women being regarded as incomplete men, nineteenth-century conceptions of gender attributed distinct physiological, intellectual, and psychological differences to women and men. Many evangelicals thus ascribed to women an inborn morality and virtue that befitted them to preach as "Sisters in Christ" and "Mothers in Israel"; this attitude reflected the (white, middle-class) republican motherhood ideology that was prevalent at this time.[56]

The leadership opportunities afforded to women by evangelical groups did not last, however:

> During the eighteenth century, many dissenting New Light, Separate, and Baptist churches had allowed women to speak during worship services, but as the new nation was born, they traded their early egalitarianism for greater political power and influence. Later, during the early decades of the nineteenth century, the Christian Connection, the Freewill Baptists, the Methodists, the African Methodists, and the Millerites allowed more than one hundred women to preach, but as they grew from small, marginal sects into

thriving middle-class denominations, they began to rewrite their histories as if these women had never existed. By the 1830s and 1840s, few clergymen wanted to be reminded of the visionary, often uneducated women who had traveled across the country thundering out their condemnations of sin.[57]

As a result of these changes in attitude and church policy toward women preachers and because of this unwillingness to preserve their contributions in historical records, the tradition of women's preaching has been fractured, as Brekus observes: "Cut off from their collective past, women struggled to defend their right to preach without ever realizing that others had fought the same battles before them."[58]

This tradition of evangelical women's religious leadership in America includes Shaker women. Within the Shaker tradition, women usually did not preach. According to Marjorie Proctor-Smith, men and women sat together during worship services in Shakerism's early years; however, beginning in 1782 at the Shaker community at Harvard, Massachusetts, the sexes were separated during worship, sometimes occupying different rooms. In addition, a sermon was added as a regular feature of the services, an activity in which only male members, usually elders, engaged. The separation of men and women during worship had significant ramifications for women's public speaking. Since men delivered the sermons, and sermons were the events that sometimes generated public debate with non-Shakers, Shaker women were often effectively excluded from participation in these public forums. Though the Shaker founder, prophet, and spiritual mother, Ann Lee, engaged in public speaking and preaching, other women were not expected to follow her example. Not until 1796, when Lucy Wright assumed the position of Shaker "Mother," would another woman enjoy a comparable public role.[59]

As Shaker worship services became more structured, the public roles of women in worship diminished. Though the ministry was comprised of both elders and eldresses, it was the elders who "'addressed' or 'exhorted' the worshippers, who delivered 'discourses' to the visitors, who indicated the commencement of dancing, and who signified the end of the meeting.[60] It was only during moments of free 'testimony' and exercise of individual 'gifts' that a woman's voice might be heard."[61] Proctor-Smith attributes the Shakers' identification of public speaking with men and spiritual gifts such as prophesying and singing with women to the dual nature of Shaker life and theology. In keeping with the traditional division of labor within Shaker communities, it was assumed that men, not women, would be more apt to bring to these societies a knowledge of public speaking. In addition, training women in public speaking might have brought the sexes together in ways that would have been deemed improper to Shaker order. Moreover, Shaker theology's dualism, which upheld separate spheres for men and women, would not have supported variance from traditional gender roles. The Shakers' belief that women's sphere was more "spiritual" than men's would have thwarted the efforts of women who wished to exercise unconventional skills such as public speaking.[62]

In light of these restrictions placed upon women's public speaking and preaching, Rebecca Jackson's preaching assumes even greater significance. Perhaps she was granted this privilege because she was regarded by the Shakers as "an authentic 'prophet.'" Jean Humez explains that during her first residence with the Shakers at Watervliet from 1847 to 1851, Jackson often preached at Sabbath meetings, which were open to the public, and her talent was acknowledged.[63] Jackson's uncompromising commitment to following the dictates of her divine inner voice may also account for her public preaching; if she felt divinely led to preach, she would have done so, regardless of conventional Shaker practices.

Within the Methodist tradition, the historical controversiality of women's preaching and leadership is well established. Rosemary Skinner Keller asserts, for example, that "[t]he 'woman issue,' in a multiplicity of forms, was the most controversial question confronting the General Conferences of the Methodist Episcopal Church from 1869 until shortly after the turn of the century." C. Eric Lincoln and Lawrence H. Mamiya add, "[T]his issue continues to be a controversial one for the Black Church."[64] At the heart of this contentiousness lay the issue of women's ordination. Bettye Collier-Thomas defines ordination as follows: "Ordination is the process by which a preacher's ministry is officially legitimated by a religious tradition. It is a credentialing process that enables one to participate fully in a tradition, to acquire certain rights, and to assume certain responsibilities denied to an unordained minister. It provides authorization for a minister to pastor a church and to ascend to other positions in a religious organization's hierarchy." Both black and white women faced difficult challenges in winning this right. As originally conceived, the Discipline of the Methodist Episcopal Church barred women from ordination; it would not be until 1956 that women would gain clergy rights in this denomination.[65]

In the Methodist Episcopal Church, the first major challenge to this exclusionary practice came in 1880, when Anna Oliver addressed the twenty-third quadrennial General Conference in Cincinnati. Oliver attended Boston University, enrolling in the School of Theology and successfully earning a bachelor's degree in sacred theology in 1876.[66] In this same year, she assumed pastoral duties at a Methodist Episcopal church in Passaic, New Jersey. It was a struggling young church in which she received assistance from Amanda Berry Smith. Of the two women's work with the church, a local newspaper reported that "Passaic is having a lively time; what with stirring up sinners and Christians on the one hand, and on the other, two women in the pulpit, and one black, the buzzing glows apace!"[67] Despite a significant increase in church membership from twenty-five people to more than 125, Oliver was removed from her pastorate by the Newark Annual Conference and replaced by a male minister the following year.[68]

In 1879, Oliver took over the pastorate of Willoughby Avenue Methodist Episcopal Church in Brooklyn, New York, which flourished under her leadership. In the spring of the following year she approached the Methodist Church's highest legislative body, the General Conference, to press the case for her ordination.[69] In a pamphlet she prepared and distributed to all 399 male delegates of the conference, Oliver laid out her reasons for pursuing ordination:

> I have made almost every conceivable sacrifice to do what I believe God's will. Brought up in a conservative circle in New York city [*sic*] that held it in disgrace for a woman to work, surrounded with the comforts and advantages of ample means, and trained in the Episcopal Church, I gave up home, friends and support, went counter to prejudices that had become second nature to me, worked for several years to constant exhaustion, and suffered cold, hunger and loneliness. The things hardest for me to bear were laid upon me. For two months my own mother did not speak to me. When I entered the house she turned and walked away. When I sat at the table she did not recognize me. I have passed through tortures to which the flames of martyrdom would be nothing, for they would end in a day; and through all this time and to-day, I could turn off to positions of comparative ease and profit. However, I take no credit to myself for enduring these trials, because at every step it was plain to me, that I had no alternative but to go forward or renounce my Lord.[70]

Further support for Oliver's ordination came when two of the conference delegates separately presented to the body a petition by the members of the Willoughby Avenue Methodist Episcopal Church, requesting that their pastor be ordained.[71]

Oliver was to learn her fate five days later, when reports from the Judiciary Committee and the Committee on Itinerancy were presented. Both committees upheld the church's Discipline in its exclusion of women from ordination. Oliver returned to the Willoughby Avenue church, making her pulpit available to supporters of women's rights within the church as well as to women involved in the suffrage and temperance movements. The church suffered financially, however, and closed its doors in the spring of 1883. Oliver traveled to Europe to nurse her failing health; she died in Greensboro, Maryland, in 1892.[72]

Women's exclusion from the ranks of the clergy led many women to seek other avenues in which to exercise their gifts of leadership. One important organization within the Methodist Episcopal Church that provided such an outlet was the Woman's Foreign Missionary Society (WFMS), the denomination's first national women's organization, which led the way in sending unmarried female missionaries abroad. Founded in 1869, the WFMS represented an officially sanctioned separate sphere for women's work within the church that kept them from encroaching on the governing and decision-making power of male clergy and laymen but also enabled them to exercise leadership and authority within this circumscribed sphere.[73]

The goals of the WFMS were "to evangelize and educate women of non-Christian countries and to create for themselves an autonomous society which could provide purpose, sisterhood, and avenues for leadership and service to its members." India and China were the first two countries to which missionaries were sent by the society, which believed that the evangelization of native women was an important step toward Christianizing these countries since women were regarded as crucial agents in the conversion of their families. The WFMS also stressed the importance of educating native women, to promote not only Christianity and the English language but also literacy in their own languages, as well as to teach the history and geography of their own countries, arithmetic, sewing, needlework, and cooking. Many women were also trained to be doctors and nurses. The women of the WFMS gained a greater sense of purpose, identity, and self-esteem through their work with the organization. They also developed bonds among themselves and with the women whom they served abroad.[74]

The struggles that women have engaged in to gain ordination in the AME Church are long-standing. Though they were granted the right to be licensed as local preachers in 1884 at the General Conference,[75] the church's refusal to ordain women was upheld until 1948, when they were given the right to be ordained as deacons; it was not until 1960 that they attained ordination rights for the position of elder. As was the case in the Methodist Episcopal Church, the male ministers' fear of women's encroachment on their domination of the ministry lay behind this restrictive policy. In addition, a racial component also influenced the men's stance. Since the ministry was one of the few occupations to which black men could aspire that granted them a degree of status in a racist culture, they were reluctant to share this domain with women.[76]

Women preachers in the AME Church were also perceived to be threatening because they believed that their main qualification for preaching lay not in ordination or formal education, but from inspiration received directly from the Holy Spirit. Asserting such credentials defied "the authority of the hierarchal episcopal system taken over nearly unaltered from Anglo-American Methodism and also conflicted with some of the most important policy decisions being made by the church's national leadership," such as raising clerical education standards and suppressing certain "ecstatic or spirit-inspired practices" that were deemed to be "heathenish." Moreover, women preachers were often critical of the church's rising materialism; particular targets of their critiques were AME leaders and members who were more highly educated, dressed stylishly, enjoyed the social opportunities afforded by the church, supported festivals and fairs, endorsed the music of choirs and instruments, "and were in general less interested in living a life centered wholly on religious experiences and values."[77]

Despite the ban on women's ordination, many black women within the AME tradition believed they were divinely ordained to preach the gospel, women who challenged the church's exclusionary practices. They pressured the church to reflect more egalitarian roles for women in its polity or organizational and governing structure. Jarena Lee was the first woman to challenge this structure when she, at age twenty-four, sought a preaching license from Richard Allen in 1809. At that time, the AME Church had not yet been established, but Allen, who would found the church in 1816, and who in 1809 was pastor of Bethel Church of Philadelphia, denied Lee the license. Lee, confident of her call, preached anyway. She would approach Allen again for a license in 1817, after the organization of the AME Church had been made official and Allen had been selected as its bishop. Once again, she was not permitted a license, but she was allowed to hold prayer meetings and to exhort in her home. In addition, Allen arranged for her to speak in several churches in Pennsylvania and permitted her to accompany him and other ministers at meetings held in New Jersey and New York. He even cared for her son while Lee engaged in a two-and-a-half-year period of travel.[78]

Besides Jarena Lee, many other black women in connection with the AME Church preached without ordination or license during the antebellum period, including Sophie Murray, who was highly regarded in Philadelphia and described as the "first evangelist of Bethel." Elizabeth Cole is another woman of Philadelphia known for her evangelistic work. In New Jersey, Rachel Evans earned praise as "a preacheress of no ordinary ability," who "could rouse a congregation at any time." She in fact was thought to have greater preaching ability than her prominent husband. In Washington, D.C., Harriet Felson Taylor gained the distinction of being "'First Female Exhorter and Local Preacher' of Washington's Union Bethel Church." Although Zilpha Elaw was not a member of the AME Church, her preaching did bring her into contact with the church. Jualynne Dodson points out that in her spiritual autobiography, Elaw was undoubtedly referring to Bethel AME Church when she states, "I visited Baltimore [1828] . . . and attended a conference of the coloured bretheren, by whom I was very kindly received; . . . a great and effectual door of utterance opened to me."[79]

The 1884 General Conference became the venue for the AME male clergy's first official reaction to the women who were preaching without church sanction. Though Nathan Ward and others presented a petition in favor of authorizing them to preach, it was defeated. In 1888, efforts to gain official acceptance of women's preaching were renewed when the Daughters of Zion, an AME women's society, petitioned the General Conference for the right of women to obtain preaching licenses. The petition was denied; however, four years later, the issue was again raised at the 1852 General Conference. The delegates of the conference (all of whom were male) decided by a large majority to uphold their stance of denying women preaching licenses.[80]

Despite these negative responses to women's efforts to gain ministerial authority, they continued to preach and to lodge petitions for ordination and licensing. It is probably due to this tenaciousness that male church leaders created alternative outlets for women's service within the organizational structure of the church. For example, delegates of the 1868 General Conference required local pastors to nominate a Board of Stewardesses for their congregations. Stewardesses were not ordained, however; they were responsible for attending to the needs of women in the church and helping the pastor, stewards, and class leaders. Stewardesses were very much under the control of churchmen; their nominations could be opposed or confirmed by stewards. Moreover, steward-esses could be removed from service by a steward and the pastor; stewardesses, however, had no such power in appointing and retaining stewards.[81]

The creation of the position of stewardess did not dissuade women from honoring their calls to preach. Amanda Berry Smith was one of the most well-known. Others included Margaret Wilson and Emily Calkins Stevens of the New Jersey Annual Conference of the AME Church. Wilson was a native of Baltimore, Maryland, who experienced a calling in 1870. She continued with her ministry until 1883, when she was assigned to the Haleyville Mission by the New Jersey Conference. Calkins Stevens believed herself to be called to the ministry three times, the third occasion being in 1882. The following year, she was granted a local preaching license by Bishop John Mifflin Brown. It is not clear, however, whether this license was written or verbal.[82]

At the 1884 General Conference, women were granted the right to be li-censed to preach as evangelists, but not to be ordained. This step was taken in order to exercise a measure of control over women evangelists who had already been given preaching licenses by some ministers, despite church policy to the contrary. Licenses given to women prior to 1884 were retroactively approved. All licensed evangelists became subject to the authority of the Quarterly Con-ference of the church to which they belonged. Further, those women who had been allowed to pastor churches were restricted to evangelistic activities. How-ever, licensing women to preach as evangelists had the effect of increasing the number of women pursuing the path of spreading the gospel.[83]

The widespread success of women's preaching and the desire to diffuse the threat that this success posed to male privilege in the ordained ministry led the church to make a third change in its organizational structure to accommodate women's service. In addition to the positions of stewardess and licensed fe-male evangelist, the church established the position of deaconess at its General Conference of 1900. Unlike deacons, however, deaconesses were not ordained. Their role was to address community social welfare needs. Though it is sig-nificant that the church was compelled by women's preaching success to make three organizational changes, these concessions nevertheless left intact the dy-namics of power based on gender.[84]

The AMEZ Church was the first Methodist denomination to grant voting rights and ministerial ordination to women. This meant that as of 1876, women had an official voice on denominational issues in their local churches, and they were able to vote at the Quarterly and Annual Conferences. The church ordained Julia Foote and Mary Small as deacons in 1895, thus becoming the first black denomination to do so. Moreover, the AMEZ Church took historic action in 1898 when it ordained Mary Small as an elder, a move no other Methodist denomination, black or white, had undertaken. The ordinations of Foote and Small had significant implications for the role of women within the church and society more broadly. Small's ordination, in particular, sparked national controversy and debate.[85]

In developing the concept of radical spiritual motherhood, I drew upon a model of spiritual maternity characterizing a contemporary group of holy women—antebellum Catholic nuns. The administrative, teaching, and caretaking roles adopted by nuns in the public sphere may be regarded as another example of women's religious empowerment that can be examined alongside women's efforts to gain preaching and ordination rights.

By 1860, there were 160 convents in America. Many Protestants feared the increasing presence of convents because of the nuns' religious affiliation and because the nuns frequently were not born in America; moreover, many Protestants perceived the nuns as defying the ideals of the "cult of true womanhood" and republican motherhood, since they rejected motherhood and marriage for their own lives and supposedly attempted to convert Protestant children and encourage Protestant daughters to join their organizations.[86] Underlying male opposition to convents was a fear that nuns were eroding patriarchal power by rejecting traditional forms of domesticity. Protestant women were alarmed by the prospect of nuns taking over roles reserved for American mothers, namely the roles of caretaker, educator, and religious instructor of children; in place of American mothers, nuns would thus become the nation's new cultural and moral judges. American Catholics, however, insisted that nuns and American motherhood were complementary within the domestic ideology.[87]

Though Protestants and Catholics held similar views on domesticity, a major point of contention was the Catholic belief that devoting oneself to a holy life was superior to marrying, and thus virginity was more valuable than motherhood for women. But Catholics felt this belief to be consonant with the maternity espoused by the domestic ideology because most women did not aspire to a religious life but instead chose to adopt the traditional roles of wife and mother. Moreover, even women who selected a chaste religious life could practice spiritual maternity, stemming from their identity as spiritual "brides of Christ" and from their engagement in moral reform, orphan care, teaching, and nursing. Further, the nuns' holy calling and their commitment to the vows of obedience and chastity fundamentally reflected the cult of true womanhood's tenets of submissiveness, purity, and piety.[88]

On one level, nuns did violate some of the institutions and forms of domesticity by rejecting motherhood, marriage, and home. The convent, which functioned as substitute for the nuclear home, offered women unparalleled opportunities for public participation. As some of the first nineteenth-century American women to permanently work in the public sphere, they set examples for the female-dominated nursing and teaching professions. Unlike most women in antebellum America, nuns held powerful and influential positions as convent superiors, academy directors, and hospital administrators.[89]

But their progressive roles in the public sphere did not inspire nuns to alter their values. They did not challenge the exclusivity of the male domain of the Catholic clergy and power structure, nor did they critique female subordination to men in general. Nuns essentially complied with the domestic ideology's definitions of gender roles and differences, and tried to instill these ideals in other women. Their trailblazing participation in the public sphere only served to produce new versions of conventional roles; they extended the definition of the female sphere but did not interrogate that domain's validity. By engaging in spiritual maternity, nuns did not subvert domesticity but instead carried out its purposes and complied with its beliefs about the nature of women.[90]

Though Catholic nuns were subordinate in relation to male church authorities, they nevertheless garnered the respect of these leaders because of their significant influence within Catholic communities and their valuable charitable work in the broader society. On occasions when disagreements occurred between a community of nuns and a bishop, the nuns were not passive but asserted their rights, which were protected by the community's constitution. During the discussions that took place in the process of negotiation or arbitration, the nuns were treated as equals, not subordinates. Besides constitutional protection, nuns also sometimes drew upon the leverage they had in order to check a bishop who occasionally tried to overstep the bounds of his authority. When it was deemed necessary, nuns sometimes threatened to join another diocese, thus raising the specter of withdrawing the valuable services they provided. In these cases, the nuns usually won.[91]

Two successful orders of black nuns were established during the antebellum period. The Oblate Sisters of Providence was founded in 1829 in Baltimore, Maryland, and the Sisters of the Holy Family was founded in 1842 in New Orleans, Louisiana. The Oblate Sisters of Providence was started by four members of a Haitian refugee colony in Baltimore: Elizabeth Lange, Marie Madeleine Balas, Rosine Boegue, and Almeide Duchemin Maxis. The women were encouraged to found the order by the French priest Jacques Hector Nicholas Jouber, who pastored the chapel in which the Haitians worshiped. Lange and Balas had already begun a free school for girls in their home prior to the establishment of the sisterhood. After its establishment, the school was combined with the religious life of the community, and Lange became its first Mother Superior. A school for boys was started later, in 1852. The Oblate Sisters founded St. Frances Academy, which served local youth and drew students from Washington, Philadelphia, and other areas. During Baltimore's 1832 cholera epidemic, some of the nuns interrupted their educational mission to nurse victims of the disease. They set up orphanages after the Civil War, including the Guardian Angel Home for boys in Leavenworth, Kansas, which was established in 1888. Though the sisters expanded their mission, their main focus continued to be education, particularly for girls.[92]

The Sisters of the Holy Family was founded by Henriette Delille, who, as an adolescent, was deeply influenced by her experience of helping the French nun Soeur Ste-Marthe Fontier with her school for black girls. Delille and her friend Juliette Gaudin assisted the free black girls who attended the school during the day and the slaves who were sent by their masters at night to receive religious instruction. Delille and Gaudin were so affected by the slaves' degraded conditions and by the lifestyles of poverty-stricken blacks in New Orleans, whom they also aided, that they resolved to dedicate their lives to helping improve the lives of impoverished blacks. The women accomplished this by establishing their sisterhood, with Delille becoming its first Mother Superior. Josephine Charles joined the community in 1843 and was considered to be one of its founders. The unusual nature of the women's undertaking is expressed by Sister Audrey Marie Detiege, who asserts that a black "nun was not only a novel concept for a slave community, but for a quadroon [Delille], due to her ill-reputed social position, to become a religious was actually revolutionary." The house in which the sisters established themselves, called the Hospice of the Holy Family, functioned as a convent, a home for elderly blacks, and a shelter for those who were ill, poor, and needy.[93]

By 1898, not only had the sisterhood grown, but it had founded six institutions in New Orleans and six others outside the city. Among those in New Orleans was the Asylum of the Children of the Holy Family, which educated slaves, the poor, and orphans free of charge. They supervised the Louisiana Asylum for Negro Girls and the Lafon Orphan Asylum for Boys. A new convent was established in 1881 in a building that had been used for quadroon balls during the antebellum period. Throughout its history, the Sisters of the Holy Family have been known both for providing educational programs and for serving the poor.[94]

On a broader scale in American religious life, revivalism was the most prominent feature in the development of American Protestantism from the Great Awakening through the nineteenth century. An important part of this tradition of American revivalism was the Holiness movement, which was an "unparalleled quest for Christian holiness and a fuller understanding of the work of the Holy Spirit in the individual, the Church, and the world." The movement had its roots in the revivals of 1760 and 1762 that occurred in English Methodist societies surrounding the experience of entire sanctification. Following the teachings of Methodism's founder, John Wesley, Holiness advocates believed that every Christian needed to experience entire sanctification, or a "second blessing" subsequent to conversion that "involved the Christian's utter consecration of himself to God through Jesus Christ in the faith that God would free him from the inner disposition to willful sin and fill him with divine love." This second blessing bestowed a kind of perfection that was not absolute, but that allowed a believer to maintain a pure love for God and to develop in his or her Christian maturity, as long as he or she did not purposely and consciously violate the new relationship established with God.[95] One thus attained and sought to maintain a state of personal holiness.

From 1835 to 1865, the doctrine of entire sanctification was most effectively promoted by the "Tuesday Meeting for the Promotion of Holiness," which became the movement's focus of attention. The meetings were begun by Methodist laywoman Sarah Worrall Lankford in her home in New York City, for the purpose of encouraging those who sought entire sanctification. Lankford herself experienced the second blessing in May 1835, and in August of that year, she moved the prayer group meetings she had been sponsoring at the Mulberry Street and the Allen Street Methodist Episcopal churches to her home at 54 Rivington Street. The prayer group meetings were combined into one, becoming known as the Tuesday Meeting, with the Lankford home becoming a kind

of "house-church." These gatherings, which met for more than sixty years, became the model after which other holiness meetings were patterned.[96]

In July 1837, Lankford's sister, Phoebe Palmer, also experienced entire sanctification and took over leadership of the Tuesday Meeting after Sarah left New
York. Drawing upon her experience of entire sanctification and her scriptural
knowledge, Palmer devised a method for achieving and understanding the second blessing known as "altar theology" or "altar terminology." In elucidating
this theology, Palmer asserted that according to scripture, Christ both sacrificed
His life for the sins of humans and served as the altar upon which believers
could wholly sacrifice their hearts to God. She believed that "the divine promise of fullness of spiritual life, release from self-will and the habit of sinning
could be realized in every Christian through entire consecration of the self offered as a gift of faith upon the 'Altar, Christ.'" As a Christian consecrated his
or her life to God on the altar of Christ, he or she was liberated from any tendencies that were not rooted in love; and the believer retained this assurance of
liberation, provided he or she remained faithful and obedient to God. Palmer's
altar theology was consistent with Wesley's theology of entire sanctification,
and it gained widespread acceptance within Methodism. Of the importance
of Phoebe Palmer's ideology and practices to the development of the Holiness movement, Charles Edwin Jones asserts: "While the holiness movement
always regarded John Wesley as its great authority, the movement owed many
of its distinctive ideas and practices to Phoebe Palmer. . . . Taken over by Methodist camp meeting promoters, Mrs. Palmer's ideas were to pervade all future
Methodist debate concerning holiness."[97]

Within the Holiness movement, women were able to play prominent roles
for several reasons, such as the importance given to public testimony and the
scriptural roots of the doctrine of holiness. Holiness adherents were required
to publicly testify about the ways God had worked in their lives. Not only was
such testimony regarded as essential to publicizing Christian holiness, but it
was also considered indispensable to retaining the grace bestowed through entire sanctification. Women's as well as men's voices and experiences were therefore validated and valued through this practice. Holiness participants were also
called upon to examine their experiences in the light of biblical truths, looking
for ways in which this experience conformed to and reflected these truths.
Drawing upon personal experience to subjectively interpret scripture, and not
being limited to literal interpretations, Holiness people claimed biblical authority to challenge the status quo.[98]

Women's importance was also underscored through the emphasis placed upon the work of the Holy Spirit and upon the individual's right to experimentation. Holiness adherents believed that the sanctified individual was baptized by the Holy Spirit, which was thought to bestow "extraordinary gifts and manifestations of power" on women and men alike. Preaching was regarded as a direct gift from the Holy Spirit, rather than a humanly derived activity sanctioned by the church. The liberty to experiment was manifested in a range of worship and evangelizing forms, such as women's preaching, lay ministry, field preaching, class meetings, and camp meetings. In addition, a new type of preaching, called "Bible readings," was used that involved a speaker's reading a passage of scripture and interjecting commentary along the way. This practice enabled women and laypeople to "preach without actually giving a formal 'sermon.'"[99]

Women also benefited from the inherently reformist ways in which the Holiness movement challenged the status quo by focusing on holiness and perfection; Holiness adherents recognized ways in which the established churches fell short in meeting certain needs and fighting injustices, so they stepped in to fill these voids. An example of this is the Wesleyan Methodists' and Finneyites' support of the abolition of slavery. Further, a number of Holiness denominations worked to aid the poor, orphans, unwed mothers, and people in distress.[100]

The late nineteenth century was also distinguished by the advent of the social gospel. Vinson Synan credits the conception of this theological movement to the Massachusetts Congregational minister Washington Gladden and the Baptist minister and Rochester Theological Seminary teacher Walter Rauschenbusch. The two men desired to establish a system of "Christian Socialism" to replace capitalism and "capitalistic Christianity." They believed that only if American culture underwent a "social conversion" could such "social sins" as poverty, poor living conditions, social exclusion, and misuse of wealth be eliminated, sins that they asserted to be as evil as personal sins.[101]

The social gospel crusade was informed by the same perfectionist thought that gave rise to the Holiness movement. In fact, it was antebellum Holiness advocates who had spearheaded the drive to reform society; most postbellum social service performed by Christians had been undertaken by the Salvation Army and the Volunteers of America, both of which were perfectionist organizations. One could argue that the social gospel logically resulted from the Holiness movement since both movements believed in the perfectibility of humans. Holiness and social gospel adherents differed, though, in their beliefs about the extent to which society could be perfected; followers of the Holiness movement asserted that only with Christ's second coming and the establishment of the millennium could society truly reach a perfect state.[102]

The social gospel had a major impact on every major church in this country, especially the Methodist Church, which within the Wesleyan tradition not only promoted the sanctification of individuals to achieve personal holiness but also called for "social sanctification," or the "sanctification of the world" so as to ultimately transform it into God's kingdom. Active engagement in social reform was to be the primary means by which believers would help to bring about this transformation. William E. Boardman poignantly described the scope of this formidable goal in 1869: "No other question . . . looms up before the thoughtful Christian mind in the immediate future with such grandeur as this of the conversion of the industrial, commercial, political, educational, and social interests of the world to Christ."[103]

According to Mary Agnes Dougherty, traditional church histories usually attribute the creation of the social gospel to men—ministers, theologians, and laymen; by contrast, churchwomen's roles in originating this movement go largely unnoticed or are disregarded. Dougherty reasons that this is probably so because historians did not recognize anything significant about women's performance of service to others, a role they were traditionally expected to play. The social gospel's requirement that Christians express love for their neighbors, particularly the lowly, was deemed to be a "natural" activity for women and therefore not likely to originate a new movement in social Christianity. On the other hand, this commitment to the welfare of others required Protestant men to think and act in ways traditionally associated with women; this is what was radical. Thus, the social gospel was not officially recognized as a historic event until men evinced this sea change in attitude and behavior.[104]

Women's restoration of the position of deaconess within the polity of the Methodist Episcopal Church in 1888 marked an active effort to foster the social gospel almost twenty-five years before the recognized high point of the movement in 1912. In 1885, Lucy Rider Meyer established the Chicago Training School for City, Home, and Foreign Missions (CTS). Basing her conclusion on observations of Chicago's tenements during the home visits required of students by the school, Meyer became convinced that Christianity must devise new ways to address the problems of city life. Two years later, in an apartment near the school, the country's first Methodist Deaconess Home was established.

The diligent work of the deaconesses proved them to be activists who made important contributions to the Methodist achievements in the social gospel.[105]

Methodist women who chose to become deaconesses took as their model the biblical figure of Phoebe, who is referred to in Romans 16:1–2. A prosperous, refined, and benevolent woman, Phoebe worked for the ancient Christian Church by serving as deaconess for a Cenchrean mission near Corinth. Phoebe gave of herself generously and lovingly to serve those in need: "This tradition of Phoebe's *diakonia*—her ability to 'see the world's pain' and her desire to overcome it through personal service—was just what nineteenth-century Methodist women wanted to revive."[106]

At the same time that deaconesses served the poor by helping to fulfill their basic needs and by evangelizing them through personal examples of love-in-action, many also participated in the developing field of quantitative sociology. As the deaconesses visited the poor, they also observed the social conditions in which they lived, recording this information like social workers. As they did so, the churchwomen demonstrated their agreement with the widely accepted belief in the necessity of studying society scientifically to help solve its problems and bring about social justice.[107]

When deaconesses visited people, not only did they address physical needs, but they also listened to people's insights about why they were suffering. The stories that the churchwomen heard each day during their visits prompted them to explore the possible root causes of people's despair. With clarity and insight, the deaconesses recognized the economic injustice underlying the suffering they witnessed; sensitized by this knowledge, they refrained from "blaming the victim" or attributing people's poverty to moral degradation. Instead, their thinking resembled class analysis as they linked poverty and despair with inequities in the nation's economy.[108]

Among the issues in which deaconesses took a special interest were child labor exploitation, alcohol abuse, and prostitution. With women and children being the primary recipients of their services, deaconesses were particularly interested in the reformist work of people like Florence Kelley, who wrote child labor exposés that were included in deaconess literature. In keeping with Methodism's staunch support of temperance, deaconesses backed attempts to close taverns and established coffeehouses as alternative venues for social gatherings. The deaconesses viewed prostitution as a social problem instead of an activity engaged in by morally depraved individuals, and they preferred to address the problem preventatively rather than setting up residences for "fallen women." This approach involved frequenting railroad depots and looking for young women who seemed to be new arrivals in the city and not very confident. Deaconesses would approach these women and provide them with information about reputable boardinghouses if they had no relatives or friends with whom they could stay. In this way, the deaconesses, who referred to themselves as Traveler's Aides, tried to foil the efforts of prostitute procurers, who also targeted the depots looking for new workers; in addition, the deaconesses sought to cultivate in churchwomen a greater understanding of and open-mindedness toward prostitutes.[109]

In carrying out a "family or household ministry" (Elaw 71) in her community prior to embarking upon her itinerant preaching career, Zilpha Elaw seemed to have intuitively recognized the importance of the kind of work undertaken by deaconesses, as modeled by their ancient Christian foremother, Phoebe: "[I]t was revealed to me by the Holy Spirit, that like another Phoebe, or the matrons of the apostolic societies, I must employ myself in visiting families, and in speaking personally to the members thereof, of the salvation and eternal interests of their souls, visit the sick, and attend upon other of the errands and services of the Lord" (Elaw 67). Also partaking in a social gospel, the radical spiritual mothers are thus part of a long tradition of service that extends from antiquity to the present.

According to Ann Braude, "Spiritualism was a new religious movement aimed at proving the immortality of the soul by establishing communication with the spirits of the dead." At its height during the 1850s and 1860s, Spiritualism attracted many people who sought a way to bolster their waning faith. The ability to communicate with deceased people's spirits offered evidence that the soul was immortal, thus fostering a renewal of faith. Spiritualism's "scientific" approach to religion offered the kind of proof that many found lacking in Christianity. Spiritualists demonstrated this proof at séances, in which people were invited to participate as "investigators."[110]

Spiritualism's affirmation that people could communicate with spirits established a direct link to sacred knowledge. This religious individualism had positive repercussions for women's leadership within the movement: "Feminist scholars have found that women have been able to exercise leadership where religious authority derives from direct individual spiritual contact or experience rather than from office, position, or training." Human mediums were the vehicles through which spirits articulated sacred truths.[111]

Women who served as mediums became public leaders while still exhibiting those qualities that were deemed to be proper feminine attributes by the cult of true womanhood; women's supposed natural piousness, sensitivity, delicacy, and passivity were regarded as characteristics that made them especially well suited to receiving spirit communications. Moreover, by serving as mediums, women became religious leaders without having to negotiate formal restrictions due to their gender. The direct interaction that women had with spirits imbued them with an authority that could not be prohibited by men since there were no educational requirements for mediumship nor demands for ordination or acknowledgment by any organization. Spirits empowered women to overcome traditional gender restrictions by inspiring them to engage in public speaking, to become authors, and to travel as lecturers.[112]

First practiced in the United States, Spiritualism also gained followings in the British colonies, England, and western Europe; moreover, many people throughout the world syncretized Spiritualism with religious rites originating in Africa. Southern slaves were drawn to Spiritualism because spirit possession and mediums had also been a part of their native African cultures. Noting similarities in African and Spiritualist beliefs, Braude explains, "The West African view that ancestors have a role in the social structure and continue to merit the obligations of kinship after death predated similar beliefs among American Spiritualists." Many southern African Americans and those who migrated to northern cities after Reconstruction believed that the spirits of the dead could return to make benign contact with the living. It was during the twentieth century that significant numbers of African Americans became Spiritualists; however, there were some black mediums during the nineteenth century. Rebecca Jackson and Rebecca Perot were among them; as self-taught mediums, they routinely partook in séances in Philadelphia.[113]

The radical spiritual mothers were both extraordinary and representative. They were extraordinary in the ways that they lived out their callings to preach the gospel, yet the material conditions of their lives were representative of the poor and working-class black women of their time; moreover, the social activism and benevolent work in which they engaged linked them to other women doing similar work. Further, the radical spiritual mothers' preaching and the obstacles they faced because of this unconventional work placed them within a larger tradition of nineteenth-century evangelical women preaching in America. In the next chapter, I explore the nature of radical spiritual motherhood.

2

POWER AND TRANSFORMATION
IN RADICAL SPIRITUAL MOTHERHOOD

In this chapter, I theorize the concept of radical spiritual motherhood as an empowering subjectivity constructed by nineteenth-century African American female spiritual autobiographers Rebecca Jackson, Amanda Berry Smith, Jarena Lee, Zilpha Elaw, and Julia Foote following their experiences of sanctification. "Radical spiritual motherhood" is a term that I apply to a particular pattern of behavior that draws upon and transforms the conventional roles that were assigned to women by nineteenth-century domestic ideology. In explaining the characteristics of this kind of subjectivity, I argue that it is revolutionary in enabling these writers to reconceptualize power from a protofeminist perspective in the midst of a rigidly patriarchal culture; in allowing them to claim sexual autonomy and physical freedom within a society that declared female bodies to be the property of men and that asserted "virtuous black woman" to be an oxymoron; and in authorizing them to actively participate in a public sphere that was hostile to blacks and proscriptive to women of all races. Specifically, I show how this subjectivity was grounded in the material circumstances of nineteenth-century free black women, thus investing these writers with a particular consciousness that informed their use of religion as a tool for critique and transformation. I explore the ways in which these authors reconceptualized and appropriated power from within the context of their identities as radical spiritual mothers. And I discuss the relationship between radical spiritual motherhood and biological motherhood.

Radical spiritual motherhood is an expansive conception of maternity that extends the scope of the biological family to regard all humans as potential recipients of maternal care, both spiritual and material. This care may include spiritual sustenance such as that provided through preaching and prayer or material support such as that given to the poor and the sick. The authors were not, however, restricted to nurturing roles but also functioned as leaders and intellectuals who actively participated in the public sphere. And, since they did not remarry after the deaths of their husbands, instead choosing to maintain their physical, emotional, and sexual autonomy, celibacy was an important part of this kind of maternity.

Prior to becoming itinerant preachers, the domestic ideology to which the radical spiritual mothers sought to adhere was the cult of true womanhood. It may seem contradictory that working-class black women would attempt to adhere to standards designed for middle-class white women, particularly since the economic reality of most antebellum African Americans required that women work outside the home in order for their families to survive, and since many black women were engaged in public activities to benefit and "uplift" black communities. Nevertheless, many black women and men believed that adopting conventional gender roles and embracing white middle-class values conferred a measure of respectability. Thus many African Americans adopted these values as a conscious strategy to combat the negative stereotypes about them that originated in slavery, to highlight their status as free men and women, and to gain acceptance by whites.[1]

This emphasis on cultivating respectability continued into the post-Reconstruction era during a period of heightened violence against African Americans, segregation, and disenfranchisement. For example, Evelyn Brooks Higginbotham explains that members of the Woman's Convention, an organization of black Baptist women founded in 1900 as an auxiliary to the black male–dominated National Baptist Convention, espoused a "politics of respectability" aimed not only at challenging racism but also at reforming what they perceived to be negative behavior and attitudes among blacks:[2] "Through the discourse of respectability, the Baptist women emphasized manners and morals while simultaneously asserting traditional forms of protest, such as petitions, boycotts, and verbal appeals to justice. Ultimately, the rhetoric of the Woman's Convention combined both a conservative and a radical impulse."[3]

Also concerned with the notion of respectability during the post-Reconstruction era was the National Association of Colored Women (NACW), an organization of black women's clubs founded in 1896. Of utmost importance to the NACW was transforming the image of black women. Damaging perceptions of black women as being immoral and sexually promiscuous were prevalent and had their roots in slavery, when black women were used as breeders to reproduce human property for their owners; enslaved women's sexual exploitation along with the practices of denying slaves the legal right to marry and breaking up their families further added to the degradation of black women. Black women were faulted with failing to live up to the tenets of the cult of true womanhood. Members of the NACW thus regarded themselves as the defenders of black womanhood. Adopting the motto "Lifting As We Climb" to link self-help with helping others, the NACW tried to inculcate middle-class values in the lower-class masses, and in particular placed great emphasis on the importance of chastity to combat the sexual stigma that black women had acquired.[4]

Three specific aspects of the cult of true womanhood that are transformed through the adoption of radical spiritual motherhood are the designation of the private sphere as the proper domain for women; the requirement that married women cede control of their sexuality to their husbands; and the expectation that married women gain their fulfillment through biological motherhood and serving their husbands. Though the private sphere was one in which women were traditionally granted circumscribed power, radical spiritual mothers were divinely authorized to move freely between the private and the public spheres to preach the gospel. The authors further capitalized on their God-given right to public intervention by using their mobility and visibility to address social and political issues such as slavery, racism, and sexism.

The writers' sexual empowerment stemmed from their insistence upon the right to control their own sexual destiny by remaining single upon the deaths of their husbands and by subsequently practicing celibacy. Rebecca Jackson took this practice a step further by insisting upon celibacy within her marriage. What is innovative about the writers' practice of celibacy is that they undertook it independently of any institutional mandates governing their sexuality. Catholic nuns, for example, took a vow of chastity as part of the requirements of their religious order. These writers, however, took matters into their own hands and declared their bodies to be their own, to be used solely for God's work. In claiming this right they not only undermined the patriarchal prerogative of male control of the female body, but they implicitly critiqued racist assumptions about black female sexuality by insisting upon their unavailability for exploitation by white men (and black men).

Though radical spiritual motherhood draws upon biological motherhood for patterns of maternal nurturing, the authors were not bound by the constraints of biological motherhood. They sometimes, for example, legitimately left their children in the care of relatives or friends in order to fulfill their ministerial obligations. Thus, spiritual motherhood takes precedence over biological motherhood if the latter interferes with the fulfillment of the authors' itinerant missions. Biological motherhood influences spiritual motherhood through the identity-shaping relationships that occur between the authors and their children and between the authors and their own mothers.

What did it mean for these women to engage in the practice of radical spiritual mothering? In its broadest sense, it meant taking care of the spiritual needs of the family of God—that is, all of the people with whom the writers came in contact during their travels. Addressing the spiritual needs of their symbolic extended families involved moving freely among the private and public spheres to perform a multiplicity of tasks, such as caring for the sick, feeding the hungry, leading prayer meetings, preaching to large assemblies, engaging in informal one-on-one teaching, and counseling those with personal problems. Because the spirit cannot be nurtured unless the basic needs of the body are met, they necessarily took a holistic approach to ministering to familial needs. What was required was the ability to relate to people from all walks of life, from all races and classes. And since their authority was frequently challenged due to their race and gender, they also had to be able to identify, critique, and transform oppressive racial and gender practices. In short, the radical spiritual mother performed traditional nurturing roles but was also divinely authorized to act as a leader and intellectual in the public sphere.

Radical Spiritual Motherhood and Theories of Subjectivity

To help conceptualize the nature of the identities constructed by the radical spiritual mothers as both historical and literary subjects, I have drawn upon several theories of subjectivity; these include the theories of audience-oriented, universal/embodied, migratory, and interstitial subjectivity.

The public nature of the radical spiritual mothers' spiritual performances as preachers is significant. Not only do they perform for God, for whom they must ultimately demonstrate their effectiveness at fulfilling the calling for which they were chosen, but they must also perform for those who are critical of them as women daring to transgress the gender boundaries that cut them off from the male privilege of preaching. For these critical spectators, their performances must be especially convincing. Such is the case when Jarena Lee spontaneously leaps to her feet during a sermon to displace a male preacher whose spiritual power is flagging:

[T]he Rev. Richard Williams was to preach at Bethel Church, where I with others were assembled. He entered the pulpit, gave out the hymn, which was sung, and then addressed the throne of grace; took his text, passed through the exordium, and commenced to expound it. The text he took is in Jonah, 2d chap. 9th verse,—"Salvation is of the Lord." But as he proceeded to explain, he seemed to have lost the spirit; when in the same instant, I sprang, as by an altogether supernatural impulse, to my feet, when I was aided from above to give an exhortation on the very text which my brother Williams had taken. (Lee 44)

Lee's performance is brilliant, not only because she attributes her actions to a higher power, thus preempting the censure that was likely to come from those who may have viewed her behavior as inappropriate for a woman, but also because during her extemporaneous exhortation, she effectively appropriates the text chosen by the minister to defend her call to preach: "I told them that I was like Jonah; for it had been then nearly eight years since the Lord had called me to preach his gospel to the fallen sons and daughters of Adam's race, but that I had lingered like him, and delayed to go at the bidding of the Lord, and warn those who are as deeply guilty as were the people of Ninevah" (Lee 44). Identifying herself with the reluctant prophet Jonah, Lee further builds her credibility with her audience, whom she thoroughly convinces of her power and authority: "During the exhortation, God made manifest his power in a manner sufficient to show the world that I was called to labour according to my ability, and the grace given unto me, in the vineyard of the good husbandman" (Lee 44). By asserting that her exhortation is "sufficient to show the world" that her call to preach the gospel is authentic, Lee eloquently claims divine sanction for the public nature of her ministry. She is essentially declaring that "all the world's a stage" for her powerful spiritual performances and that God Himself has ably groomed His protégé. Though Lee fears she may be thrown out of the church for what she has done, she is reassured by Bishop Richard Allen, who is present in the audience, when he admits that "he now as much believed that [she] was called to that work, as any of the preachers present" (Lee 45).

The public, performative subjectivity cultivated by the radical spiritual mothers may be characterized as a kind of "audience-oriented subjectivity." A term originated by Jürgen Habermas and elucidated by Glenn Hendler, an audience-oriented subjectivity is formed in relationship to an audience for which it performs; moreover, there is a "calculated theatricality, epitomizing an 'audience-oriented subjectivity.'"[5] As an indicator of their preaching power, the radical spiritual mothers frequently describe the impact they have upon their audiences. Zilpha Elaw, for example, poignantly describes her ability to elicit powerful emotional responses from her listeners:

> On one occasion, a number of persons, amounting to between twenty and thirty, presented themselves in the chapel, in great distress and deep penitence on account of their sins. The excess of their emotions were such, that the order of worship was suspended; for some were calling upon the name of the Lord, some were groaning to receive the atonement of Jesus, while others were rejoicing in his salvation and giving glory to God. (Elaw 106–7)

The extent to which the radical spiritual mothers can captivate, inspire, and elicit such responses from their listeners is a gauge by which they can measure their effectiveness as instruments of God. Though they attribute their power to God, and their identities as preaching women are authenticated by Him, their subjectivities are nonetheless partly constituted through their relationship with their audiences; engaged in a dynamic reciprocity, the radical spiritual mothers not only aid their listeners by helping to bring about repentance, conversion, and sanctification, but they are in turn aided through their audiences' corroboration of their power, authority, and identities as authentic spiritual leaders.

As the radical spiritual mothers engage in self-representation through the act of writing their narratives, they ultimately textually perform for their reading audiences, whom they also wish to convince of their gifts and callings, and whom they want to instruct and inspire to greater faith through their personal stories. Thus, these holy women are significant historical subjects who performed for the audiences that witnessed their preaching and works, and they are also literary subjects cogently fashioned for the reader's enlightenment and interpretation.

Richard Douglass-Chin also recognizes the importance that public performance plays in the lives and texts of these evangelists; however, he draws a distinction between performance and "(per)formance": "By '(per)formance' I mean a profound self-fashioning that demystifies and challenges the 'performance' of black womanhood prescribed and/or described as 'natural' by hegemonic discourses."[6] One of the "hegemonic discourses" to which he refers is the cult of true womanhood. As mentioned, this ideology was specifically designed to govern the behavior of white women; however, it was the standard to which many black women aspired and by which they were judged by many black men. Women who deviated from this standard were often considered to be "unnatural" women: "The 'unnatural woman' is the black woman preacher, litigator, speaker in the public domain who challenges the tenets of 'true (natural) womanhood.'"[7] Zilpha Elaw's and Jarena Lee's "breaking up housekeeping" and leaving their children with relatives and friends so that they could pursue their callings to preach is an example of the challenge they posed to prevailing gender conventions.[8] Thus, their (per)formances as preachers challenge the role they are expected to perform as "good" mothers who remain at home to care for their children.

Nineteenth-century ideologies of the subject firmly shackled the black woman's voice to the constraints of her body. Sidonie Smith describes two interdependent histories of subjectivity that were prevalent during the nineteenth century—those of universal subjectivity and embodied subjectivity. Universal subjectivity grew out of Enlightenment notions of the self as unitary, rational, and transcendent. This universal self, as disembodied consciousness, could exist only if it rejected the chaotic passions associated with the body. As privileged originator of knowledge, meaning, and truth, the Enlightenment self maintained its universality (and exclusivity) by establishing normative standards of gender (male), race (white), class (middle), and sexuality (heterosexual). Anyone not meeting these standards was marginalized and perceived as essentially body. Embodied subjectivity therefore makes the existence of universal subjectivity possible. Unlike the universal/male subject, a different type of selfhood is attributed to women—an essential selfhood that is burdened by the body. Woman's destiny is determined by her biology, and she must gain her fulfillment by living for and through others in the assigned social roles of wife, mother, daughter, and sister. She may escape negative associations with the body to the extent that she represses sexual desire and individual identity, subjects herself to man's authority, and serves others selflessly. Because she cannot determine her own destiny, she cannot truly exercise agency.

The discourse of the embodied woman specifically creates the subjectivity of bourgeois white women because just as the universal subject defines himself against those who are not white, male, middle-class, and heterosexual, so the embodied subject creates her identity by excluding women who are not white, middle-class, and heterosexual. Working-class women, lesbians, and women of color are perceived as even more embodied and, as such, possess no possibilities of escaping the stigma of the body, even through repressive and selfless behavior.[9]

According to these ideologies, the radical spiritual mothers, as historical subjects who were black, female, and working-class, would have been considered hyperembodied, but these evangelists, as literary subjects, used their embodied status to their advantage to help textually construct their authority as women of God. When, for example, they depict themselves as falling ill as a sign of God's displeasure and then as being providentially restored to health to signify a renewed relationship with Him, or when they represent themselves as wearing their bodies out in the service of God, the radical spiritual mothers make some of their strongest arguments for their spiritual authority. In other words, some of their most eloquent arguments for their spiritual power are made as they embody their texts in strategic ways.

As itinerant preachers, the radical spiritual mothers frequently depicted their bodies in motion; indeed, itinerancy played a key role in the development of their identities as evangelists. This identity development was a gradual process, taking place within the many contexts in which these writers found themselves on their travels. The concept of "migratory subjectivity" that Carole Boyce Davies presents in *Black Women, Writing and Identity* is a useful model for understanding how this process worked. Davies argues for a more complex understanding of black women's experience and writing, one that recognizes the various locations that inform the construction of subjectivity and the production of writing: "If we see Black women's subjectivity as a migratory subjectivity existing in multiple locations, then we can see how their work, their presences traverse all of the geographical/national boundaries instituted to keep our dislocations in place. This ability to locate in a variety of geographical and literary constituencies is peculiar to the migration that is fundamental to African experience as it is specific to human experience as a whole."[10] Though migration is not an experience unique to black people, as Davies indicates above when she characterizes it as a "human experience," migration has certainly played a significant historical role in shaping the identities and consciousness of blacks, as Davies suggests above when she refers to the "migration that is fundamental to African experience."[11] For example, the forced migrations of the Atlantic slave trade during the African diaspora and the Great Migration of African Americans from the South to northern cities during the early twentieth century as they sought greater economic opportunities and relief from racial oppression are two events that have had lasting psychological and spiritual impact upon African Americans. These journeys, driven mainly by economic and social imperatives, were part of the collective history of the radical spiritual mothers, and they add nuance to the spiritual imperatives driving these religious women's quests to do God's work.

Rejecting the notion that black women's experience and writing can be reduced to any particular geographical location, Davies asserts that black female subjectivity is renegotiated as movement takes place among the contexts of these various sites. This process of renegotiation captures the dynamics of the subjectivity of radical spiritual mothers. As these authors traveled throughout the United States and the world to minister to their spiritual families, they frequently encountered people and circumstances that disrupted the identities they had constructed for themselves, forcing them to reevaluate their assumptions about who they were. Zilpha Elaw's sojourns in the slave states exemplify such disruptions of identity. Her understanding of herself as an empowered agent of God is assailed by the degrading perceptions of whites who encounter her. She survives these "identity crises" by reasserting the subjectivity she has constructed for herself against the object status that others project upon her.

In further elucidating the concept of migratory subjectivity as it applies to black women and their writing, Davies suggests a purposefulness to the act of migrating as well as a resistance to physical, ideological, and discursive confinement. She also suggests the migratory subject possesses dynamic and improvisational qualities.[12] It could be argued, however, that these are qualities that have been exhibited not only by black women, but also by people from diverse races, ethnicities, nationalities, genders, and sexual orientations. In spite of this, the concept of migratory subjectivity is nevertheless useful for understanding how the radical spiritual mothers, as working-class black women, constructed themselves as historical and literary subjects.

In formulating her ideas about black female subjectivity, Davies draws upon the discourse of borderlands delineated in the work of Gloria Anzaldúa,[13] explaining that the Chicana feminist "talks about border spaces as locations or sites of contest, of flux, of change. The new mestiza consciousness is one of 'crossing over,' 'perpetual transition,' plural personality which resists unitary paradigms and dualistic thinking (pp. 77–91). Thus, borders are those places where different cultures, identities, sexualities, classes, geographies, races, genders and so on collide or interchange."[14] Throughout their travels, the spiritual writers found themselves crossing a variety of borders, both internal and external. These women were divinely authorized to traverse racial, gender, class, and ideological boundaries. Moreover, through divine empowerment, they were able to cross psychological boundaries that defined them as powerless, as nonpersons, into a new consciousness that enabled them to regard themselves as valuable human beings with an important purpose. By boldly crossing a myriad of borders, they double-crossed those who negatively defined them.

Davies's approach is one of reconnection. She is concerned with exposing the false separations that have been imposed upon black women located in different geographical locations, resulting in the marginalization of both their experiences and their texts. She seeks to redefine identity away from marginality and exclusion by "re-connect[ing] and re-member[ing]" and "bring[ing] together black women dis-located by space and time."[15] The kinds of textual representations that the authors construct in their narratives of their complex relationships with enslaved and free, middle-class and poor black women speak to the implicit project of re-connecting, of re-membering communities of women separated by time and space. Not only are radical spiritual mothers concerned with making connections with other black women, but they also welcome opportunities to form unions with women and men of other racial groups who share their visions of a world transformed through spiritual enlightenment. The texts themselves participate in the practice of forging connections, of building community through the action they invite their readers to take. Joycelyn Moody reminds us that "through the participatory act of reading, contemporary readers become part of the protagonist's community, bound by each text to a collective duty to nurture and preserve the integrity of the black American woman."[16]

Finding supportive communities was all the more crucial given that the radical spiritual mothers were interstitial subjects. Here, I draw upon William Andrews's sense of the term "interstitial" as he discusses African American autobiographies written from 1850 to 1865. He uses the term "interstitial autobiographers" to describe those who "depict themselves as 'betwixt and between' standard identifying classifications and norms, whether they are recalling their situations in the South or the North. In the cracks and crevices of the social hierarchy, the interstitial figure creates his own fluid status and unlikely freedom."[17] Not only were the radical spiritual mothers positioned "'betwixt and between' standard identifying classifications and norms" as women pursuing the unconventional role of itinerant preacher; they were also located between the temporal and spiritual worlds as they claimed divine power in their lives and ministries. This slippery and confounding in-betweenness could be both liberating and isolating. For example, when Zilpha Elaw informs her church class of her calling, she is ridiculed and shunned: "[A]fter I commenced the work of the ministry, I was a person of no account, and ever had been; and I became so unpopular, that all our coloured class abandoned me excepting three. Like Joseph, I was hated for my dreams; and like Paul, none stood with me" (Elaw 83). The lives of the radical spiritual mothers were not easy, but their commitment to God and His ministry helped sustain them through difficult times; Elaw thus continues: "This treatment, however painful, by no means damped my ardour in the work to which I had been called. I still continued my Master's work, and great crowds assembled every Lord's day to hear me" (Elaw 83).

In chapter 1, I discussed the spiritual maternity of antebellum Catholic nuns. The kind of spiritual maternity exemplified by the nuns originated in their symbolic matrimonial relationship with Christ and in the teaching and caretaking roles these women took on in the larger community. Though they renounced biological motherhood, they acquired a kind of extended family made up of the people whom they served as teachers and caretakers. In the case of the spiritual autobiographers, however, I argue that radical spiritual motherhood originated in the experience of sanctification. Although the writers did not declare themselves to be brides of Christ, through sanctification they did dedicate themselves completely to God. In doing so, they, like the nuns, committed themselves to engaging in a life of service to the larger community. They, too, acquired extended spiritual families. Zilpha Elaw, for example, calls the five-year period following her sanctification at a camp meeting her "family or household ministry" (Elaw 71), which she describes as follows:

> [I]t was revealed to me by the Holy Spirit, that like another Phoebe, or the matrons of the apostolic societies, I must employ myself in visiting families, and in speaking personally to the members thereof, of the salvation and eternal interests of their souls, visit the sick, and attend upon other of the errands and services of the Lord; which I afterwards cheerfully did, not confining my visits to the poor only, but extending them to the rich also, and even to those who sit in high places in the state; and the Lord was with me in the work to own and bless my labours. (Elaw 67)

In this passage, not only does Elaw link herself with an ancient tradition of spiritual mothers (that is, Phoebe and the apostolic-era matrons), but she also reveals the power of the radical spiritual mother to minister to the needs of people from all walks of life.

These Protestant spiritual writers, unlike the Catholic nuns, have no orders of chaste holy women to guide their behavior. The only vows they take are their individual pledges to God to serve Him faithfully, acting according to the dictates of their own inner voices. Theirs is a self-styled identity that draws upon and validates their unique experiences as black women called to do God's work. This is one sense in which the kind of spiritual motherhood they practice is "radical." But more important is the bold approach they take to critiquing the sexism exhibited by male church authorities, which the nuns fail to do.

Jarena Lee, for example, delivers a cogent critique of this sexism after she is denied a license to preach by the AME church leader, Richard Allen:

> O how careful ought we to be, lest through our by-laws of church govern-ment and discipline, we bring into disrepute even the word of life. For as unseemly as it may appear now-a-days for a woman to preach, it should be remembered that nothing is impossible with God. And why should it be thought impossible, heterodox, or improper, for a woman to preach? seeing the Saviour died for the woman as well as the man.
>
> If a man may preach, because the Saviour died for him, why not the woman? seeing he died for her also. Is he not a whole Saviour, instead of a half one? as those who hold it wrong for a woman to preach, would seem to make it appear. (Lee 36)

Lee illuminates the fallacy of man-made church laws in their ability to paradox-ically render ineffectual the very power of God to be inclusive and empowering to all people, male and female.

Lee's assertion that Christ died for women as well as for men implicitly reflects liberation theologies' belief in Christ as the liberator of all oppressed groups. She understands the importance of His redemptive role to the lives of poor black women like herself and predicates her right to preach upon this re-demption. Lee goes on to assert the primacy of women's preaching by arguing that the very first preacher was in fact Mary Magdalene, who announced the resurrection of Jesus to his disciples (see John 20:11–18). She places a woman at the center of the Christian tradition by identifying the resurrection as the climax of Christianity. For those who argue that Mary was not a true preacher, she deconstructs the ideology that defines the meaning of preaching:

> But some will say, that Mary did not expound the Scripture, therefore, she did not preach, in the proper sense of the term. To this I reply, it may be that the term *preach,* in those primitive times, did not mean exactly what it is now *made* to mean; perhaps it was a great deal more simple then, than it is now:—if it were not, the unlearned fishermen could not have preached the gospel at all, as they had no learning. (Lee 36–37)

In speaking of the way in which preaching has been made to take on a particular meaning, Lee shows an awareness of the power that those in positions of domination have to define not only words and concepts but reality. Particularly problematic for Lee and other women preachers was the controversial movement led by Daniel Alexander Payne, beginning in 1842, to raise the educational standards of African Methodist Episcopal ministers. Payne, a longtime advocate for education who later became bishop in 1852, opposed the charismatic preaching of unlearned ministers. This stance put him at odds with many church members, but it was particularly troublesome for Lee and other female preachers who asserted the legitimacy of their ministries, which were based on the direct inspiration of God, rather than on any kind of formal training.[18]

The consciousness that informed the behavior of the radical spiritual mothers was cultivated, I believe, amid the material circumstances of their lives. Their awareness of the ways in which racism, sexism, and classism converged to undermine their efforts to create for themselves and their families stable and fulfilling lives guided their use of religion as a powerful tool with which to critique oppression stemming from the church, marriage, domestic ideology, and other social institutions.

Low-paying and unstable employment for black men made it necessary for most married women to work outside the home to supplement the family income. While most women worked during the day as domestics in the homes of white families, many others lived at the residences of their employers, sometimes keeping their children with them. To further diminish the family's financial burden, it was also common for children to be bound out as indentured servants.[19] Jarena Lee, for example, was only seven years old when she moved sixty miles from her parents in order to become a servant maid. Twelve-year-old Zilpha Elaw was placed in service by her father after her mother died. Julia Foote was a servant girl as well. And according to Nancy Hardesty and Adrienne Israel, Amanda Smith lived apart from her second husband for much of their marriage for economic reasons, with Smith living and working in Greenwich Village while her husband lived with his employer in Brooklyn.[20] Therefore, it was not uncommon for family members to be separated by economic necessity. The result was a kind of elasticity of the domestic sphere that stretched the definition of the normative nuclear family structure. I suggest that when some of the spiritual autobiographers left their children in the care of relatives or friends so they could more freely pursue their itinerant preaching careers, they were in fact drawing upon this pattern of domestic elasticity. These writers used what was initially a practice resorted to out of economic need to transgress the rigid gender boundary that cut women off from public ministry.

Black women's work outside the home—or more accurately, outside their own homes and in the homes of others—created for them a more fluid relationship between the public and private spheres that disrupted the demands of the dominant domestic ideology that sought to confine women to their own homes to care for their own children and husbands. I use the term "serial domesticity" to describe black women's movement between their homes and those of their employers to suggest that the spiritual autobiographers made use of this familiar pattern when embarking upon their itinerant preaching missions. In traveling from house to house or church to church (houses of God), they also engaged in the practice of serial domesticity. The difference between these women and other free black women is that the former were not driven by economic necessity but were ministering to the spiritual needs of their extended spiritual families.

Because of the very limited educational opportunities available to blacks during the nineteenth century, none of the authors received extensive schooling. Remarkably, Foote had only two months of formal education; Lee and Smith had only three months. Jackson was not educated but claimed she attained literacy as a divine gift at a late age. All of the authors, nevertheless, were able to write their own narratives.[21] Despite this lack of formal education, each writer receives her education as a spiritual leader, not formally through theological training, but through her own diligent efforts to educate herself and through the direct instruction of an indwelling spirit. In a sense, the radical spiritual mother may be regarded as a kind of spiritual organic intellectual who arises from her community without formal training, but who nonetheless makes important contributions through her leadership and organizational activities.[22] The sophistication with which Lee expounds the scriptures on the issue of preaching reveals her intellectual engagement with theology. Yet she is very much an activist intellectual, thoroughly engaged with the social and political concerns of the communities she serves.

What are some of the particulars of the material circumstances of these women's lives that came to inform their thoughts and actions as radical spiritual mothers? As working-class black women, economic insecurity and poverty were a fact of life for most of them. Amanda Smith, for example, often notes her status as a poor washerwoman who must struggle to support herself and her children, all of whom die except for a daughter. She seems to have received only limited financial support from her husbands during two unhappy marriages. On one occasion, while a widow from her second marriage, Smith faced a particularly trying situation when her money had dwindled to thirteen cents, and she was forced to make some difficult choices:

> My little girl was at school, and when she came home the first thing she would say was, "O, Ma, I am so hungry; have you got any bread?" So I had done without any dinner, and saved the piece of bread I had, so that when my child would ask me for a piece of bread I might have it to give her. I thought I couldn't stand it, to have her ask for bread and have none to give her; so, though I was very hungry, I did without. (Smith 150)

These kinds of hardships invested the author with a sensitivity to human suffering that translated into an ability to minister with compassion in her role as a spiritual leader. Moreover, the consciousness that arises from her own class status enables her to assess with clarity the dynamics of class in a variety of contexts, as when she later becomes involved in missionary work in West Africa:

> I do not know if the Colonization Society thinks so or not; but most of the white people think, and some colored people, too, I am afraid, especially those who go as emigrants, that all the Americo-Liberians are on perfect equality with each other in all their social relations; and that, because they are a colored republic, and an independent colored government, that they are all as one. But they never made a greater mistake; for in that republic there is grade and caste among them almost equal to that that is found among the upper-ten colored folks in America. So that the ignorant emigrant does not strike the highest and best grade of society when he first gets there. (Smith 463)

The ability to assess and critique power dynamics, whether in relation to class, race, gender, or the complex interworkings of all three, was crucial for the radical spiritual mother, not only for her own self-preservation and development but also to her process of envisioning empowering alternative models of human interaction, in opposition to the oppressive modes that she lived with on a daily basis.

The economic uncertainties with which these women lived did not disappear once they adopted the identity of radical spiritual mother, but rather these were incorporated into a new understanding of their relationship to divine power. As itinerant spiritual leaders obliged to go wherever and whenever the divine voice within led them, they were dependent upon the goodwill of those whom they served to provide shelter, food, and if necessary, money. The fulfillment of their material needs was thus attributed to providential care, an understanding that bestowed on them a degree of psychological assurance that they lacked prior to becoming radical spiritual mothers. Such assurance should not be underestimated, given the strains with which most black women labored to provide for themselves and their families. Smith cites many incidents in which she attributes material sustenance to God:

> After I got to England, the first money that was given me, about three days after, was five pound sterling and something over, equal to about twenty-five dollars. Some ladies at Keswick, said to Mrs. Johnson, "Who supports Mrs. Smith?" Of course they didn't tell me this, but they asked Mrs. Johnson all about it. She told them that I just trusted the Lord to supply all my needs, and so it went around quietly.
>
> Mrs. J. came to me one morning and said to me, "Amanda, it is wonderful how the Lord is putting it into the hearts of the people to help you financially. Several have come to me and put in my hand money for you."
>
> I thanked her very much. (Smith 262)

Zilpha Elaw, who must also support a daughter on her own after her husband dies, arrives at a similar understanding of God's providential care as she begins her life as an itinerant preacher. Though she starts by preaching in her hometown of Burlington, New Jersey, she is reluctant to travel more broadly until she has earned the means to pay her debts. However, it is only through itinerancy that Elaw regains financial stability: "It never occurred to me that I should receive a single penny in this work; but when I was willing, I ought to say—made willing to go just as I was, as the apostles of old, without purse or scrip, then the Lord made my way straight before me, and dealt bountifully with me. . . . In the first three weeks I obtained every particle that I wanted, and abundance of silver to proceed on my journey with" (Elaw 89).

Rebecca Jackson enjoyed greater economic stability than the rest of the spiritual writers; she lived with her husband in her brother's home with his family, and it is likely that she managed her own finances as a seamstress. But the rising racial tensions and violence occurring in Philadelphia from her childhood through the time of her conversion in 1830 was a material reality that profoundly impacted her consciousness, as is revealed in many of her dreams.[23] In constructing her identity as a radical spiritual mother, it is imperative for Jackson to learn to "act in ways that will earn and invite divine protection from the constant, debilitating threat of sudden violence, both natural and human."[24] One of the most frightening threats of violence comes from her own husband when she declares that she will no longer continue sexual relations with him after she comes to a new understanding of the sinfulness of sexuality through her experience of sanctification. Through the "gift of foresight" (Jackson 145), which she earns though strict obedience to her divine inner voice, she is able to elude his attempts on her life.

The material conditions of the radical spiritual mothers' lives informed their racial consciousness as black women, which aligned them with the antebellum black nuns. Recognizing the tremendous needs of enslaved and free blacks, the Oblate Sisters of Providence and the Sisters of the Holy Family both specifically focused their efforts on providing for their educational and social welfare. Moreover, the Oblate Sisters expressed their racial consciousness by adopting St. Benedict the Moor as one of the community's secondary patron saints. Cyprian Davis explains, "Benedict, who died in 1589, had been canonized in 1807 as a statement of opposition to the slave trade."[25] Further, the sisterhood was enrolled in the Association of the Holy Slavery of the Mother of God, with each nun receiving a small chain to symbolize this pious act. Davis suggests that this may symbolically link the nuns' African ancestry and slavery with a symbol for slavery, the chain.[26]

Though the radical spiritual mothers were concerned about the spiritual well-being of all people, they seemed to evince a particular social consciousness for African Americans that encompassed both their spiritual and material needs. For example, according to Hardesty and Israel, Amanda Smith founded an orphanage in 1899 for black girls in Harvey, Illinois, that came to be known as the Amanda Smith Industrial School for Girls.[27] Moreover, "[i]t was the only Protestant institution for African American children in Illinois at the time."[28] The facility burned down in 1918, however, just three years after Smith died.[29] Similarly, prior to embarking upon her itinerant preaching career, Zilpha Elaw had opened a school for black children who were not allowed to attend white schools (Elaw 85).

Although the radical spiritual mothers consciously resisted racial stereotypes, they at times reflect the extreme difficulty of completely liberating themselves from particular cultural symbols, such as the equation of whiteness with goodness and blackness with evil. Julia Foote, for instance, joyfully declares: "Jesus' blood will wash away all your sin and make you whiter than snow" (Foote 189). The possession of a complex double-consciousness may help to explain how these evangelists, as black women, accept the negative values attached to blackness. In *The Souls of Black Folk*, the scholar, civil rights leader, novelist, and essayist W. E. B. Du Bois (1868–1963) coins the term "double-consciousness" to refer to African Americans' consciousness of possessing a dual identity that is both African and American and often psychically difficult to reconcile. It is also an awareness that one is constantly judging oneself by the standards of the dominant culture, which, as Du Bois notes, can result in inner conflict and self-alienation: "It is a peculiar sensation, this double-consciousness, this sense of always looking at one's self through the eyes of others, of measuring one's soul by the tape of a world that looks on in amused contempt and pity. One ever feels his two-ness,—an American, a Negro; two souls, two thoughts, two unreconciled strivings; two warring ideals in one dark body, whose dogged strength alone keeps it from being torn asunder."[30]

Related to double-consciousness is the notion of "masking," in which the radical spiritual mothers sometimes engage as a self-protective device in the presence of those possessing greater power, especially whites, to preserve their own sense of power. Regarding the role that masking has historically played in the lives of African Americans, Pearlie Peters explains: "A deceptive role-playing and a shrewd survival strategy, masking has historically been used by blacks in the presence of whites to maintain some semblance of empowerment in a racially prejudiced society. Masking . . . hides the true feelings, frustrations, cleverness, and sophisticated ambiguities of identity held by the mask wearers when they are in racial conflict or competition."[31]

Related to the concept of masking is the "culture of dissemblance," in which the radical spiritual mothers and enslaved women alike engaged to preserve a sense of self-worth. These women may thus be placed within a tradition of nineteenth-century black women who constructed positive alternative subjectivities to counter the deeply entrenched negative images imposed upon them. Darlene Clark Hine describes this impulse among black women: "[W]hat I propose is that in the face of the pervasive stereotypes and negative estimations of the sexuality of black women, it was imperative that they collectively create alternative self-images and shield from scrutiny these private empowering definitions of self."[32] Hine asserts that the construction of these positive identities was part of a culture of dissemblance that black women created in the face of severe racial and sexual oppression. She defines dissemblance as "the behavior and attitudes of black women that created the appearance of openness and disclosure but actually shielded the truth of their inner lives and selves from their oppressors."[33] The prevalence of the rape of black women and the threat of rape lay at the root of the creation of this culture.

The most institutionalized form of the culture of dissemblance occurred with the founding of the National Association of Colored Women (NACW). With a membership of fifty thousand by 1914, the NACW became the largest protest organization in African American history, even surpassing the enrollment of the National Association for the Advancement of Colored People (NAACP) and the National Urban League. The NACW's main objects of attack were the negative stereotypes and derogatory images of black women's sexuality. To combat these images, many NACW members felt it necessary to deemphasize, and even deny, sexual expression.[34] As growing numbers of black women became more economically secure and better educated, they had greater access to birth-control information. Hine suggests that many urban middle-class aspirants chose to limit their reproduction in response to the social stigma attached to having many children. The period between 1915 and 1945, when hundreds of thousands of black women migrated out of the South, may have been the first time that large numbers of black women had the choice not to bear children.[35]

Hine explains that through dissemblance, black women cultivated secret personae that allowed them to function within a hostile racist, sexist, and classist culture. Adopting these undisclosed selves enabled them to effectively perform domestic work in white households, to persevere through domestic violence directed toward them by under- or unemployed spouses, to bear and raise children, to found institutions, to support churches, and to participate in social service activities.[36] The radical spiritual mothers and enslaved women, as early creators of the culture of dissemblance and as foremothers of the NACW members, developed positive, empowered personae in and through their texts as well as in their daily lives. Representing their resistance to sexual oppression in their narratives was part of the strategy that both enslaved women and the radical spiritual mothers used to construct empowered alternative subjectivities. It was important for both groups to depict themselves as agents who successfully struggled to control their own bodies and their own destinies. Frances Smith Foster points out the ways in which male and female emancipatory narrators differ in their portrayals of women in slavery. Unlike male writers, who usually represent women as helpless victims of physical and sexual violence, female narrators emphasize their ability to endure and persevere in the face of intense oppression. Moreover, women do not allow the violence committed against them to define their lives, but rather they celebrate the ways in which they engage in struggles against oppression and the manner in which they ultimately achieve their freedom.[37]

One might question the authenticity of the radical spiritual mothers' texts if they in fact engaged in the culture of dissemblance in their lives and in their narratives. But the culture of dissemblance was about creating and protecting the truth about who black women were and fending off the racist and sexist lies that were perpetuated about them. Through assertive acts of self-definition, black women preserved the truth about themselves: that they are strong, valuable, capable human beings. So ironically, black women—including the radical spiritual mothers—used dissemblance to foster their authenticity.

In taking on the identity of radical spiritual mother, the spiritual autobiographers reconceptualized power and their relationship to it. One important strategy for accomplishing this, which linked them to their old identities as women defined by more traditional gender roles, was to draw upon familiar domestic images to articulate a growing sense of their legitimacy as instruments chosen to do God's work. Initially, they seemed to espouse a theory of power similar to that held by writers of sentimental fiction and by members of various religious groups, such as the New York City Tract Society, which were involved in a widespread evangelical movement to reform the nation's morals. This theory of power asserted that "all true action is not material, but spiritual; that one obtains spiritual power through prayer; and that those who know how, in the privacy of their closets, to struggle for possession of their souls will one day possess the world through the power given to them by God."[38] And retire to their "closets" is exactly what these authors did. For Jackson, her special place for prayer was the garret of her home. Jarena Lee spoke of a secret place to which she withdrew in times of crisis. And Amanda Smith frequently retreated to her room for communion with God. All of the writers invested the home with a special significance as a sacred space in which the terrestrial and the celestial converged. Smith, for example, displays this attitude of reverence for the home and for the traditional work that she performed within it in the following passage:

[T]hough your hands are employed in doing your daily business, it is no bar to the soul's communion with Jesus. Many times over my wash-tub and ironing table, and while making my bed and sweeping my house and washing my dishes I have had some of the richest blessings. Oh, how glad I am to know this, and how many mothers' hearts I have cheered when I told them that the blessing of sanctification did not mean isolation from all the natural and legitimate duties of life, as some seem to think. (Smith 103)

Not only does Smith assert the compatibility of motherhood and spirituality, but she marks the domestic sphere as a privileged space in which women's work has the potential to become a ritual of communion with the divine. She invites mothers to explore the links between the domestic and the divine and to experience the inner strength and solace that these connections accord.

Coming to Terms with Power and Publicity via Domesticity: The Dreams of Rebecca Jackson

Though the spiritual autobiographers valued the power that could be garnered through communion with God in the home, they nevertheless differed from the sentimental writers and the religious groups in a fundamental way in theorizing power. Unlike the heroines of sentimental fiction who could not venture beyond the private spaces of the home, these writers all received divine authorization to intervene in the public sphere to preach the gospel. Accepting this knowledge was not always easy, however. Living in a culture in which women were generally barred from public participation and in which the words and presence of black women were not valued, the writers found this God-ordained power and publicity difficult to reconcile. I have said that one important strategy that the radical spiritual mothers used to articulate a growing sense of their legitimacy as instruments chosen to do God's work was to draw upon familiar domestic images, which linked them to their old identities as women defined by more traditional gender roles; in particular, they drew upon domesticity to help them come to terms with the power and publicity associated with their new roles as itinerant preachers. All of the radical spiritual mothers do this.[39] However, I think that Jackson gives a particularly unique perspective on this process that we do not get nearly as extensively from the other authors—namely the perspective offered by her dreams; by exploring her dreams, we get a glimpse into Jackson's rich inner life and the way that she draws upon this life to help her negotiate important changes in her external life.

Jackson seems to use her dream life to come to terms with her new role as a radical spiritual mother and the personal power and mobility that accompany this identity. In particular, dreams with domestic imagery are central to the process of reformulating her relationship to power and publicity. By focusing on two dreams that draw upon domestic imagery, I will show how they are central to this process. These dreams are "Dream of the Cakes" and an untitled dream that I call "Housekeeping in Philadelphia."

In recounting "Dream of the Cakes," which Jackson has three months after experiencing sanctification at a prayer meeting, she tells of inviting a woman from her Covenant group to join her as she makes some griddle cakes. She describes in detail the location and appearance of her cooking facilities as well as the process involved in preparing the cakes:

> I sat down on a low stool before the griddle. It laid on two bricks, the fire under it. It stood in the northeast corner of the room on the floor. The fireplace was on the west side of the room. However, I greased the griddle, put on a little batter, about a tablespoonful. It run all over the griddle, a beautiful brown on both sides, though I did not turn it. And in a moment the people ate it all up—they were all white. (Jackson 99)

Each time she places a tiny bit of batter on the griddle, it expands greatly and is quickly devoured by a crowd of white people that appears suddenly out of nowhere. As each of three cakes is made, the crowd increases until a multitude is present. The positioning of the griddle on the floor seems to mirror the low status her work within the home is accorded. Later, when she leaves her husband to pursue an itinerant preaching career, she gives some indication of the frustration she has felt in trying to be a good wife: "I was commanded [by God] to tell Samuel I have served him many years, and had tried to please him, but I could not" (Jackson 147). Her own low position on the stool seems to reflect her deteriorating position within the family after she becomes convinced that God has chosen her for special work. Her ascetic rituals, her vivid dreams and visions, and her refusal to bend to the authority of her husband and brother have begun to alienate her from her family. Her husband and brother do not understand her behavior and even question her sanity: "'I [her husband, Samuel] never seen such a woman. The people will think she has killed somebody.[40] I think she is agoing crazy.' 'I [her brother, Joseph] have been afraid of that some time, Brother Samuel'" (Jackson 87).

The griddle's distance from the fireplace seems to pose a problem for Jackson initially, as is suggested by her use of the word "However." Perhaps she usually prepares griddle cakes at the fireplace. If this is the case, then it would

seem that her separation from this main source of heat could present an obstacle to her cooking, just as her growing alienation from family, church, and
community (the main sources of support and identity) could cause a personal
crisis. To become detached from all that is familiar and from all that has given
her life meaning is a frightening situation to face. However, with God's help,
she is able to do so, just as she is able to continue making the cakes despite the
griddle's distance from the fireplace. The cakes' turning "a beautiful brown on
all sides" without her having to turn them suggests the intervention of a supernatural force to aid her cooking. Similarly, with divine intervention in her life,
nothing seems impossible to her.

In continuing the description of the dream, Jackson speaks of how she and
the woman looking on sample the cakes:

> They ate it all, except a little piece about one inch in length, a half an inch in
> width. This little piece lay before my right foot in the ashes. It was all I seen.
> I picked it up and said, "Let us taste it. They ate it so good." I broke it and
> put the piece in my mouth. It was the sweetest I ever tasted. I gave her the
> other, said, "Here, taste. No wonder they ate it up!" (Jackson 99)

Though Jackson knows that the cakes must be good since the people eat them
so quickly, she is not fully aware of the impact of her cooking until she actually tastes for herself. This suggests the importance of self-awareness, of being
in tune with her inner voice, to her future effectiveness as a spiritual leader. So
crucial is this need to obey the divine voice within that she makes a covenant
with God in 1831 to heed its guidance in all that she does: "I will obey Thee in
all things, in all places, and under all conditions" (Jackson 85).

"Dream of the Cakes" represents a symbolic transformation of the domestic
task of cooking into the power to provide religious truths to a multitude seeking spiritual sustenance. In this regard, Jackson takes on the role of a spiritual
mother who provides for the spiritual health of her "children." Not only does
she use a domestic task to prefigure future power and publicity, but she also
revises and feminizes the powerful biblical image of Christ feeding the multitude, thus effectively casting herself in the role of Messiah. As God performs
a miracle through His son by multiplying loaves and fishes, so He effects a
miracle through His daughter by multiplying cake batter.[41]

Besides the parallel with Christ's feeding of the multitude, one can also
detect echoes of the Genesis story of Eve's temptation to eat of the tree of the
knowledge of good and evil. When Eve, tempted by the serpent, sees that

the fruit of the tree is good, she eats of it and then gives some to Adam. Similarly, after tasting the alluring griddle cakes herself, Jackson gives some to the woman who accompanies her. Just as Eve's eyes are opened to a godlike consciousness of good and evil, Jackson's eyes have also been opened. She too realizes that she possesses godly insight that will set her apart from all who have known her. Moreover, just as Eve is driven from the Garden of Eden because of her transgression against God, Jackson too must leave her home for daring to transgress the code of wifely submission set for her by nineteenth-century domestic ideology.[42]

Jackson tells of actually meeting the people she sees in her dream when she travels to Marcus Hook, Pennsylvania, in 1833 to begin her itinerant preaching career: "So I went, and when I got there the house was full, and all around the door, and they were nearly all white people. . . . And while I was speaking, I saw that this was the people that ate off of the griddle and out of the ashes in 1831" (Jackson 126–27). Offering further insights into this dream, Jackson states, "[The dream of the cakes was unfolded to me the first time I went to Marcus Hook—the people who ate my first, second, and third cakes attended my first, second, and third meetings there. The cakes that I baked represented the testimony of truth that those people received from me]" (Jackson 130).[43]

It is significant that the people Jackson feeds in the dream and leads in her waking life are white. Her emphasis on their racial identity may be an effort to trace a visual and discursive trajectory of her influence among whites, which culminated in her residence and leadership in the white Shaker commune at Watervliet, New York. The Shakers are the group to which she is divinely led because only they share her controversial religious ideals. For a woman whose views were deeply contested within her own black community, from which she became alienated early in her career, it would seem plausible for her to legitimate her close association with whites through dream representations.[44]

"Dream of the Cakes" functions as a kind of psychological transitional space that allows Jackson the opportunity to assert her growing spiritual power while at the same time preserving an image of herself as a dutiful housekeeper. I call it a transitional space because she has not yet dissolved her marriage and struck out on her own. The dream thus gives her a chance to visually "try on" power before letting go of the traditional image of herself, just as Lee tries on the role of preacher within a domestic space before taking on the role of a public preacher. At the same time, the domesticity of the dream gives spiritual power a kind of immediacy and concreteness that Jackson can easily grasp.

"Housekeeping in Philadelphia" is a dream that Jackson has much later in her career, in 1850, after she has joined the predominantly white Shaker commune in Watervliet, New York. According to Humez, at this point in her life, Jackson has become dissatisfied with the level of commitment that the Shakers have shown in addressing the needs of blacks, and she has also become wary of Paulina Bates, who assumed leadership as eldress of the South Family in Watervliet in 1848. In particular, Bates has refused to grant permission to Jackson to pursue missionary work among blacks in Philadelphia.[45]

Like "Dream of the Cakes," "Housekeeping in Philadelphia" also functions as a psychological transitional space, but in some ways, the stakes are higher at this point in Jackson's career because she is no longer just trying to come to terms with the role of preacher; she is trying to envision herself as the eldress of a predominantly black and female Shaker community that she founded in 1858 in Philadelphia, a role with even greater authority. Early in her career, Jackson faced daunting opposition from family, friends, church members, and church leaders. At this stage in her career, she still faces opposition initially, but this time it comes from Shaker leaders, namely Paulina Bates. Employing the domestic imagery of a mother caring for her children, Jackson uses this dream to envision herself as the "head of household" of the Philadelphia Shaker community and to psychologically prepare herself for this role:

> On the morning of the 15th, I dreamed that I was housekeeping in Philadelphia, and had around me a little family of spiritual children, and among them was Susan Thomas and Rebecca Perot.[46] I was busy at the table, preparing something to eat, and somebody came and told me they wished me to take a young child and care for it until it was four years old, and then somebody else would take it and keep it until it was eight. For its mother was a poor girl.
>
> While they talked, I heard the child crying. And I wanted Susan and Rebecca to hasten and get their work done, and go out and bring the child. I felt ashamed of them, because they did not do their work. At length the child ceased crying, while I was talking to some who wished to hear what I was saying. When I considered how long the child had ceased crying, I started off in a hurry, just as I was, with my hands from the dough, thinking the child had cried itself to death.
>
> I went up 7th Street to Spruce Street and up Spruce to 8th.[47] And on the right hand, going down 8th, stood a box about four feet long, on four legs, and in it was the child. When I went to it, it looked at me and smiled. I took

it up and pressed it to my bosom, and it nestled its little face in my neck. Oh, how I loved it! I said, "Keep it four years! My! I will keep it forever!—It shall be my own child." It was a darling boy, yea, a proper child. I brought it home and took care of it. And oh, how I loved it! So healthy a child in every respect, I have not seen for many a day. (Jackson 218–19)

As the head of the Shaker community in Philadelphia, Jackson was known as "Mother Rebecca" by her followers, and her dream seems to anticipate this maternal role. It is an important role that cannot be delegated to anyone else, as is suggested by Jackson's dismay with Thomas's and Perot's failure to attend to the crying child. The child whom she is charged with caring for ceases to cry at the moment Jackson "was talking to some who wished to hear what [she] was saying," thus suggesting the respect accorded her voice; this voice, a reflection of the authority she will have as a Shaker eldress, is one that people desire to hear. That the baby ceases to cry at the sound of her voice suggests its power to bring solace to those whom she wishes to serve in Philadelphia. Not only might the child represent a "crying need" for outreach among African Americans in Philadelphia, but he may also symbolize Jackson's own need to move beyond the authority of the Watervliet community in order to take on a greater leadership role as eldress of her own community.

The number four and a multiple of four (eight) seem to have significance in this dream. This may be reflective of Shaker theological conceptions of God and Christ. God is believed to be both male and female, as is Christ, thus positing a kind of holy quaternity that is represented in familial terms:

> It is admitted by us all that the attributes ascribed to Deity, some are considered masculine, some feminine; and hence comes the idea of father and mother of the universe. We admit the revelation of these attributes of The *Eternal Unity* by son and daughter; that is to say, *God as Father,* or the *fatherly character of God* was *revealed by the Son, Christ Jesus,* and *God as mother,* or the *motherly character of God* was *revealed by the daughter (Ann Lee).*[48]

Robley Edward Whitson describes this foursome as "the extension of the human analogy for the Godhead to its fullest—male/female, father/mother, son/daughter."[49]

Jackson's waking thoughts following her dream are just as significant as the dream itself, and offer further insights:

I then awoke, and after I awoke I loved the child still. In the evening of
February 15th, as I went to draw down the curtain, I thought I would look
out first and see if there was a new moon. And I saw the new moon over
my right shoulder. Oh, I thought, that was good! Then I recollected it was
the evening of my birthday, and what I had prayed for the day before, and
how the Lord had this morning encouraged me in my dream, and I loved
my darling boy still.[50]

This is indeed a spiritual dream, which greatly encourages me. I am
fifty-five years old today. Nineteen years of this I have spent in the service
of God, in obedience to my call to the Gospel. Thirteen years thereof, *I have
dedicated my soul and body to the Lord in a virgin life,* for which I do this day
lift up my heart, my thought, my mind, my soul, with all my strength, in
thanksgiving to God, who in His unbounded mercy has looked upon me,
the least of all His people, and has shown me such great things, and has
given me such great faith to patiently wait upon the Lord, and to know His
voice from all others. Glory! Glory! Glory! to God the Father, and to Holy
Mother Wisdom, and to my Blessed Savior, and to my Blessed Mother Ann
Lee, who in mercy thus looked upon poor helpless me. (Jackson 219)

The language and tone of the latter half of the second paragraph is uncannily
reminiscent of Mary's Magnificat, the song of praise sung to God by the virgin
Mary for blessing her with the privilege of bearing His Son, Jesus Christ.[51] In
"Dream of the Cakes," Jackson identifies with Jesus Christ; now it seems she
is identifying with His mother. Mary bore a child who was immaculately conceived. Likewise, the idea of starting a Shaker community in Philadelphia is
an immaculate conception (with "conception" in this case meaning an idea), as
Jackson credits God with implanting this idea in her mind, through her divine
inner voice: "After I was gathered home to Zion [Watervliet], I expected to
stay forever. But before many days, it was made known to me that I had yet a
greater work to do in the world, and I must return to the world" (Jackson 249).
In other words, the Philadelphia community is God's and Jackson's "brain-
child." Jackson's emphasis on her faithful living of a "virgin life" through the
practice of celibacy strengthens the biblical parallel. And the gender of the baby
in the dream mirrors that of Christ. Moreover, the baby's appearance in a box
is reminiscent of the manger in which Christ was born.[52] Jackson ends her waking recollections by praising the "holy quaternity" referred to above.

If Jackson did in fact have Mary's Magnificat in mind as she wrote this journal entry, she made some significant revisions to reflect the realities of her racial identity within nineteenth-century American culture. For example, while Mary self-effacingly refers to "the humble state of his servant,"[53] Jackson describes herself as "the least of all His people." This low social status was certainly true of black women at this time. Moreover, Mary recognizes the elevated status she will enjoy as the mother of Christ, as she declares, "From now on all generations will call me blessed."[54] By contrast, as the mother of God's "brain-child," Jackson will be affirmed in a way that only a black woman could fully appreciate. That is, she will be able to shed the negative maternal label of "mammy" that was prevalently imposed upon black women during the nineteenth century and will become a spiritual mother worthy of reverence in the eyes of many.[55] Thus, this dream is not only empowering; it is ennobling.

That Jackson has this dream on her birthday is significant; like the new baby, her new identity as mother of her own Shaker community is symbolically being born. And she joyously embraces this new identity, just as she lovingly nestles the child in her bosom. Her observation of the new moon over her right shoulder after she awakens also seems to affirm this developing identity; in language that echoes God's affirmation of His new creation in the book of Genesis, Jackson pronounces the goodness of the creation of a new, empowered identity: "Oh, I thought, that was good!"

The Relationship between Biological and Radical Spiritual Motherhood

Though radical spiritual mothers located the source of their spiritual power outside of themselves, in the celestial realm, they in fact participated in a kind of spiritual collaboration with God that foregrounded and legitimized the material and spiritual conditions of their lives as the context in which this power was made manifest. As editors of emancipatory narratives encouraged their subjects to represent themselves in specific ways to further the abolitionist cause, so the Divine Editor, God, inspired these writers to represent their lives in particular ways. Thus, their appropriation of power as economically poor women, and their ability to restructure traditional roles as a result of possessing this power, is represented as implicitly receiving divine authentication.

I have said that radical spiritual motherhood is a transformative identity, one that alters the conventional roles that ordered these women's lives. The process of reconceptualizing power, therefore, involved reaching back and drawing upon significant experiences that shaped their lives prior to sanctification. One such experience was that of biological motherhood. All of the authors had bio-logical mothers, of course. Smith, Elaw, and Lee were biological mothers; Foote and Jackson were not. Although Rebecca Jackson was not a biological mother, she was a surrogate mother, responsible for taking care of her brother's six children. Biological motherhood played a significant role in the development of radical spiritual motherhood through the identity-shaping relationships that the authors (except for Foote) had with their children and with their own moth-ers. Through the experiences of mothering and being mothered, these writers learned a great deal: they gained valuable insights into oppressive power rela-tions and acquired tools for critiquing and transforming these relations; they came to cultivate and value early spiritual gifts; they gained an understanding of the importance of being true to one's voice; and they learned some sobering lessons about the difficulties of privileging spiritual maternity over biological maternity to fulfill their callings as itinerant preachers.

Julia Foote's mother has a significant presence in her text. The maternal model that her mother brings to her daughter's life visibly shapes and strength-ens the author's identity by providing a pattern that Foote sometimes revises and applies to her own life and at other times uses to define herself in opposition to. What she gains from this relationship is an independent spirit that was criti-cal to her ability to resist sexist opposition to her ministry. From the beginning the reader is made aware of the indelible mark that Foote's mother stamped on her memory and her psyche, as she presents in the first paragraph a moving ac-count of a brutal whipping her mother received at the hands of a cruel master while she was enslaved. The woman's offense was refusing to make her body sexually available to her master and reporting his indecent conduct to his wife. Following the whipping, the master washed her back with salt water and left her to wear the same whip-slashed garment for a week, at the end of which time it stuck securely to her back. Her mistress then ripped the garment from the slave woman's back along with her skin, leaving it raw (Foote 166).

This story of maternal suffering passed on to her daughter leaves a sear-ing impression on the author's mind that seems to contribute to an attitude of defiance and independence that was so crucial to fulfilling her future calling to preach the gospel. In what appears to be a deliberate attempt to rewrite the tragic scene in which her mother is whipped and "skinned," Foote narrates an incident in which she herself was whipped as a girl by a woman with whom she was living. The woman wrongfully accused her of stealing some pound cakes and whipped the girl on her back with a rawhide when she refused to confess to taking the cakes. Rather than face another promised whipping the next day for an act she did not commit, Foote carries the rawhide to a woodpile, chops it into pieces, and throws it away (Foote 175–76). In committing this act of defiance as a girl, Foote evinces an early determination to defy unjust authority. She repeats this pattern of defiance throughout the text as she struggles against sexist male church authorities who attempt to prevent her from exercising her gift to preach. Moreover, in writing about the incident as a mature author, Foote demonstrates a desire to appropriate and reformulate her mother's whipping into a context from which she can create meaning for her own experience. The skin that is forcibly removed from her mother's back is figuratively reclaimed by the daughter who envelops herself with a thick skin of resistance that she can draw upon again and again.

Though it is clear that Foote deeply respects her mother and honors the struggles she has had to face throughout her life, it is also apparent that there is an underlying need to challenge and even subvert maternal authority in order to create for herself that identity with which she perceives to be divinely ordained. Foote sometimes represents her mother as an obstacle to this process by showing her to be ignorant of important spiritual matters, a source of inappropriate advice, and even a roadblock to her daughter's spiritual growth. For example, central to attaining this growth was being able to achieve sanctification. When Foote informs her mother that she wants to visit an old couple that has experienced sanctification in order to gain further information about this process, her mother responds, "No, you can't go; you are half crazy now, and these people don't know what they are talking about" (Foote 185). Though Foote is reluctant to disobey her mother, she visits the couple anyway and is eventually sanctified. In this instance and in others, the writer privileges her own comprehension of her spiritual condition and destiny over that of her mother. Thus it is sometimes within the context of these tensions within the mother-daughter relationship that Foote forges her identity and authority as a woman called to do God's work. Though Foote does desire her mother's approval, it is ultimately the approbation of the heavenly Father that preempts that of the earthly mother.

Julia Foote may have figuratively reclaimed her mother's skin, but she rejects the self-effacement and ignorance that the older woman cultivated in slavery. The author must temper the experiences of slavery that her mother has bequeathed to her by transforming demeaning qualities so that they may be productively integrated into her own life. Early in the narrative, Foote recounts an incident in which her mother is humiliated in a segregated church. It was the church's policy for blacks to wait until all whites had been served communion before they could partake of it. Foote's mother approached the communion table, not realizing that two white people had not yet been served. She was abruptly halted by a white woman who asked, "Don't you know better than to go to the table when white folks are there?" Foote then comments: "Ah! she did know better than to do such a thing purposely. This was one of the fruits of slavery" (Foote 167). It is the bitter fruit of humiliation that Foote repeatedly refuses to swallow when dealing with people who attempt to break her spirit. Refusing to be whipped is one example. But she is particularly tenacious in responding to those who try to subdue her spiritual gifts. The most critical example of such an instance is when she is excommunicated from her church for preaching.

Despite the desire of many people to hear Foote preach, her minister, Rev. Jehiel Beman of the African Methodist Episcopal Zion Church of Boston, staunchly opposes her. When church members attempt to circumvent his censure by opening their own homes to her, he threatens them with excommunication. Foote eventually resorts to holding meetings in her own home but is summoned to appear before the minister and a committee for refusing to abide by the church's rules of discipline. When she is notified the following day of her dismissal, she delivers a letter to members of an AME Zion Conference, stating the details of the circumstances surrounding this dismissal. She asks for an impartial hearing but is dismayed when the Conference members react by throwing her letter under the table. Foote, painfully aware of the injustice served her because of her gender, declares: "[T]here was no justice meted out to women in those days. Even ministers of Christ did not feel that women had any rights which they were bound to respect" (Foote 207).[56]

Foote matches the visceral response of her would-be spiritual saboteurs with rational discourse befitting that of a spiritual organic intellectual. Logic and wit are her tools of defense. In the chapter following the narration of her excommunication, she critiques the double standard to which her opponents hold her and presents scriptural justification for a woman's right to preach: "I read that on the day of Pentecost was the Scripture fulfilled as found in Joel ii. 28, 29; and it certainly will not be denied that women as well as men were at that time filled with the Holy Ghost" (Foote 208). She is much more sarcastic in speaking of the precedent that the Apostle Paul set in entreating help for those women who worked with him: "When Paul said, 'Help those women who labor with me in the Gospel,' he certainly meant that they did more than to pour out tea" (Foote 209).

In the process of negotiating an identity in the context of her relationship with her mother, Foote does receive her mother's blessing for her life's work—something that the author seems desperately to need. When she visits her parents in Binghamton, New York, after preaching in various cities in the Northeast, her mother comments, "[W]hen I first heard that you were a preacher, I said that I would rather hear you were dead." But the woman then adds, crying: "My dear daughter, it is all past now. I have heard from those who have attended your meetings what the Lord has done for you, and I am satisfied" (Foote 212). This acknowledgment by the mother of the daughter's most important choice in life can be read as a kind of transition in their relationship, a transition in which daughter now becomes spiritual mother because she has surpassed the elder woman in spiritual wisdom. Further, when the older woman becomes so feeble that she must live with Foote in Cleveland, this completes the role reversal, since she must now take care of the older woman's physical needs as well as those of a spiritual nature.

Amanda Berry Smith offers a much more positive portrayal of her relationship with her mother. Among the things that Miriam Berry bequeaths to her daughter is a courageous spirit, a concern for the oppressed, and a precedent for public speaking. Like Foote's mother, Mrs. Berry had lived through slavery, but rather than exhibiting a desire to transform or reject her mother's experiences, Smith evinces a deep pride in her maternal legacy. One recollection by the author, in particular, is illustrative of the fondness that marked the mother-daughter bond. In this incident, Smith (as a child) and her mother anxiously await the return of Mr. Berry, who is away on an extended visit with his brother: "I would make an excuse to stay with her. Sometimes I would cry and say I was sick. Then she would call me to her and let me lay my head in her lap; and there is no place on earth so sweet to a child as a mother's lap. I can almost feel the tender, warm, downy lap of my mother now as I write, for so it seemed to me" (Smith 25).

To illustrate her mother's courageous spirit, Smith proudly describes an incident in which she thwarts the efforts of some fugitive slave catchers. At the time her family was living near New Market, several of these men burst into their home in pursuit of a runaway slave that the family unknowingly was harboring (the slave pretended to be a man en route to a camp meeting). The slave catchers eventually capture the slave after beating her father, trampling her and her siblings, and nearly killing her mother. A few months later, more slave catchers come to their home in pursuit of another fugitive. This time Miriam Berry rushes to the door with a cane, pushes her husband aside, and chastises the startled men. The next morning Mrs. Berry goes to New Market to spread the news of how these men had been harassing her family, revealing all of their names. The leading doctor of New Market encourages her to speak out publicly against the men, which she does:

> [S]he stood on the stepping stone at Dr. Bell's, right in front of the largest Tavern in the place. There were a lot of these men [slave catchers] sitting out reading the news. The morning was a beautiful Fall morning, and she opened her mouth and for one hour declared unto them all the words in her heart. Not a word was said against her, but as the spectators and others looked on and listened the cry of "Shame! Shame!" could be heard; and the men skulked away here and there. By the time she got through there was not one to be seen of this tribe. (Smith 34)

Not only is this occasion a triumph for the Berry family, but it also marks a maternal precedent for public speaking that Smith can draw upon for her preaching. The courage and commitment that Mrs. Berry exhibits in her speaking is reflected in her daughter's public career.

Unlike Foote, who shows her mother to be an obstacle to her spiritual development, Smith represents both parents as supportive of her efforts to grow spiritually. When she joins the Methodist Church at age thirteen, her parents also join the same church and revival class in order to support their daughter's new life.

Smith's relationship with her own children is illustrative of the ways in which biological motherhood informs radical spiritual motherhood. In particular, through the death of her favorite child, she comes to a new understanding of her relationship to divine power. Smith bore five children, but only her daughter Mazie lived to maturity. Her son Will was her favorite child. She believed him to be the "brightest and most promising" (Smith 122) of all of her children and consecrated him to God, promising to raise him to become a minister. The child thrives for the first few months of his life but then sickens and dies. Before his death, God comes to her in a voice, giving her the opportunity to save the child if she so desires. Smith, wanting to demonstrate her complete obedience to divine authority, places the will of God above her own. With words and feelings of anguish that echo those of Jesus as he cries out to God in the Garden of Gethsemane prior to his impending crucifixion, Smith sacrificially chooses His will over her Will: "'Oh, Lord, Thy will is so sweet, I only say Thy will be done.' . . . About two o'clock the next morning little Will fell asleep in Jesus, in my arms" (Smith 124).[57] To be able to say, and truly mean, "Thy will be done" is for Smith the essence of sanctification.

For some readers, it may be problematic that a mother would be willing to sacrifice the life of her own child to prove her faithfulness.[58] But perhaps Smith really did not have control over the destiny of her son but instead constructed some agency for herself by representing herself as being in the position to choose. Because of the unhealthy setting in which she lived, it is likely that she really did not have a choice. Adrienne Israel explains that the rented basement room in which she lived at the time in Greenwich Village was constantly damp, and in the winter was cold, thus possibly contributing to her child's death from bronchitis.[59] Israel further adds that "[e]ven though Greenwich Village was relatively healthy compared with other parts of the city, the areas of the Village inhabited by blacks quickly became overcrowded and unhealthy."[60] For a poor black washerwoman coping with the harsh realities of daily life in nineteenth-century northern urban America, possessing some degree of agency, even if it is textually constructed, is a step toward self-empowerment. Moreover, claiming the power to represent oneself favorably in a text flies in the face of the cruel stereotypes strategically manufactured to crush the spirit of black women.

For Zilpha Elaw, the decision to adopt spiritual maternity was interestingly facilitated by her own daughter. The author is careful to reproduce her child's words of encouragement to "break up housekeeping" as she grapples with the idea of pursuing the life of an itinerant minister: "'Now, mother, what is the matter?' for she was aware of the great anxiety of mind I had so long been labouring under, and she said all she could to comfort me; and added, 'If I were you, I should not mind what any person said, but I should go just as I had arranged to go, and do not think any thing about me, for I shall do very well'" (Elaw 89). What better sanction could Elaw receive for an unconventional life that is antithetical to the constraints of domesticity? Elaw then takes her little girl and leaves her in the care of relatives so that she may begin her itinerant ministry, remaining away from her child for seven months.

The complex relationship between biological and spiritual motherhood is poignantly illustrated during an occasion when Elaw is preaching at a camp meeting and precipitates the conversion of her own daughter. As Elaw addresses the crowd, her daughter is inspired by the scripture that her mother expounds: "Oh, that there were such an heart in them, that they would fear me, and keep all my commandments always, that it might be well with them and with their children forever" (103). Elaw records her daughter's emotional response to her message: "Oh, Lord! have mercy upon me, for I can hold out no longer. Oh, Lord! have mercy upon me" (103). In this dramatic moment, Elaw's relationship with her daughter is transformed: Her biological daughter has now become her spiritual child, thus joining the countless other spiritual children that the preacher has acquired since redefining her identity as a religious leader. The secondary role that biological parenting has taken to spiritual parenting seems to be even further diminished by this transformation of the relationship. Indeed, Elaw does not even attend to her child during this emotional time, but instead leaves her in the hands of friends: "[A]nd though my position would not allow me to leave the pulpit, to go and pour the oil of consolation into her wounded spirit, yet, thank God, there were abundance of dear friends present who were ready for every good word and work" (103). The fact that Elaw never names her daughter in her text seems to further undermine the status of the biological mother-daughter relationship and places the girl more firmly within the ranks of the preacher's spiritual children.

As Elaw describes her daughter's conversion experience, she declares that it "occurred in the midst of listening hundreds, and it produced a most thrilling sensation upon the congregation" (103). It is as if the author wants her readers to know that the new relationship she has precipitated with her daughter received mass approbation by the onlooking crowd. This implied mass approval, coupled with the fact that there are people willing to step in and attend to her child where it would have been appropriate for Elaw herself to care for her, would doubtless be quite affirming for a woman daring to live out such an unconventional calling. Elaw goes on to assert that "[m]any a mother strongly felt with me on that occasion" (103). The author thus successfully redefines maternity in a self-empowering manner and at the same time exploits the symbolic power of biological motherhood, garnering the support of many other (conventional) women.

Throughout her narrative, there are many instances where Elaw exploits this symbolic power of biological motherhood by highlighting the maternal roles she plays in connection with her ministry. For example, in describing the success she has had in ministering to people in England, she says, "I have travelled in several parts of England, and I thank God He has given me some spiritual children in every place wherein I have laboured" (Elaw 141). Elaw has been fruitful in multiplying devoted followers of Christ. In this passage, she suggests the procreative role of God, who gives her spiritual children, thus displacing reproductive labor with spiritual labor. And for this labor, she receives both divine and human approbation.

While Elaw's daughter helps to facilitate her transition from biological mother to spiritual mother, Jarena Lee reflects the challenges of being a biological mother and trying to be true to her calling as a spiritual leader. When Lee's husband dies, she is left to care for two young children on her own. While she is developing her preaching skills by holding meetings at a nearby house for six months, she takes care of her very sick son. She does not mention what has happened to her other child. When she is called for her first itinerant assignment about thirty miles away—a week-long preaching engagement with Methodists —she leaves her son with friends to care for him in her absence. After this successful mission, she returns home to find that her son is safe. She then begins to seriously consider "breaking up housekeeping" in order to pursue a full-time itinerant preaching career (Lee 46).

Though Lee believes there is a spiritual imperative to "break up housekeeping" so that she can devote herself full-time to preaching the gospel, there seems to be an internal struggle to privilege spiritual maternity over biological maternity. Though Lee makes it seem unproblematic for her to leave her sick child with friends (and to later leave him with her mother) so that she can go preach, there are clues in her narrative that suggest otherwise. For example, according to Lee, it takes an act of God to keep her from thinking about her sick child while she is away: "[D]uring the whole time, not a thought of my little son came into my mind; it was hid from me, lest I should have been diverted from the work I had to, to look after my son" (Lee 45). And when she returns home and finds him safe, she refers to her son as "it," as if to depersonalize him, perhaps making it easier for her to contain her emotions about leaving a sick child behind and to ultimately divest herself from the role of biological mother: "I now returned home, found all well; no harm had come to my child, although I left it very sick. Friends had taken care of it which was of the Lord" (Lee 46). And the fact that she does not mention the fate of her other child is telling. Perhaps the child has died, and the subject is too painful for her to discuss. She does mention, however, that she suffered the loss of five family members, including her husband, within a six-year span (Lee 40, 41). For a woman who has lost five family members in a short span of time and who has a child who is very sick, it would be understandable if she chose to omit painful details about the death of a child. Moreover, her silence about the child also seems to rhetorically downplay her biological maternity. Thus, for Lee there seems to be an unspoken emotional cost to privileging radical spiritual motherhood over biological motherhood, a cost perhaps too difficult to admit to her readers. Lee in fact seems to be engaging in textual masking in order to conceal some of the emotional costs of radical spiritual motherhood.

As a surrogate mother, Rebecca Jackson has her own challenges to face. At times she represents her brother's children as being part of a daily routine of exhausting labor that she must perform; at other times, she shows the children as facilitating or attesting to her spiritual power. To illustrate the first quality, Jackson relates:

> The exercise I used brought my system down very low. I sewed all day, having the charge of my brother and his four children,[61] and my husband to take care of, and see that the house was keep [*sic*] in good order, done all their sewing, keep them neat and clean and took in sewing for my living, held meeting every night in some part of the city, then came home. And after Samuel would lay down, I would labor oft times till two or three o'clock in the morning, then lay down, and at the break of day, rise and wait on the Lord, according to the covenant I made January the 30, Friday morning. And fasting the three days, Monday, Tuesday, Wednesday—at evening of each day I would take a little bread and water. This brought my system low, yet I had strength to do my daily duty. (Jackson 86)

Part of this rigorous routine involves the necessities of taking care of a large family and working outside the home to help support the family. And part of this routine involves cultivating a spiritual life through fasting, communing with God, and fellowshipping with other believers, which Jackson also considers to be a necessity, not a luxury. Jackson shows that though she is a divinely led woman, she is not a superwoman who can "do it all" without detrimental physical consequences. She credits her inner voice with leading her to break away from her family to begin traveling on her own as a preacher. But on some level, she no doubt realizes that the traditional maternal (and wifely) roles she is expected to play will not allow her to fulfill her heart's desire to become a full-time spiritual leader. She has to choose, and she chooses God over biological family.

By contrast, Jackson also shows how her brother's children facilitate her spiritual development on an occasion when she is recovering from a serious illness. Despite this illness, she believes she is led to attend a camp meeting and thus requests her husband to help her prepare for the trip by getting needed items for her. When he refuses because he does not think she should go, her niece helps her (Jackson 112).

On another occasion, her brother's youngest child, nine-year-old John, attests to Jackson's spiritual power when she helps him to be converted before he dies of consumption. Jackson has a vision of the head and wings of a child and hears a spirit voice telling her that the child has consumption and will die from it; she thus knows that he is sick before he knows it himself. When John weakens and is near death, he expresses concern about the fate of his soul; believing himself to be wicked, he greatly desires to be converted before he dies. Jackson earnestly works to bring this about, visually seeing that the gift of conversion is near:

> And I saw the gift lowering over his face [in form like a silver cord].[62] I cried, "John, believe!" "I do believe, Aunt!" "John, believe!" "I do believe, Aunt!" "John, believe! The blessing is over your head!" And as I said it the third time, it fell on his face. And he answered every time, and as it fell on his face, he called out, "Glory to God! Aunt, the Lord has converted my soul!" He clapped his little hands. "Aunt Rebecca, let us praise the Lord for what He has done for my poor soul! Oh, did I think He would save my poor soul— such a wicked child as I was?" (Jackson 117)

Following this dramatic scene of conversion, John confesses all of his sins before Jackson and his father. In three days, he is dead. Jackson's role in precipitating her nephew's conversion attests to her power as a developing spiritual leader; moreover, her prophetic and visionary powers are displayed, powers that will play a central role in her life as a radical spiritual mother.

Jackson represents her relationship with her own mother ambivalently; at times, she shows her to be someone who suppresses her voice in the articulation of her dreams, which she had since childhood. By contrast, she also portrays her as a source of vocal empowerment. In regard to her mother's acting as a repressive force to her voice, Jackson relates an occasion when, at ten years old, she had an impressive yet disturbing dream, which she told to her mother. In the dream, her mother and all of her siblings had been killed; Jackson gathers up all of their spirits and brings them to heaven to present to God. She thinks she is in heaven to stay, but is told by God to go back to earth because He has "a great work" for her to do; she returns to earth with much sorrow and reluctance (Jackson 234–37). Jackson describes what happens when she tells this dream to her mother:

In the morning I told my dream to my mother, and she told her friends—
and it was thought to be a remarkable dream for a child ten years old. I had
been accustomed to dreaming from early childhood, and like a child I told
them in the morning. Mother would sometimes send me out to play, and
tell me if she ever heard me tell that again, she would whip me. I went out
when she told me, but instead of playing, I would go and seclude myself in
some corner of the yard and there ponder upon what I had seen in the night
before. (Jackson 237)

Not only is Jackson's early propensity for dreaming and dream analysis evident
here, but so is her need to freely express those dreams to others, which her
mother thwarts. Jackson as an adult was divinely led to carefully record her
dreams and experiences in a religious journal, to be shared with other Shakers
for their instruction; but beyond divine motivation, perhaps the imperative to
record and share her dreams is partly derived from this early suppression of
voice. Jackson, as a child and as an adult, seems to need to freely express her
dreams and to have those dreams affirmed.

In a later journal entry, Jackson records a similar experience that occurred
when she was six years old and told her mother of a dream in which she saw
her stepfather dead and burning inside a Dutch oven, probably representing
hell. She is troubled by this dream, and when her mother asks her what is
wrong, she replies, "I saw Daddy last night in the bad place, and the naughty
man had him all afire in a dutch oven" (Jackson 239). Her mother responds by
saying, "Get up this minute and go along out to your play! And if I ever hear
you say such a thing again, I will whip you!" (Jackson 239). Sometime later
Jackson's mother is informed that her husband has drowned at sea; this knowledge leads her to ask Jackson about her dream:

[M]y mother called me, took me in her lap, pressed me to her bosom, and
said, "Now, tell me what you dreamed a good while ago, about your father."
I began to cry and said, "You will whip me if I tell." She kissed me and said,
"No, I will not whip you my dear child. Tell me all about it." She was weeping all this time, so I told her the dream. She said, "Your father is dead."
She put me down. And I heard her tell her friend that the day previous to
the night I had the dream, he got drunk at sea, and fell overboard, and was
drowned. (Jackson 239–40)

This dream and the one she had at age ten reveal Jackson's early prophetic abilities; she seems to suggest that her mother's strong negative reactions to her dreams result not only from their disturbing details, but also from her mother's awareness that her daughter possesses the power to foretell the future through these dreams:

> It was not because she was an unkind mother that she threatened to whip me, for she was one of the best of mothers, and I bless the memory of her. She was buried Christmas 1808–and I was fourteen years old, the 15th of the next February. My mother had a presentiment of her death from the dream I have related, that occurred when I was ten years old, and she believed all the children would die before me. After her death, it was often mentioned by my older brother Joseph that I would outlive them all. He died in September 1843. I write this April 14, 1854, in my sixtieth year. (Jackson 240)

I believe these interactions between Jackson and her mother impact Jackson's identity as a radical spiritual mother by helping her to affirm her spiritual power of prophecy; moreover, these interactions help Jackson to recognize the importance of being true to her voice and honoring her inner life, of which dreaming is a central part.

Showing her mother in a different light, Jackson represents her as empowering her voice later in life after she has begun to preach; this occurs when Jackson performs the miracle of restoring a blind woman's sight. The woman heard that Jackson was to preach and had a desire to hear her; she is brought to Jackson, who feels compassion for her:

> I was moved to go and lay my hand on her head in love. I got up and went, and as soon as I done it, I was commanded to sing, hold my right hand on her head, my left on her left shoulder. And I sung three heavenly songs,[63] and while I sung the third, the power of God fell upon her and she cried out, "Oh, that I could see you my dear child, for I know your voice! What is your name?" I told her. My mother and her used to belong to band meeting together when I was a child. It was my mother's voice she heard in me. (Jackson 133)

As Jackson continues to sing with her hands on the woman, the latter's sight is restored. The laying on of hands together with Jackson's singing precipitates a miraculous healing; in fact, it seems to be the singing that carries the real power, since it is during the third song that the woman receives her sight. For the woman, Jackson seems to be channeling her mother's voice and the power it evokes.

Cultivating the identity of radical spiritual mother amid the material realities of nineteenth-century African American women was a complex process that involved reaching back to familiar domestic roles, reconceptualizing one's relationship to power and publicity, and envisioning a dynamic life of spiritual leadership and community. This process was challenging, bringing about external conflicts with those who opposed the unconventional roles these women sought to adopt, as well as causing internal conflicts as these women struggled to come to terms with their developing identities. The radical spiritual mothers faced racial, gender, and class discrimination, yet they drew upon these experiences to help them cultivate a larger vision of a world transformed through individual and social sanctification. It is their experiences of personal sanctification as a dramatic transformative force in their lives that I explore in the next chapter.

3

SANCTIFIED LADIES

Transformation of Vision and Voice in the Narratives of
Amanda Berry Smith, Julia Foote, and Jarena Lee

In this chapter, I explore the empowering and transformative nature of sanctification in the lives of Amanda Berry Smith, Julia Foote, and Jarena Lee since
it is through this spiritual experience that the radical spiritual mothers gain
the power and authority to reinvent themselves as women of God.[1] For them,
sanctification was not an unattainable abstract ideal but an integral part of their
everyday lives, lives in which racism, sexism, and economic uncertainty were
very real. By "walking the talk" of sanctification, the radical spiritual mothers
found an effective means of coping with these realities while proclaiming the
uplifting message of God's promise of salvation to all. Sanctification altered
the radical spiritual mothers' vision; seeing through sanctified eyes, they were
able to envision themselves as chosen women who were uniquely set apart
to do God's work. Moreover, sanctification altered the radical spiritual mothers' voices. Emboldened by the power of God, each woman came to possess a
"Mouth-Almighty" that was capable of articulating divine truths to people from
all walks of life.[2]

Entire sanctification,[3] according to John Wesley, the founder of Methodism,
may be defined as "[p]urity of intention, the imitation of Christ, and whole-
hearted love of God and our neighbor."[4] One who is fully sanctified completely
surrenders one's will to God, and wholly devotes one's life to Him. Moreover,
people who are fully sanctified are believed to be completely liberated from sin;
they do not commit inward sin (harbored in the heart or mind) or outward sin
(reflected in acts and words). This is so because fully sanctified individuals are
released from the root of sin, or original sin, which Christians believe imbued
humans with a sinful nature.[5]

Wesley believed that perfection was a state that Christians could attain during their lifetimes, but it was not an absolute perfection that prevented them
from making mistakes. Rather, it was a relative perfection that took into account

the limitations of earthly life and the shortcomings that naturally accompany the human state.[6] Because humans were created with free will, they could always choose to willfully disobey God, and thus sin, but through Christian perfection, believers could be "delivered from the *necessity* of voluntary transgressions by living in moment-by-moment obedience to God's will."[7] This meant that for fully sanctified Christians, sin was no longer sovereign in their lives.[8]

Entire sanctification, a gift bestowed by God upon believers based on their faith rather than their works, represents the most advanced stage in the process of Christian salvation, which occurs as follows: "1) The operation of prevenient grace. 2) Repentance previous to justification. 3) Justification or forgiveness. 4) The New Birth. 5) Repentance after justification and the gradually proceeding work of sanctification. 6) Entire sanctification."[9]

Grace is love and protection that is freely given to humans by God.[10] Prevenient grace is that which was offered to Adam and Eve following their commission of the sin of disobedience in the Garden of Eden and their subsequent corruption. This grace was meant to draw the original humans back to God, restoring the divine image with which they were created, and reestablishing a loving relationship with God. Prevenient grace is offered to all humans, and it is each individual's choice whether or not to accept it in faith.[11] Prevenient grace may also be defined as God's grace "coming before" one believes in Christ; it is "preparatory" or "assisting" grace.[12]

One who accepts God's prevenient grace becomes aware that he or she is guilty of sinning against Him. This awareness of sin leads to a deeper level of self-knowledge from which the believer becomes convinced that he or she deserves to be condemned by God because of his or her transgressions. Repentance then results from this conviction, and the Christian is then prepared for the stages of justification and the New Birth, which occur simultaneously and instantaneously.[13]

With justification one gains acceptance by God, and is forgiven of one's sins; with the New Birth, a Christian is born anew in the spirit of God. This means that sin no longer has a predominant place in his or her life. To further distinguish between justification and the New Birth, the former involves an objective change because it marks an alteration in one's relationship with God. The latter involves a subjective change since a person is fundamentally transformed from within; that is, he or she essentially becomes a new person who has been born again and restored to God's image.[14]

Following the New Birth, a Christian experiences a process of gradual

growth and development in his or her spiritual life. This period, called sanctification, is marked by an increased awareness of the sin that remains in a believer's life and the knowledge that his or her will is not yet wholly subordinate
to that of God. Thus, the Christian repents again, this time with the cognizance
that he or she has been accepted by God. The believer can then experience the
ultimate stage of salvation—entire sanctification, which occurs instantaneously.[15]
When one is entirely sanctified, one is "baptized, or filled, with the Holy Spirit,"
which "brings added power to conquer sin, to love others, and to witness for
Christ."[16]

Attaining entire sanctification does not conclude an individual's spiritual
development; he or she continues to grow in love and grace, and to cultivate a
close relationship with Christ, whose mind and character he or she gradually
comes to imitate. The indwelling Holy Spirit guides the believer in this gradual
process of conforming to the likeness of Christ.[17] The essence of sanctification
is love; it is "receiv[ing] grace to love God with your whole heart and to love
your neighbor as yourself."[18] Further elucidating the meaning of sanctification,
Melvin Dieter explains: "The fundamental meaning of the word *sanctify* is 'to
set apart,' or 'to consecrate'; it is derived from the Hebrew qādaš, meaning 'to
separate' or 'to divide.' It means to remove persons or things from the realm of
the profane and to set them apart to God. They become thereby 'holy.'"[19]

In terms of textually representing this process of Christian salvation in nineteenth-century American evangelical Protestant conversion narratives, Virginia
Brereton has noticed a predictable pattern:

> (1) life before the conversion process began, when narrators more or less ig-
> nored the question of salvation; (2) a period when narrators became acutely
> aware of their sinfulness and of the possibility they would be damned for-
> ever; (3) the surrender to God's will in conversion proper, during which
> converts felt the oppressive sense of sinfulness lifted and gained confidence
> or at least hope that they were saved; (4) a description of the narrator's
> changed behavior and attitudes, resulting from conversion; and (5) an ac-
> count of periods of discouragement and low spiritual energy followed by
> renewals of dedication.[20]

In reading the narratives of Smith, Foote, and Lee, one witnesses many attributes of sanctification that inform their transformations of vision and voice,
including their surrender of personal will to that of God; their desire to wholly

devote their lives God's service, particularly through their acceptance of their calls to preach the gospel; and their consciousness of being set apart for God's use. It is these characteristics that I explore further in this chapter.

Amanda Berry Smith was sanctified in 1868 while attending a service at Green Street Methodist Episcopal Church in New York.[21] She was particularly drawn to this church because she had learned that its minister, Rev. John S. Inskip, had himself experienced the second blessing.[22] On that day, Rev. Inskip delivered a sermon on sanctification based on the biblical verse Ephesians 4:24: "And that ye put on the new man, which after God is created in righteousness and true holiness" (Smith 75).[23] As Inskip begins his sermon, Smith feels as though he is speaking directly to her as he says, "There are a great many persons who are troubled about the blessing of sanctification; how they can keep it if they get it" (Smith 76). Smith's narrative describes how Inskip draws her in with imagery that she can readily relate to as a hardworking washerwoman:

> "When you work hard all day and are very tired,"–"Yes," I said, and in a moment my mind went through my washing and ironing all night,–"When you go to bed at night you don't fix any way for yourself to breathe,"–"No," I said, "I never think about it,"–"You go to bed, you breathe all night, you have nothing to do with your breathing, you awake in the morning, you had nothing to do with it."
>
> "Yes, yes, I see it."
>
> He continued: "You don't need to fix any way for God to live in you; get God in you in all His fullness and He will live Himself." (Smith 76)

The minister's description of the natural, autonomic manner by which a sanctified individual maintains his or her relationship with an indwelling deity resonates poignantly with Smith, evoking a physical response in her:

> "Oh!" I said, "I see it." And somehow I seemed to sink down out of sight of myself, and then rise; it was all in a moment. I seemed to go two ways at once, down and up. Just then such a wave came over me, and such a welling up in my heart, and these words rang through me like a bell: "God in you, God in you," and I thought doing what? Ruling every ambition and desire, and bringing every thought unto captivity and obedience to His will. How I have lived through it I cannot tell, but the blessedness of the love and the peace and power I can never describe. (Smith 76)

This dramatic response in which Smith experiences "God in [her] . . . Ruling every ambition and desire" marks the moment in which she is sanctified. Her inner dialogue seems to reflect the complete surrender of personal will to God's will that is characteristic of the sanctified individual. It is this same attribute that later enables her to relinquish her son, Will, to God's will to take the sick child in death. As a result of adopting this attitude of surrender, she does indeed seem to "put on [a] new self," as the text from Ephesians suggests. Among the changes that are evident in this new self is a heightened critical consciousness of her worth as a black woman.

In particular, Smith experiences a radical change in her racial perceptions. She explains that prior to becoming sanctified, "Somehow I always had a fear of white people—that is, I was not afraid of them in the sense of doing me harm, or anything of that kind—but a kind of fear because they were white, and were there, and I was black and was here!" (Smith 80). The fear that Smith describes alludes to the vast social and political gulf that divided blacks and whites during this period in history. But through sanctification, and in particular, through a new comprehension of a Bible verse that came to mind as she was sanctified, she is able to intellectually and spiritually bridge this gulf. The verse that comes to Smith's mind is Galatians 3:28: "There is neither Jew nor Greek, there is neither bond nor free, there is neither male nor female, for ye are all one in Christ Jesus" (Smith 80). Of this verse, Smith declares: "I had never understood that text before. But now the Holy Ghost had made it clear to me. And as I looked at white people that I had always seemed to be afraid of, now they looked so small. The great mountain had become a mole-hill" (Smith 80). The indwelling Spirit acquired by individuals through sanctification has provided Smith with divine insight that enables her to debunk the myth of white racial superiority.

This seems to be a significant psychological reorientation that is necessary for Smith to effectively carry out the work that God later calls her to do as a preacher among people of a variety of races and walks of life. Moreover, the expression of love that is said to be the essence of sanctification includes love of self. This self-love is bound up with Smith's racial identity and is poignantly expressed several times throughout her narrative in her references to African Americans as being "the royal black." For example, Smith describes an occasion on which she has a conversation with a woman who asks her if she thought that all black people would rather be white. Though Smith admits that being black can sometimes be "inconvenient," she makes it clear that she is quite proud of who she is: "No, we who are the royal black are very well satisfied with His [God's] gift to us in this substantial color. I, for one, praise Him for what He has given me, although at times it is very inconvenient" (Smith 117).

Though sanctification may enable Smith to attain a more realistic image of whites, it does not completely quell her racial insecurities, nor does it protect her from suffering indignities because of her race. Sanctification does, however, help to imbue her with inner strength to deal with these trials. Smith comments that people often remark on how well she seems to be treated as a black person. To this, she responds, "[I]f you want to know and understand properly what Amanda Smith has to contend with, just turn black and go about as I do, and you will come to a different conclusion" (Smith 116). Regarding the value of sanctification in helping Smith to live with the challenges of being black in America, she then comments to her readers, "And I think some people would understand the quintessence of sanctifying grace if they could be black about twenty-four hours" (Smith 116–117).

Smith includes many incidents in her narrative that illustrate the trials she must deal with as a black woman, and the ways that sanctification strengthens her to cope with these trials. For example, while attending a camp meeting in Kennebunk, Maine, she becomes a "gazing stock" to whites who are attending the meeting, because she is the only black person there:

> It was one Sunday. There had been a great crowd all day, and everywhere I would go a crowd would follow me. If I went into a tent they would surround it and stay till I came out, then they would follow me. Sometimes I would slip into a tent away from them. Then I would see them peep in, and if they saw me they would say, "Oh! here is the colored woman. Look!" Then the rush! So after dinner I managed to get away. I went into a friend's tent and said, "Let me lie down here out of sight a little while." (Smith 183)

Smith hides under the bed until the people go away. Not surprisingly, she is very upset by this incident. To cope with it, she goes into the woods by herself, turns to God, and prays, "Help me to throw off that mean feeling, and give me grace to be a gazing stock" (184). In answer to her prayer, a thought comes to her regarding an occasion on which she herself joined a crowd of people that was gazing through a window at a picture. In a dialogue that unfolds between Smith and God, God employs the Socratic method in order to help Smith effectively deal with her pain:

"The other day when you were carrying the clothes home you saw a crowd standing and looking in at a window on Broadway, New York, at a picture."

"Yes."

"And you went up with the crowd and looked at it too."

"Yes."

"You heard the remarks of the people, and the approvals and dis-approvals."

"Yes." I said.

"Did that picture say anything?"

"No."

"Did it injure its beauty?"

"No, Lord; I see it."

I got up and went on double quick to the tent. I praised the Lord. I laughed, and cried, and shouted. It was so simple, and yet so real. The next morning at the eight o'clock meeting I got up and shouted, "I have got the victory! Everybody come and look at me! Praise the Lord!" (Smith 184)

In this revelatory moment, Smith seems to acquire what bell hooks would call an "oppositional gaze," or a kind of critical spectatorship cultivated through a conscious resistance to the dominant order.[24] She does not defiantly return the gaze to the crowd that objectifies her, but rather she appropriates it to underscore her own self-worth, thus inherently shifting the power relationship between herself and the crowd in her favor. She in fact "change[s] the joke and slip[s] the yoke" by redefining the meaning with which the gaze is invested:[25] in the transformative hands of Smith, a gesture meant to demean and objectify now becomes a tool for self-glorification. In this instance, Smith literally embodies sanctification's distinctive quality of being set apart for God's use; through the inspiration of the indwelling Holy Spirit, she sets herself apart from the crowd in order to manifest God's power to transform despair into joy by bringing about a critical change in perception.

Not only do Smith's perceptions change as a result of her sanctification, but so does her voice. Recalling an occasion at a camp meeting during which Smith is conscious of her reticence during prayer meetings, she describes how God aids her in coming to voice: "I had not been accustomed to take part in the meetings, especially when white people were present, and there was a timidity and shyness that much embarrassed me; but whenever called upon, I would ask the Lord to help me, and take the timidity out of me; and He did help me every time" (Smith 174). Regarding the role that early Methodism played in helping women to find their voices, Diane H. Lobody explains that this religion was particularly instrumental in encouraging women to openly speak about their experiences: "Early Methodism provided a structure—a grammar and a rhythm—by which believers could order and organize their worlds in a new way. A significant evidence of the power of that remarkable grammar and rhythm was the unsilencing of women."[26] The structures that fostered this expressiveness included call-and-response preaching, which encouraged listeners to testify, shout, sing, pray, and sob; love feasts, during which participants shared a ritual meal and spoke about the ways that God's love affected their lives; and class meetings, which were intimate and ordered gatherings where members were counseled about their soul's condition, and where they prayed aloud and told of personal difficulties, conflicts, and hopes. Some members also belonged to praying bands.[27]

Praying bands were among the many contexts in which the voices of the radical spiritual mothers were cultivated and fine-tuned. Within these small, intimate groups of believers, members shared their deepest feelings and spiritual concerns. Band members were expected to bare their souls for their own and for their group's spiritual growth and development. According to *The Doctrines and Discipline of the African Methodist Episcopal Church*, the scriptural basis for the formation of these bands lay in the biblical command to "[c]onfess your faults one to another, and pray one for another, that ye may be healed [James 5:16]."[28] Thus, the willingness to speak openly and candidly was essential for spiritual health and wholeness. A description of the procedures of AME praying bands gives valuable insight into the role and character of these groups, which were segregated by gender and marital status. Among the procedures that specifically pertain to speaking and eliciting members' candid responses include the mandates:

4. To speak, each of us in order, freely and plainly the true state of our souls, with the faults we have committed in tempers, words, or actions, and the temptations we have felt since our last meeting.

5. To end every meeting with prayer, suited to the state of each person present.

6. To desire some person among us to speak *his* own state first, and then to ask the rest in order, as many and as searching questions as may be, concerning their state, sins, and temptations.[29]

Within a confidential, confessional atmosphere, members were held account-
able to each other for sharing and sifting through the daily details of their lives
for their spiritual implications. The act of testifying, or of attesting to the ways
that God intervened in one's life and the faith that resulted from this intervention, was an important ritual that was a regular facet of these prayer meetings.
As one of the "[f]our pillars of the Afro-Christian religious tradition" identified
by Cheryl Townsend Gilkes,[30] testifying was particularly important for the psychological survival of black women, for whom oppression and suffering were a
daily fact of life.[31] Belonging to a praying band required members to trust one
another implicitly with their innermost thoughts, feelings, and doubts. Members' willingness to be vulnerable and transparent was tested prior to being
admitted into a band by being subjected to questions such as the following:

6. Do you desire to be told of your faults?
7. Do you desire to be told of *all* your faults, and that plain and home?
8. Do you desire, that every one of us should tell you, from time to
   time whatsoever is in our heart concerning you?
9. Consider! Do you desire we should tell you whatsoever we think,
   whatsoever we fear, whatsoever we hear concerning you?
10. Do you desire, that in doing this, we should come as close as pos-
    sible, that we should cut to the quick, and search your heart to the
    bottom?
11. Is it your desire and design, to be on this and all other occasions, en-
    tirely open, so as to speak without disguise, and without reserve?[32]

In addition, four particularly searching questions were to be asked of each
member at every meeting:

1. What known sins have you committed since our last meeting [?]
2. What particular temptations have you met with?
3. How were you delivered?
4. What have you thought, said, or done, of which you doubt whether
   it be sin or not?[33]

Smith belonged to a praying band with three women who would meet together at her house. The procedure of their meetings closely followed that described above: "We generally took turns about; one would open by giving out

a hymn, reading a chapter and then praying. Then we would tell each other our joys or sorrows, our victories and defeats, if we had any, and if Satan had buffeted us, how we bore up or if we yielded under the pressure, etc., and then we would advise each other and pray for each other" (Smith 143).

The praying bands thus offered an ideal setting and procedure for confession, prayer, and encouragement. Members of the bands did not always live up to this ideal, however. For example, Rebecca Jackson tells of organizing a small weekly meeting in her home that included a woman whose spiritual sincerity she doubted. The woman did not use these occasions as an opportunity for self-disclosure, but rather as a chance to reveal the sins of others:

> When she first began to come to see me, as seeking after spiritual light, I found her first work was to bring the sins of her friends. After she would lay them all before me, I would get up and lock the door. "Now, Sister, come. You must pray for them till you can feel that love and pity for their soul that you feel for your own soul. Without this you can never be saved." So when she found she had to pray for the people's sins when she brought them to me, she soon quit bringing them. This I done to her and everybody else that brought the sins of others. (Jackson 106)

The divine affirmation that Amanda Smith receives as a child of God through the experience of sanctification combined with the validation of voice she receives in her praying band helps to prepare her for the most important role she is called to accept—that of itinerant preacher. Smith's and the other radical spiritual mothers' acceptance of this role is the ultimate expression of the sanctified individual's willingness to wholly devote his or her life to God. Smith experiences this call in 1890 at the Fleet Street AME Church in Brooklyn while listening to a sermon by Rev. Gould:

> I was sitting with my eyes closed in silent prayer to God, and after he had been preaching about ten minutes, as I opened my eyes, just over my head I seemed to see a beautiful star, and as I looked at it, it seemed to form into the shape of a large white tulip; and I said, "Lord, is that what you want me to see? If so, what else?" And then I leaned back and closed my eyes. Just then I saw a large letter "G," and I said: "Lord, do you want me to read in Genesis, or in Galatians? Lord, what does this mean?"

Just then I saw the letter "O." I said, "Why, that means go." And I said "What else?" And a voice distinctly said to me "Go preach." (Smith 147–48)

Later in her preaching career while addressing a gathering in Bangalore, India, where she had been engaging in missionary work, Smith boldly takes on the biblical text that has traditionally been used to silence women in the church, that is, 1 Corinthians 14:33–35: "As in all the churches of the saints, the women should keep silence in the churches. For they are not permitted to speak, but should be subordinate, even as the law says. If there is anything they desire to know, let them ask their husbands at home. For it is shameful for a woman to speak in church."[34] On this particular occasion, Smith speaks in response to male church officials from Plymouth, England, who had written to her and admonished her about the inappropriateness of women preaching; these men actually wanted her to preach against women's preaching! Smith recalls this occasion with subtle wit and sarcasm:

But the good Plymouth brethren were much disturbed, because I was a woman, and Paul had said, "Let your women keep silence in the churches." So they had nice articles in the daily papers; then they wrote me kind letters, and bombarded me with Scriptural texts against women preaching; pointed out some they wished me to preach from. I never argue with anybody—just say my say and go on. But one night I said I would speak on this subject as I understood it. Oh, what a stir it made. The church was packed and crowded. After I had sung, I read out my text: "Let your 'men' keep silence in the church," quoting the chapter and verse (1 Cor., 14: 28) where Paul was giving directions so as not to have confusion—one to speak at a time, while the others listened. And then one was to interpret, and if there was no interpreter, they should keep silence in the church. So I went on with my version of it. We had an excellent meeting, and the newspaper articles stopped, and the letters stopped, and I went on till I got through. (Smith 321)

To defuse the biblical injunction against women speaking in church, Smith's strategy is to place the proscriptive passage within its broader scriptural context; that is, she effectively reminds her audience that the passage prohibiting women's speaking in church is contained in a section of the Bible in which the Apostle Paul instructs the church of Corinth on how to conduct worship in an orderly fashion. To achieve and maintain this order, it is also necessary for men to keep silent at appropriate times. On this occasion, Smith uses her Mouth Almighty, which has been sanctified, amplified, and validated by God, as well as honed and strengthened within the sacred space of her female praying band, to deliver a cogent feminist exegesis to counteract a historically antifeminist text; in so doing, she effectively silences some of her harshest critics.

Not only is Smith moved to find her voice through sanctification, but she inspires other women to find their own: "I felt the Lord laid it on me to give a bit of my own personal experience, how God converted and sanctified my heart, so I spoke, and the power of the Spirit seemed to come mightily upon all the people. Oh, what a stir; they wept and sobbed, and one woman was so baptized that she cried out and could not restrain herself" (Smith 261). The impact that Smith's powerful message has upon many people is far-reaching and long-lasting. Years later, while traveling by train in Liverpool, she meets the woman whom she had affected so deeply:

> "Do you remember the morning you spoke at Broadlands [England] and gave your experience?"
> "Yes."
> "Do you remember some one crying out?"
> "Yes."
> "Well," she said, "that was I. Oh, God filled me that morning and I have never gotten over it, the trials have been severe, but Oh, I have been saved and kept and am full of praise to-day. I am glad to see you, praise the Lord." (Smith 261)

While sanctification is important in Smith's narrative, it thoroughly pervades the spiritual autobiography of Julia Foote; in fact, the author asserts that her whole purpose for writing her spiritual autobiography is to attest to the power of sanctification in her life and to exhort her readers to pursue this second blessing for themselves: "My object has been to testify more extensively to the sufficiency of the blood of Jesus Christ to save from all sin. . . . My earnest desire is that many—especially of my own race—may be led to believe and enter into rest . . . sweet soul rest" (Foote 163). Foote's desire for this "sweet soul rest" begins as an indeterminate longing for something beyond the blessing she had experienced when she was converted at age fifteen: "I needed something more than what I had, but what that something was I could not tell" (Foote 184).

She learns about sanctification from an elderly couple that have themselves been sanctified and have greatly benefited from the experience. She prepares to receive the second blessing by "going many times to my secret place of prayer, which was behind the chimney in the garret of our house" (Foote 186). Like Rebecca Jackson, for whom the garret also served as a personal site of prayer and meditation, Foote invests this private space with spiritual significance.

While at home in agony over her spiritual condition, she is visited by the old woman from whom she had learned about sanctification, a woman she refers to as "that dear old mother in Israel" (Foote 186). The woman reads and explains to Foote a number of scriptural passages regarding sanctification. As she does so, Foote is gradually enlightened about its meaning: "All this had been a sealed book to me until now. Glory to Jesus! the seals were broken and light began to shine upon the blessed Word of God as I had never seen it before" (Foote 186).

Two days later, Foote is sanctified: "The glory of God seemed almost to prostrate me to the floor. There was, indeed, a weight of glory resting upon me. I sang with all my heart, 'This is the way I long have sought, And mourned because I found it not'" (Foote 186–87). It is significant that the "dear old mother in Israel" helps Foote to be reborn into the life of Christ. In a sense, she is a surrogate mother for Foote's own mother, who discouraged her daughter from pursuing sanctification because she believed that it could only be experienced by people who were close to death. The "mother in Israel" thus helps to midwife a radical spiritual mother into being.

Not only is Foote's identity transformed at the moment of sanctification, but so is her vision; with sanctified eyes, she witnesses a series of visions that gradually help her to come to terms with her calling to preach the gospel, a calling that she is initially reluctant to accept: "I took all my doubts and fears to the Lord in prayer, when, what seemed to be an angel, made his appearance. In his hand was a scroll, on which were these words: 'Thee have I chosen to preach my Gospel without delay.' The moment my eyes saw it, it appeared to be printed on my heart" (Foote 200). Foote, still beset by doubt and fear, does delay her ministry. It would take a second angelic visitation to convince her of her destiny: "Nearly two months from the time I first saw the angel, I said that I would do anything or go anywhere for God, if it were made plain to me. He took me at my word, and sent the angel again with this message: 'You have been chosen to go in my name and warn the people of their sins.' I bowed my head and said, 'I will go, Lord'" (Foote 202). In a third vision, on a Sabbath evening, Foote is ritually prepared for her new role by God the Father and Son themselves, along with a host of angelic attendants. In this vision, she is led by the same angel that appeared in the first two visions to a large tree, under which God the Father, Son, and Holy Spirit are all sitting, along with a group of angels. God the Father allows her to choose whether or not she wants to obey His calling. When she assents, she is led to a silvery pool of water where Christ takes her by the hand and strips her of her clothing. He then proceeds to bathe her in the warm water:

> During this operation, all the others [the Holy Spirit and the angels that have gathered by the water] stood on the bank, looking on in profound silence. When the washing was ended, the sweetest music I had ever heard greeted my ears. We walked to the shore, where an angel stood with a clean, white robe, which the Father at once put on me. In an instant I appeared to be changed into an angel. The whole company looked at me with delight, and began to make a noise which I called shouting. We all marched back with music. When we reached the tree to which the angel first led me, it hung full of fruit, which I had not seen before. The Holy Ghost plucked some and gave me, and the rest helped themselves. We sat down and ate of the fruit, which had a taste like nothing I had ever tasted before. When we had finished, we all arose and gave another shout. Then God the Father said to me: "You are now prepared, and must go where I have commanded you." I replied, "If I go, they will not believe me." Christ then appeared to write something with a golden pen and golden ink, upon golden paper. Then he rolled it up, and said to me: "Put this in your bosom, and, wherever you go, show it, and they will know that I have sent you to proclaim salvation to all." He then put it into my bosom, and they all went with me to a bright, shining gate, singing and shouting. Here they embraced me, and I found myself once more on earth. (Foote 203)

In this solemn yet joyous vision, Foote is ritually cleansed, reborn, and charged with an awesome mission. Sexual undertones of Foote's being disrobed and bathed by Christ are certainly suggested in this scene. More significant, however, is the way that the scene can be read as a spiritual countertext to her mother's story of being washed with salt water following the brutal whipping she received by her master for refusing his sexual advances.[35] The salt water was probably intended to prevent her lacerated flesh from decaying, thus preserving his property and his domination over her. In Foote's countertext, how-ever, the brutal earthly master is supplanted by a loving heavenly master, who bathes Foote with pure water to ritually cleanse and prepare her for service as a preacher. The earthly master wounds, humiliates, and dominates the mother; whereas the heavenly master affirms, uplifts, and liberates the daughter.

Foote's acceptance by the triune God and her transfiguration into angelic form are particularly affirming for a black woman who would not ordinarily be highly valued in her culture. The biblical scene in the Garden of Eden in which Adam and Eve disobey God by eating of the tree of the knowledge of good and evil is rewritten in this vision, with the Holy Spirit freely offering Foote the fruit; she thus symbolically receives the fruit of the Spirit, which she will draw upon for spiritual power in her preaching. Though the music she hears may be otherworldly, the shouting and singing of the heavenly company seem to reen-act a style of worship with which Foote would have been familiar in the African Methodist Episcopal churches she attended. God and the angels thus seem to want to make her feel at home in their world, and to help her transition back into the earthly realm that she will help transform with her newfound power.

Though Foote is aware that she has God's approval for her preaching, she nevertheless understandably anticipates disbelief and disapproval of her gifts from people on earth. Christ therefore offers her a golden letter to verify the divine authority she has been given to preach the gospel. This validating letter almost seems to be as necessary to Foote in dispelling insecurities about herself as it is to those who may question her authority. Sanctification has thus helped Foote to envision herself as a woman who has been made holy and who has been set apart for God's use.

Being set apart for God's use sometimes literally meant standing apart from others who were critical of the behavior of those who had been sanctified or who were skeptical about the nature of sanctification itself. For example, Foote's second blessing leads to a rift between her and her husband, who quips to his wife, "Julia, I don't think I can ever believe myself as holy as you think you are" (Foote 196). Like Rebecca Jackson's husband, George Foote accuses his wife of being crazy because of her spiritual zeal and threatens to either send her back home to her family or "to the crazy-house" (Foote 196). Foote refers to the wall that develops between her and her husband as "an indescribable some-thing between us—something dark and high," a barrier that distorts her vision of him: "From that time I never beheld my husband's face clear and distinct, as before, the dark shadow being ever present" (Foote 196). Shortly after this,

George Foote goes off to sea for six months, precipitating a period of emotional and spiritual struggle for Foote: "The day my husband went on ship-board was one of close trial and great inward temptation. It was difficult for me to mark the exact line between disapprobation and Christian forbearance and patient love. How I longed for wisdom to meet everything in a spirit of meekness and fear, that I might not be surprised into evil or hindered from improving all things to the glory of God" (Foote 197). During this period of trial, Foote finds solace in the awareness that when her earthly husband fails her, she can turn to a divine husband for comfort and support: "While under this apparent cloud, I took the Bible to my closet, asking Divine aid. As I opened the book, my eyes fell on these words: 'For thy Maker is thine husband' [Isa. 54: 5]. I then read the fifty-fourth chapter of Isaiah over and over again. It seemed to me that I had never seen it before. I went forth glorifying God" (Foote 197). Though Foote is unable to see her husband clearly, her eyes are opened to a text that speaks directly to her circumstances. The fifty-fourth chapter of Isaiah that she repeatedly reads figuratively portrays the nation of Israel as a wife who has been abandoned by her husband. The people of Israel have been severely punished by God for their disobedience; however, God's compassion for His people leads Him to restore them to their former glory. The figurative representation of this promised restoration is that of a husband who returns to the wife he has abandoned to pledge his eternal love and protection. In addition, the wife is portrayed as a barren woman who will become fruitful when her husband returns:

> "Sing, O barren woman,
> you who never bore a
> child;
> burst into song, shout for joy,
> you who were never in labor;
> because more are the children of the
> desolate woman
> than of her who has a husband,"
> says the Lord.[36]

As the symbolic husband of Israel, God promises to multiply His people's descendants, who will spread out far and wide to reestablish a mighty nation. All of this resonates deeply with Foote, who is also childless and feels abandoned by her husband. The words and images of this scripture help to sustain her un-til her husband returns from sea. Moreover, this scripture seems to foreshadow the role that Foote will play as a radical spiritual mother since this identity ex-pands the conception of maternity so that all humans become potential children of the radical spiritual mother as she nurtures their spirits, minds, and bodies. So for the childless Foote, this scripture indeed bespeaks her future: "more are the children of the desolate woman than of her who has a husband."

Further, in her husband's absence, Foote uses her time advantageously to prepare herself for her future role: "Having no children, I had a good deal of leisure after my husband's departure, so I visited many of the poor and for-saken ones, reading and talking to them of Jesus, the Saviour" (Foote 198). Anticipating her role as a radical spiritual mother, Foote freely ministers to her spiritual children in the absence of biological children.

Richard Douglass-Chin interprets this section of Foote's narrative as part of a recurring rhetorical strategy throughout the text in which Foote represents herself as a meek woman who purposefully uses biblical scripture in her de-fense: "Such a strategy is a mode of 'signifying'—the speaker's apparent mean-ing is not to be taken merely at face value; it points to a subtle, unspoken mean-ing, nevertheless understood by everyone present."[37] What she is signifying on, Douglass-Chin asserts, is the cult of true womanhood since her childlessness and alienation of her husband directly undermine the roles of devoted mother and supportive wife that the cult prescribes for the proper woman.[38]

Foote's appropriation of God as her surrogate husband helps to provide further insight into the intimacy with Jesus Christ that is portrayed in the above vision in which she is ritually cleansed and prepared to preach the gospel. One way to interpret her passive acceptance of Christ's disrobing and bathing of her and placing the letter of authority in her bosom is that she is allowing someone she loves and trusts to perform a caretaking role that honors and nurtures her body and her soul. The water in which Jesus bathes her is described as warm and is no doubt soothing; the letter placed in her bosom is not only designed to lend Foote credibility but to protect her from those who think she is overstep-ping her bounds as a woman. As a "bride of Christ" in this particular vision, she is entitled to and receives His loving care and protection. Moreover, it is the goal of all sanctified individuals to develop an intimate relationship with Christ since it is His nature and His character that they strive to emulate through their daily walk of faith.

The conflicts with her earthly husband are just some of the many trials that

Foote must face as a sanctified Christian. In fact, trials are expected to accompany the experience of the second blessing. Amanda Smith offers an explanation of why this is so: "It is, I believe, first, to develop the strength and muscle of your own soul and so prepare you for greater service, and second, to bring you into sympathy with others, that are often sorely tempted after they are sanctified, so that you can help them" (Smith 92). In other words, sanctified individuals need to be "toughened up" in order to be useful to God, even if this means being subjected to criticism for one's devotion to Him and His work. Further, trials cultivate a necessary sensitivity to those who are suffering similar difficulties, so that the believer can be supportive of them. Foote provides her own insights into the difficulties to which believers are at times subjected:

> God permits afflictions and persecutions to come upon his chosen people to answer various ends. Sometimes for the trial of their faith, and the exercise of their patience and resignation to his will, and sometimes to draw them off from all human dependence, and to teach them to trust in Him alone. Sometimes he suffers the wicked to go a great way, and the ungodly to triumph over us, that he may prove our steadfastness and make manifest his power in upholding us. Thus it was with me. I had trusted too much in human wisdom, and God suffered all these things to come upon me. He upheld me by his grace, freeing me from all care or concern about my health or what man could do. He taught me to sit patiently, and wait to hear my Shepherd's voice; for I was resolved to follow no stranger, however plausibly he might plead. (Foote 225)

Among the afflictions to which Foote refers in this passage is one that threatens to silence the voice that she has so carefully cultivated for the service of God; she suffers from a throat ailment that leaves her unable to preach for several years (Foote 224, 227–28) . Foote faults herself for trusting in the advice of doctors and friends instead of relying upon God for healing. She credits sanctifying grace for bringing about her recovery: "When I had well nigh despaired of a cure from my bodily infirmities, I cried from the depths of my soul for the blood of Jesus to be applied to my throat." She then continues, "I looked to my God for a fresh act of his sanctifying power. Bless his name! deliverance did come, with the balm, and my throat has troubled me but little since" (Foote 228).

Like Smith and Foote, Jarena Lee also finds her voice and vision irrevocably altered by the experience of sanctification. She is sanctified six months after her conversion, and like Foote, Lee is "led to believe that there was yet a greater work than that of pardon to be wrought in me" (Lee 34). Impressed by what she learns about sanctification from a man who has himself been sanctified, Lee actively seeks the second blessing but is not successful at attaining it until a day on which she has labored particularly long and hard in prayer: "When I arose from my knees, there seemed a voice speaking to me, as I yet stood in a leaning posture–'Ask for sanctification.' When to my surprise, I recollected that I had not even thought of it in my whole prayer. It would seem Satan had hidden the very object from my mind, for which I had purposely kneeled to pray" (Lee 34). Once Lee regains her focus and asks God specifically to sanctify her, the results are dramatic: "That very instant, as if lightning had darted through me, I sprang to my feet, and cried, 'The Lord has sanctified my soul!'" (Lee 34). After announcing this, however, she is conscious of the presence of Satan, who, having failed to foil her attempts at praying for sanctification, is lingering to persuade her that she did not get what she prayed for, arguing, "No, it is too great a work to be done" (Lee 34). Not to be undone by the devil, a competing spirit commands Lee to "Bow down for the witness–I received it–*thou art sanctified!*" (Lee 34). Lee rushes into the house to proclaim her victory. It is an emotional rendering of an experience that is beyond human description: "I stood perfectly still, the tears rolling in a flood from my eyes. So great was the joy, that it is past description. There is no language that can describe it, except that which was heard by St. Paul, when he was caught up to the third heaven, and heard words which it was not lawful to utter" (Lee 34).[39]

Lee directly links her experience of sanctification with her calling to preach the gospel:

> Between four and five years after my sanctification, on a certain time, an impressive silence fell upon me, and I stood as if some one was about to speak to me, yet I had no such thought in my heart. But to my utter surprise there seemed to sound a voice which I thought I distinctly heard, and most certainly understood, which said to me, "Go Preach the Gospel!" I immediately replied aloud, "No one will believe me." Again I listened, and again the same voice seemed to say, "Preach the Gospel; I will put words in your mouth, and will turn your enemies to become your friends." (Lee 35)

Like Foote, Lee fears that people will not believe that she has been chosen by God to preach His word. And like the prophet Jeremiah, Lee receives God's promise that He will put words into her mouth;[40] she will thus attain a Mouth Almighty capable of articulating the Truth so plainly and powerfully that her enemies will be converted into friends. As if to prepare her voice for its destiny and to reconcile her to her emerging identity as a radical spiritual mother, Lee envisions herself as a preacher while dreaming the following night: "I took a text, and preached in my sleep. I thought there stood before me a great multitude, while I expounded to them the things of religion. So violent were my exertions, and so loud were my exclamations, that I awoke from the sound of my own voice, which also awoke the family of the house where I resided" (Lee 35).

The process of Lee's coming to voice as a preacher is gradual. When she approaches Rev. Richard Allen to inform him of her call to preach the gospel, he denies her a preaching license because there is no provision in the Methodist Church Discipline for women's preaching. Lee is relieved because the burden of her calling has been temporarily deferred, and yet she also finds that "a love of souls had in a measure departed from me; that holy energy which burned within me, as a fire, began to be smothered" (Lee 36). She finds herself beset with doubts about the fate of her soul and fears a fall from grace. It is a vision that assures her that her soul's eternal destiny is secure:

> [T]here appeared a form of fire, about the size of a man's hand, as I was on my knees; at the same moment, there appeared to the eye of faith a man robed in a white garment, from the shoulders down to the feet; from him a voice proceeded, saying: "Thou shalt never return from the cross." Since that time I have never doubted, but believe that god will keep me until the day of redemption. (Lee 37–38)

Lee lets her readers know that the power of sanctification has been integral to maintaining this assurance: "From that time, 1807, until the present, 1833, I have not yet doubted the power and goodness of God to keep me from falling, through sanctification of the spirit and belief of the truth" (Lee 38).

In 1811, Lee marries a minister, Rev. Joseph Lee, and puts her own preaching on hold. During her marriage, she suffers a serious illness that she describes as "a state of general debility" (Lee 40). William Andrews suggests that this illness resulted from her efforts to sublimate her passion to preach by marrying a minister.[41] Lee asserts that her strong desire to preach is what kept her alive. Though Lee is unable to exercise her spiritual gifts to their fullest extent at this point in her life, she does effectively engage in a domestic ministry while stricken with illness: "[A] desire to warn sinners to flee the wrath to come, burned vehemently in my heart, when the Lord would send sinners into the house to see me. Such opportunities I embraced to press home on their consciences the things of eternity, and so effectual was the word of exhortation made through the Spirit, that I have seen them fall to the floor crying aloud for mercy" (Lee 40). Though Lee's body is in a weakened state, her will and her spirit are strong. Her home, a space that prefigures her later serial domesticity as an itinerant preacher, serves as a site where her preaching voice can be cultivated through her exhortations. Lee's description of God as One who sends people to her home suggests that He is a collaborative partner who subversively undermines the restrictions placed upon her spiritual gifts by Richard Allen. God wants His partner to lie low for the time being, all the while gaining in spiritual strength.

Lee is assured by God that her time for healing and preaching will come in time; she gains this assurance through a dream:

> I thought I saw the sun rise in the morning, and ascend to an altitude of about half an hour high, and then become obscured by a dense black cloud, which continued to hide its rays for about one third part of the day, and then burst forth again with renewed splendour.
>
> This dream I interpreted to signify my early life, my conversion to God, and this sickness, which was a great affliction, as it hindered me, and I feared would forever hinder me from preaching the gospel, was signified by the cloud; and the bursting forth of the sun, again, was the recovery of my health, and being permitted to preach. (Lee 40)

Following this dream, Lee prays to God and receives a confirming response: "Ye shall be restored to thy health again, and worship God in full purpose of heart" (Lee 40). Of this divine reply, Lee asserts, "From that very time I began to gain strength of body and mind, glory to God in the highest, until my health was fully restored" (Lee 40).

About eight years after Lee requested permission to preach from Richard Allen, she feels a renewed conviction that she must follow her calling; Lee approaches Allen again, this time requesting the privilege of holding prayer meetings in her home and exhorting people, which she is granted. By this time, her husband has passed away, and she must care for their two young children on her own. As she recounts this period in her life, Lee interrupts the narrative thread to relate the circumstances by which she helps to bring about the conversion of "a very wicked young man" (Lee 42). This incident is significant for charting the evolution of her voice.

Lee describes the youth as a black man who regularly attends her prayer meetings for the purpose of disrupting them and criticizing her denomination. The young man, however, becomes ill with consumption. When Lee visits him during his final days for the purpose of facilitating his conversion, she is received by him with indifference. On a second visit, Lee is accompanied by two women from her church; after the women's earnest prayers on his behalf, he is more receptive and invites them to return. Two days later, Lee is urgently sought by the young man's sister as he is on the verge of death and specifically requests Lee's presence. Taking one of the churchwomen with her, she goes to his bedside. Lee selects a hymn appropriate for his condition and begins to sing, "[b]ut there seemed to be a *horror* in the room—a darkness of a mental kind, which was felt by us all; there being five persons, except the sick young man and his nurse" (Lee 43). The palpability of this unearthly presence causes everyone to stop singing except for Lee, who continues "in a dull and heavy manner, though looking up to God all the while for help" (Lee 43). She suddenly feels a surge of energy, and a glimmer of light begins to pierce the darkness of the disturbing presence. When she finishes the hymn, the group kneels to pray. "While calling on the name of the Lord, to have mercy on his soul, and to grant him repentance unto life," it occurs to Lee that she should not cease until the young man's soul is converted and saved (Lee 43):

> Now, while I thus continued importuning heaven, as I felt I was led, a ray of light, more abundant, broke forth among us. There appeared to my view, though my eyes were closed, the Saviour in full stature, nailed to the cross, just over the head of the young man, against the ceiling of the room. I cried out, brother look up, the Saviour is come, he will pardon you, your sins he will forgive. . . . We rose up from our knees, when lo, his eyes were gazing with ecstasy upward; over his face there was an expression of joy; his lips were clothed in a sweet and holy smile; but no sound came from his tongue; it was heard in its stillness of bliss, full of hope and immortality. Thus, as I held him by the hand his happy and purified soul soared away, without a sign or a groan, to its eternal rest. (Lee 43–44)

In order to facilitate this conversion, Lee calls upon God's name, importuning Him to save the soul of the young man. Hers is an impassioned, insistent voice that helps to bring about salvation on the man's behalf. Not only this, but her sanctified voice has the power to drive the "horror" from the room and displace it with glory: "But as for me, I was filled with the power of the Holy Ghost—the very room seemed filled with glory" (Lee 44).

After relating this account, Lee returns again to discussing her renewed conviction that she must preach the gospel. She describes the occasion on which she suddenly jumped up and took over for Rev. Richard Williams when he lost the spirit in the middle of his sermon. Even after Richard Allen witnesses this inspired performance and is convinced that Lee has indeed been called to preach, coming to terms with the power of her voice as one that is destined for public expression is still a gradual process for Lee: "The next Sabbath day, while sitting under the word of the gospel, I felt moved to attempt to speak to the people in a public manner, but I could not bring my mind to attempt it in the church. I said, Lord, anywhere but here. Accordingly, there was a house not far off which was pointed out to me, to this I went" (Lee 45). Just as Rebecca Jackson's domestic dream imagery helps her to come to terms with her evolving identity as a radical spiritual mother and the power and publicity associated with this identity, the domestic sphere functions as a training ground for Lee's public voice. It is an early link in a developing chain of serial domesticity.

After Lee receives permission from Richard Allen to pursue her calling to preach, she cannot bring herself to begin publicly in the church. So she holds a meeting at a nearby house instead; the home thus becomes a "house-church" in which she hones her preaching skills:[42] "My congregation consisted of but five persons. I commenced by reading and singing a hymn, when I dropped to my knees by the side of a table to pray. When I arose I found my hand resting on the Bible, which I had not noticed till that moment" (Lee 45). Lee represents herself as unconsciously stumbling upon the Word that has been right in front of her all along. She must reclaim the vision that had been bestowed upon her years ago when she was sanctified so that she can once again envision herself as woman set apart for God's use—and this involves seeing and interpreting His Word: "It now occurred to me to take a text. I opened the Scripture, as it happened, at the 141st Psalm, fixing my eye on the 3d verse, which read: 'Set a watch, O Lord, before my mouth, keep the door of my lips.' My sermon, such as it was, I applied wholly to myself, and added an exhortation" (Lee 45). Even as she purposefully "takes a text," Lee still hesitates to accept agency for the scriptural choice, as is suggested by the words, "as it happened." And she is self-deprecating in her description of her ability to preach a sermon, as is clear by the disclaimer "such as it was." Accepting a God-given role that has been heretofore suppressed is not an easy task for Lee, and is one into which she must grow.

The verse on which she bases her sermon and her application of its meaning to herself is appropriate for one coming voice who will have a significant influence on a great number of people; though her sermon may seem to be invoking a kind of divine censorship of her verbal expression, she in fact seems to be emphasizing the need to live out the true spirit of sanctification; that is, to be "completely identified with God in thought, word, and deed."[43] In entreating God to "[s]et a watch, O Lord, before my mouth, keep the door of my lips," Lee is asking that her complete identification with God be made evident through the words she speaks. She also seems to be asking God to fulfill His promise to put His words in her mouth.

At the close of her service, Lee offers to preach again the following week if a home is made available, "when one answered that her house was at my service" (Lee 45). At this second meeting of her house-church, her growing spiritual power is made manifest: "Some wept, while others shouted for joy. One whole seat of females, by the power of God, as the rushing of the wind, were all bowed to the floor at once, and screamed out. Also a sick man and woman in one house, the Lord convicted them both; one lived, and the other died. God wrought a judgment—some were well at night, and died in the morning" (Lee 45).

Lee continues to hold meetings at this house for six months until she is invited to preach among the Methodists at a location thirty miles away. Her ministerial training in the domestic sphere has helped her to segue into this public venue. During this week-long preaching engagement, important developments in voice and consciousness occur. Asserting that "[t]he Lord gave his handmaiden power to speak for his great name," Lee points out that her voice is able to reach a wider range of people in terms of class: "Though, as I was told, there were lawyers, doctors, and magistrates present, to hear me speak, yet there was mourning and crying among sinners, for the Lord scattered fire among them of his own kindling" (Lee 46). But more important, this is the first preaching endeavor that has brought her away from her home and the care of her child. As stated in chapter 2, she must leave her sick son behind with friends who will care for him. When Lee returns home and finds her son safe, she evinces an important change of consciousness that indicates that her identity as a radical spiritual mother is beginning to take precedence over her identity as a biological mother: "I now began to think seriously of breaking up housekeeping, and forsaking all to preach the everlasting Gospel" (Lee 46).

Lee officially initiates the serial domesticity of a radical spiritual mother by taking her son and embarking by sea in the direction of her birthplace in Cape May, New Jersey, where she has a strong desire to go. She disembarks before reaching her hometown and gradually makes her way toward her mother's home, holding a meeting when she is about ten miles away. When she finally reaches her destination, her own mother helps to facilitate her daughter's developing identity as a radical spiritual mother by relieving her of her duties as a biological mother: "With her I left my sickly boy, while I departed to do my Master's will" (Lee 46). Lee's preaching career carries her far and wide, addressing people from a variety of races, classes, genders, and denominations. She asserts that with God's help, "My tongue was cut loose, the stammerer spoke freely" (Lee 48).

The transformative nature of sanctification upon the voice and vision of the radical spiritual mothers is profound. But beyond this, Christian perfection offers a psychological value for these women in that it acts as an "integrating force" to help them to better make sense of and adapt to life. Of this psychological value, George Dixon Greer explains:

> Judged by its influence in the lives of those who have claimed the experience, sanctification is a powerful integrating force. It stands for an ideal about which all of life is organized. For the individual it comes to mean three things: (1) continual and progressive adjustment to life situations, (2) a hopeful and expectant outlook on life as far as the individual is concerned, (3) a life filled with satisfying activity. Such qualities of life have a unifying effect. If moral conflict is the great disintegrator of personality, then sanctifying faith is the great unifier.[44]

With all of these potential benefits available to the believer through the experience of sanctification, it is no wonder that Julia Foote offers this earnest invitation to her readers in the final chapter of her narrative: "Why not yield, believe, and be sanctified now—now, while reading?" (Foote 234).

For the radical spiritual mothers, sanctification was not an abstract religious principle; it was a spiritual event that fundamentally transformed their lives. Sanctification helped them to cope with the daily struggles of life by providing emotional and psychological strength and enhancing self-esteem. Also significant were the ways that sanctification impacted their vision, enabling them to perceive themselves as favored agents of God and allowing them to envision a world transformed by God's grace. Further, sanctification helped the radical spiritual mothers to come to voice so that they could effectively spread the gospel and speak the truths that they felt divinely compelled to articulate.

Central to spreading these truths was the act of itinerancy. Therefore, in the next chapter, I examine itinerancy not only as a means for transmitting truths to the masses but also as an act central to the radical spiritual mothers' process of identity formation as migratory subjects.

4

MOVERS AND SHAKERS

Itinerancy and the Search for Community and Identity in the
Narratives of Zilpha Elaw and Rebecca Jackson

A gentleman residing in the city of Annapolis, offered me a house and a plot of
ground on condition of my residing there; but it was not meet for me to depart
from my Master's work, from considerations of worldly interest. I dared not, like
Demas, forsake my itinerating ministry, to love this present world.

—Elaw 99–100

R adical spiritual mothers were uncontainable. The divine mandate that
each woman received to travel widely and preach the gospel precluded
her physical confinement to the private sphere and her ideological constraint to
prescribed roles and ways of thinking and being. Although these women hon-
ored the private sphere as a space for self-reflection and for ritual communion
with God, it was nevertheless within the realm of the public sphere that they
were most critically engaged in the struggle against racial, sexual, and class
oppression. Because these writers were excluded from positions of power and
authority within their families, churches, and the larger society, they sought
alternative communities in which to share their gifts as intelligent, charismatic,
and powerful black women divinely chosen to carry out the work of God. In
this chapter, I argue that it is through the authors' public circulation as itinerant preachers that they most effectively engage in the process of finding and
forging communities of people who share their visions of a more just world
characterized by equality, inclusivity, and spiritual integrity.

In creating communities of faith, the radical spiritual mothers drew upon
imaginations that had been profoundly affected by the experience of sanctification, enabling them to spiritually envision these communities. The communities that they envisioned were spiritually based yet had radical social and political implications.[1] By asserting their fitness to assume positions of leadership
within these communities and by insisting upon equality among members, rad-

ical spiritual mothers soundly rejected their degraded status within the larger culture and undermined the institutionalized race, class, and gender inequities on which American society was founded and maintained.

As explained in chapter 3, radical spiritual mothers have their ontological base in the experience of sanctification; for only when each writer believed herself to be in complete harmony with the will of God did she feel fully authorized to step out of prescribed roles in order to exercise spiritual self-determination. In chapter 2, I pointed out the ways in which the material circumstances of these authors' lives invested them with a particular consciousness of the ways that racism, sexism, and classism converged to undermine their efforts to create stable and fulfilling lives for themselves and their families. But through the experience of sanctification, these women underwent a radicalization of consciousness that enabled them to view themselves as empowered agents of God and to posit a "radical egalitarianism"[2] against a cultural ethos that denied their full humanity.[3] Sanctification allowed them to formulate theologies of liberation that provided them with a set of religious tools with which to name, analyze, critique, and transform oppression. The achievement of sanctification did not signal the end of identity development for the radical spiritual mothers, however. On the contrary, they continually strove to cultivate a sense of self in relation to God and the world.

In conceiving of a new image of the world, the radical spiritual mothers desired the establishment of God's kingdom on earth. Rebecca Jackson explicitly articulates her belief that the Shakers are the divinely appointed agents responsible for ushering in this divine world order. Their desires for a spiritual transformation of society reflect the millennialist ideals that were prevalent during the nineteenth century.

The radical spiritual mothers, realizing, however, that they could not effect a full-scale transformation of American society (in which they were excluded from the rights and privileges bestowed upon citizens), sought alternative spaces in which to exercise spiritual leadership and to receive validation of their gifts. This method of creating empowered spaces for themselves made them interstitial subjects who exploited their marginality. In a radical act of self-affirmation, they placed themselves in the center and projected outward to envision communities that cut across boundaries of race, class, and gender to embrace all who professed a commitment to spiritual growth. In so doing, they in essence expressed an inclusiveness characteristic of liberation theologies.

The praxis of radical spiritual mothers fundamentally involved exercising the power to "care-in-relationship" to contribute to the material and spiritual sustenance needed by their extended spiritual families.[4] Black women have historically developed their identities within the context of community, within the context of caring for others. Possessing relational identities, radical spiritual mothers participated in a rich heritage of black collectivity: "African-American women recognize themselves not solely in isolation but in relationship to other women, to culture, and to creation. They develop individual identities by embracing the collective religious consciousness of black culture."[5] This collective orientation does not mean that black women have lost sight of themselves as individuals; on the contrary: independence, self-reliance, and the drive for self-definition have also been historically integral to black women's experiences.[6] The marginal status of the radical spiritual mothers required that they go out, and through itinerancy, "round up" people who would support them in their developing identities as powerful spiritual leaders; this action thus reflects both their desire for communal engagement as well as their need to be affirmed as individuals with unique callings.

The development of identity was a gradual process, taking place within the many contexts in which these writers found themselves on their travels. Carole Boyce Davies's concept of "migratory subjectivity" is a useful model for understanding how this process worked.[7] In the following sections, I focus on the narratives of Zilpha Elaw and Rebecca Jackson as texts that exemplify the process in which radical spiritual mothers engaged to find supportive and fulfilling communities of faith. Elaw is a "mover" who circulates broadly throughout the United States and England to deliver the message of the gospel. As she does so, not only does she have a powerful impact upon the audiences who hear her message, but she in turn is influenced by the people she meets and the circumstances she experiences. Jackson is a "shaker," not only in her religious affiliation as a member of the Believers in Christ's Second Appearing (the Shakers) but also in the radical ideology she espouses, which includes belief in celibacy and in a feminine component of the divine. She, perhaps more so than the other writers, insisted upon a community that both shared these beliefs and recognized her as an authoritative spiritual leader who lived by an uncompromising commitment to the mandates of a divine inner voice. I focus on Elaw and Jackson in particular because they represent the spectrum of the kinds of communities for which the radical spiritual mothers searched: small, supportive groups of women, often in the form of praying bands that provided spiritual and emotional support; mixed-gender prayer meetings that recognized the radical spiritual mothers' spiritual authority; camp meetings, which provided opportunities for spiritual renewal and offered large-scale venues for the authors to exercise their spiritual gifts; and, in the case of Rebecca Jackson, a permanent faith community that recognized her spiritual authority.

The Mover: Zilpha Elaw

Zilpha Elaw began her itinerant preaching career in Philadelphia in 1827 and worked her way throughout New York State. In 1828, she made a daring trip to the slave states, preaching in cities such as Annapolis and Baltimore, Maryland, Washington, D.C., and Alexandria, Virginia. She again visited the southern states in 1839. During this same year, Elaw met Jarena Lee in western Pennsylvania, where the two women formed a powerful preaching duo; of this collaborative experience, Lee comments: "[W]e enjoyed good seasons together. The greatest display of God's power seemed visible in a Protestant congregation; sister preached, and I gave an exhortation and closed, in which there was a great shout for victory."[8] Elaw also preached in the northeastern and Middle Atlantic states, and in 1840, she crossed the ocean to proselytize in London and central England. Though a member of a Methodist Episcopal Society, Elaw was never granted a license to preach but rather relied upon the promptings of her inner voice to guide her in her evangelistic pursuits.

Throughout Elaw's travels, communities of women occupy a significant presence. The various networks of women with whom she interacts not only provide her with unconventional access to power and leadership but also serve as vital material contexts for her spiritual development. Two groups that exemplify such communities are a large circle of young Methodist women who attend Elaw's ministry in Salem, Massachusetts, and a concerned band of caretakers who watch over the author during a protracted period of illness. Elaw describes the Methodist circle as a group whose unswerving commitment to a life of spiritual growth led many of them to achieve "considerable eminence in the apprehension of, and conformity to, the love of Christ, which passeth knowledge" (Elaw 119). The prominence that these women attain within (and possibly outside) the group reveals their establishment of an alternative standard of value for themselves. Within their circle they are not assessed according to standards of domesticity, but rather for their capacity to comprehend and demonstrate the love of Christ. As the woman most gifted in this capacity, Elaw is acknowledged as their leader, a title that she takes very seriously. Having been denied positions of authority in other areas of her life, she guards this distinction carefully in what almost seems to be a spiritual competition: "[T]he holy vigour and zeal with which they pressed forward after the life of God, the avidity with which they drank until they were filled with the Spirit, and the wonderful revelations God was pleased to manifest to them, provoked me to run forward in the heavenly race with increased earnestness, lest they should overtake, and leave me behind them" (Elaw 119). Notwithstanding the diligent efforts on her part, Elaw attributes her continued leadership to divine intervention: "but as the Lord set me as their leader, He sustained me as such; and an abundance of grace was given to me as His commissioned servant, to maintain my leadership" (Elaw 119).

Extending their efforts beyond the scope of the group, the women of Salem cultivate a spirit of ecumenism among the various denominations in the city by organizing monthly union prayer meetings. It is this faithful circle that helps to bring about a unified Christian community that Elaw envisions as "one fold and one shepherd; one body and spirit; one hope, one Lord, one faith, one baptism; and one God and father of all. . . . [Eph. 4:4–6]" (Elaw 117).

Throughout her text, Elaw describes incidents in which she becomes ill or suffers serious accidents. She interprets these occasions as trials administered by God in order to strengthen her faith. During many of these occurrences, she is attended by women who provide her not only with comfort and care but also with spiritual knowledge that enables her to proceed with the next step in her spiritual growth. Such a time occurs when she suffers an eight-month-long illness on Nantucket Island. Three women who attend her are a local young woman named Sarah M. Coffin, an elderly Baptist woman, and Elaw's daughter, who comes from New York to be with her mother. While praying at Elaw's bedside one evening, Sarah Coffin entreats, "Lord, of [*sic*] consistent with thy will, spare our sister Elaw, and take my life in her stead; for she is useful to thy cause, and I am but a feeble worm, and but of little worth" (Elaw 129). Sarah's prayer deeply impresses Elaw, who feels that the woman's words are "written on my heart as with an iron pen, or the point of a diamond" (Elaw 129). The sacrificial role that Sarah willingly accepts illustrates the collaboration that frequently occurs among women who work together to help midwife the identity of radical spiritual mother. The permanent inscription that this woman leaves upon Elaw's heart is a symbolic reminder of the vital role female community plays in underwriting the evolving identity of these authors.

On one particularly bleak day during Elaw's illness when she is expected to die, an elderly Baptist woman enters her room, saying: "Mrs. Elaw, I am bidden to tell you, that you will get better; God has a great work for you yet to do, and

I think you will travel some thousands of miles yet" (Elaw 129). The Baptist woman renews an earlier promise made by God to Elaw that she would preach the gospel in England. The attendant is just one of a number of women who deliver privileged spiritual knowledge to the author at critical moments of her life. Elaw's sister Hannah, for example, delivers a message that she insists she received from heaven on her deathbed, declaring that Elaw is destined to preach.

In narrating the details of Hannah's death, Elaw explains, "[S]he addressed herself to me, and informed me, that she had seen Jesus, and had been in the society of angels; and that an angel came to her, and bade her tell Zilpha that she must preach the gospel; and also, that she must go to a lady named Fisher, a Quakeress, and she would tell me further what I should do" (Elaw 73). Hannah actually extends the network of women having access to privileged spiritual knowledge for Elaw since she directs her to another woman for further instruction. Shortly after her sister's death, Elaw is visited by a woman minister (it is not clear if this is the Quakeress to whom her sister refers) who attempts to shepherd Elaw along toward her destiny of preaching:

> Soon after this [her sister's death], I received a visit from a female who was employed in the work of the ministry, who asked me if I did not think that I was called by the Lord to that work? to which I replied in the negative; she then said, "I think you are; now tell me, do not passages of Scripture often open to thy mind as subjects for public speaking and exposition? Weigh well this matter and see; for I believe that God has provided a great work for thy employment." (Elaw 75)

Like her biological sister, this spiritual sister has inside information on Elaw; she seems to read Elaw's mind, peering into its natural ability for scriptural exegesis. This visitor's role is to aid Elaw in her spiritual journey by helping her to envision herself as a public figure with spiritual authority, one who does not confine scriptural exposition to her mind but who cultivates a public voice to be used for God's service. These female messengers represent important alternative sources of knowledge against the patriarchal avenues of learning (such as seminaries) from which radical spiritual mothers are barred.

When Elaw begins to recover from her illness, Sarah Coffin informs her that she has asked a Quaker woman to pray for Elaw. In response to her prayer, the Quakeress receives the answer, "She shall get better, and in this Island shall hereafter be her home" (Elaw 130). Elaw's daughter eventually marries and settles in Nantucket, thus fulfilling the Quakeress's prediction. The role that

Elaw's daughter plays as "homemaker" is one of importance. Though traveling is central to community and identity development, the spiritual writers nevertheless express a strong need to call someplace home. For Elaw, it is Nantucket. For Amanda Smith, it is her two little attic rooms in the back of 135 Amity Street in New York (Smith 175). Home is where identity and community converge in the familiarity of God's love and care.

The boundaries between home and the public sphere are complicated as the radical spiritual mothers engage in serial domesticity, or a kind of itinerancy that involved traveling from house to house and church to church (houses of God or houses of worship) in order to minister to the needs of the family of God. As I argued in chapter 2, the radical spiritual mothers seem to draw upon familiar models of fluidity between the domestic and public spheres that have their basis in economic necessity, models they then apply to their spiritual praxis. In particular, the movement back and forth between their own homes and those of their employers provides a ready model for their house-to-house ministries. As spiritual leaders, however, they garner a measure of power, authority, and respect that they did not enjoy as secular women laboring both inside and outside the home.

Elaw actually makes her initial tentative attempts at preaching within the domestic sphere as she attends to her sister on her deathbed. After Hannah informs Elaw that she has received a heavenly message that Elaw is destined to preach, she insists that Elaw immediately begin to practice her calling by preaching to the people in the house:

> I cannot describe my feelings at this juncture; I knew not what to do, nor where to go: and my dear sister was pressingly urgent for me to begin and preach directly. . . . I was utterly at a loss what to say, or how to move; dear heart, she waited in silence for my commencing, and I stood in silence quite overwhelmed by my feelings. At length, she raised her head up, and said, "Oh, Zilpha! why do you not begin?" I then tried to say something as I stood occupied in mental prayer; but she said, "Oh! do not pray, you must preach." (Elaw 73–74)

Under the pressure of her sister's urgent entreaties to come to voice, Elaw delivers a weak but earnest command performance: "I then addressed a few words to those around me, and she was very much pleased with the attempt" (Elaw 74). Not only is this a difficult moment for Elaw as she tries to come to terms with her destined role, but it is also difficult for some of the women present to grasp, two of whom wonder about Elaw's strength and about Hannah's mental state: "[T]wo of the sisters then took me by the arm, and led me into another room; they there informed me they expected to see me sink down upon the floor, and that they thought my sister was perhaps a little delirious" (Elaw 74). Despite the uncertainty of some who are present on this occasion, it is an important opportunity for Elaw to try on her destined role in the safety of a house-church.

Joycelyn Moody views Elaw's portrayal of her sister's death as significant not only because Elaw links Hannah's passing to her calling to preach the gospel (another kind of passing–into a new identity), but also because it provides an occasion for Elaw to articulate her own theological viewpoints: "[W]hat distinguishes the event for Elaw is not that her sister was about to die. . . . Rather, she recounts Hannah's death using the Christian concepts of conversion, salvation, deliverance, exultation, and so on because the incident can teach readers about God and about the distinctive kind of relationship they could cultivate with God."[9] Thus Elaw explains, "I have been very careful, and the more minute in narrating the experience of my dear sister during her illness and death, in hope that it may possibly meet the cases of others tempted in a similar manner; that they may take encouragement from her happy and triumphant end" (Elaw 74).[10] Moody further notes that in particular, Elaw interjects into her account of her sister's illness and death a critique of those who might be skeptical of Hannah's visionary (her interaction with Jesus and angels) and prophetic (her pronouncement of Elaw's ministerial calling) experience, thus elaborating on her theology: "Elaw thus performs the work of traditional theologians: she constructs an argument in defense of Christianity rooted in personal witnessing, doctrinal concepts, and the glory of the divine."[11]

It was a particularly daring choice for a woman, especially a black woman, to declare her intentions to pursue a life of public ministry during a time when the home was deemed the proper sphere for women's work. When she believed herself to be divinely called to embark upon such work, Elaw already had one child, and she had a husband who strongly objected to her chosen course. Following her sanctification at a camp meeting, Elaw does not immediately begin traveling outside of the city in which she lives (Burlington, New Jersey) to preach the gospel. She instead engages in a five-year period of service to those in need in her community, a period that she tellingly describes as her "family or household ministry" (Elaw 71). Of this ministry, she explains:

[I]t was revealed to me by the Holy Spirit, that like another Phoebe, or the matrons of the apostolic societies, I must employ myself in visiting families,

and in speaking personally to the members thereof, of the salvation and
eternal interests of their souls, visit the sick, and attend upon other of the
errands and services of the Lord; which I afterwards cheerfully did, not confining my visits to the poor only, but extending them to the rich also, and
even to those who sit in high places in the state; and the Lord was with me
in the work to own and bless my labours. (Elaw 67)

Not only does this important work enable Elaw to transition into a full-fledged
career of public ministry, but her calling this mission a "family or household
ministry" seems to allow her a psychological connection to a role with which
she was already intimately familiar—that of a woman in charge of her own
household. Becoming a public religious leader meant fundamentally reformulating her relationship to power, and it seems that a necessary part of that refor-
mulation involved "domesticating" this power in order to justify to herself and
to others the new authority she was garnering.

Later in her ministry, Elaw makes it clear that with God's help, she is willing
to go into all kinds of houses: "Being encouraged by the smiles of my heavenly
Father, and animated to increased zeal in his holy cause, I went from house to
house and preached Christ and Him crucified to the people; I even ventured into
houses of ill fame, and exhorted the debased inmates to repent of their sins and
turn to Jesus Christ: and many of these unfortunate females became the genu-
ine disciples of Jesus" (Elaw 105). Whether she "inhabits" houses of ill repute,
houses of God, or private homes where prayer meetings are held, Elaw typically
describes her ability to attract large crowds and the strong impact her messages
have upon her audiences. Within these homes, she represents herself as being
clearly in charge of her church family, thus subverting patriarchal expectations
of authority. She explains that during services in which she presides, it was
not unusual for her to have to pause in order to allow listeners who are deeply
moved to express their emotions. One way that she seems to justify her authority is to suggest that within God's house, there is room for variation, including
such displays of emotion. Deviations from the expected order and manner of
worship are even desirable—if they demonstrate evidence of God's power. For
example, in commenting on the role of order in worship services, she explains:

Order in divine worship and in the house of God is graceful and appropriate; but the life and power of religion is not identified with, nor in propor-
tion to, the polish of the minister, the respectability of the congregation, or
the regularity and method of its services: the most abrupt and extraordi-

nary vicissitudes of weather are frequently productive of more benefit than the nicest graduated scale of temperature; and had it not been for some of these instances, in which the Almighty displayed the wonders of his victorious grace, even though the accustomed proprieties and regularity of divine service were at the time abruptly trenched upon and suspended, there are many churches now lively and flourishing, which, notwithstanding the exactness of the order of their worship, and the beauty of their arrangements, would now be but little more than so many religious automata. (Elaw 107)

In other words, it is acceptable to occasionally "shake things up" in God's house in order to breathe spiritual life into His family. Elaw perhaps envisions herself as part of this productive chaos, a part that is capable of incorporating alternative models of religious leadership within the church, specifically that of women. As an interstitial subject, she thus implicitly creates a space for herself as one who possesses legitimate spiritual authority.

The houses of God that Elaw inhabits transcend the confines of church buildings to encompass camp meetings, where domesticity and publicity are symbolically linked. It is within the contexts of American camp meetings that Elaw is able to envision God's kingdom on earth: "Oh, how I should like our dear English friends to witness some of our delightful camp-meetings, which are held in the groves of the United States. There many thousands assemble in the open air, and beneath the overspreading bowers, to own and worship our common Lord, the Proprietor of the Universe; there all arise and sing the solemn praises of the King of majesty and glory. It is like heaven descended upon an earthly soil" (Elaw 64). Perhaps for Elaw, God's heavenly kingdom represents the ultimate domestic sphere, one that is truly liberating in its promise of equality and inclusivity. She certainly would have been familiar with the Bible scripture John 14:2, in which Jesus describes for his disciples the kingdom of heaven in domestic terms: "In my Father's house are many rooms; if it were not so, would I have told you that I go to prepare a place for you?" Not only does Elaw feel it imperative to have a place prepared for her in heaven in God's house, but she also demands exalted spaces on earth; she desires places where she is recognized and respected for her spiritual gifts, places where her leadership is validated. Camp meetings provide such venues for her, as well as enable her to reconceptualize her relationship to the earthly domestic sphere.

Camp meetings were a revivalistic tool used mainly by Methodists and Baptists as a means of accomplishing religious conversions on a large scale. In particular, these denominations targeted white southern "plain-folk," a term used to describe the large numbers of southern farmers and townspeople who, prior to the Civil War, led lives that were neither wealthy nor impoverished. This group characterized the majority of antebellum southerners and was the most diligent in serving as leaders for the Methodist and Baptist denominations.[12]

Camp meetings are particularly meaningful for Elaw because it is at one such gathering that she is sanctified and at another that she begins her public ministry. The positive terms in which she speaks about these religious revivals suggest that she views them as transitory communities of faith in which she can engage in fellowship with others who are searching for deeper spiritual meaning. The location of camp meetings in "some wildly rural and wooded retreat in the back grounds of the interior" (Elaw 65) implies a marginal quality, an interstitial space, with the potential to foster human relationships that are more liberating than those defined by the larger society. Perhaps the wide-open space of the camp-meeting setting evoked for Elaw the same kinds of feelings of catharsis and freedom that the character Baby Suggs brought to the clearing in Toni Morrison's *Beloved:* "When warm weather came, Baby Suggs, holy, followed by every black man, woman and child who could make it through, took her great heart to the Clearing—a wide-open place cut deep in the woods nobody knew for what at the end of a path known only to deer and whoever cleared the land in the first place."[13] In the protected hollow of the clearing, the "unchurched preacher" Suggs teaches black people to love themselves. The gift that she offers to her burdened followers is to give them back their humanity. Like her fictional sister of the spirit, Elaw yearns to be the transmitter of healing grace for her people. Her explicit characterization of these gatherings as "like heaven descended upon earth" implies that these communities approach her ideal of the kind of society she envisions.[14]

In reality, though, camp meetings replicated the social structures of the larger culture. The organizational structure of the meetings and the roles enacted by participants served to reinscribe male dominance and racial inequality. Dickson D. Bruce explains that at the center of the clearing, where the pulpit, altar, and congregational seats were arranged, white men were separated from white women, and blacks were segregated from whites. White men and women were kept apart by a center aisle or a rail fence; moreover, whites sat in the front and blacks in the back, with the minister positioned on an elevated pulpit, high above the masses.[15]

The roles of minister and professional exhorter were held by men. Black men could be professional exhorters, but they usually addressed only other black people in the congregation. Women and children were allowed to act as convert exhorters (recent converts who exhorted others to undergo conversion); however, they usually did not make exhortations at scheduled services, as men were called upon to do, but made spontaneous appearances. Women and children could also function as "good singers and praying persons," who, through their songs and prayers, encouraged individuals who were overcome by God's power.[16]

The only time that social distinctions were suspended was during the ritual of conversion. At this time, those who sought conversion came forward and entered what was called the altar or pen, which was situated in front of the pulpit. The minister descended from his platform and joined the prospective converts (also called mourners), thus physically placing himself on equal footing with them. Joining the minister in the pen were the "good singers and praying persons," who offered further encouragement to the mourners. For a brief period, as the conversions took place, women and children enjoyed leadership roles as convert exhorters and as "good singers and praying persons." Moreover, segregation by gender was either downplayed or suspended in the pen. The only possible structural distinction retained in the pen was that of race.[17]

The details that Elaw provides regarding camp meeting procedures are accurate, yet her account is incomplete. What she chooses to emphasize and to omit is instructive. What she highlights are procedural and organizational details, such as how the meetings are published, the kinds of preparations that are made for the occasion, the physical arrangement of the site, the number of people who attend, the manner in which worship is undertaken, and the rituals that are involved in bringing the meeting to a close. She also describes the spiritual effects that the community experiences as a whole, as well as the personal enrichment she gains. What Elaw does not mention is the hierarchical nature of social relationships within the community. She instead implies that the power of God is capable of eliding social distinctions. At the camp meeting in which she begins her public preaching career, she articulates this implicit attitude while describing the effects of a powerful sermon: "When he came to the application of his discourse, there seemed not to be one person on the spot, whose eyes were not suffused with tears; both high and low, rich and poor, white and coloured, were all melted like wax before the fire" (Elaw 81). Though race, class, and gender equality do not actually exist in the community of the camp meeting, Elaw exhibits an imperative to textually construct that which is lacking. With her pen, she discursively creates a "pen" in which social distinctions are negated.

Being a member of a textually constructed egalitarian camp meeting community is not enough. Just as Elaw insists upon a position of authority within the group of women who attend her ministry in Salem, so does she desire to be recognized as a leader at the camp meeting. At the 1817 meeting, it is her dramatic sanctification and subsequent role as a "praying person" that establishes this authority. At a later camp meeting, it is the divine calling to public ministry, in the presence of other (ordained, male) ministers that launches her into a position of power.

At the 1817 camp meeting, while under the influence of a powerful sermon, Elaw sinks to the ground and undergoes an out-of-body experience: "[A]nd while I was thus prostrate on the earth, my spirit seemed to ascend up into the clear circle of the sun's disc; and, surrounded and engulphed in the glorious effulgence of his rays, I distinctly heard a voice speak unto me, which said, 'Now thou art sanctified; and I will show thee what thou must do'" (Elaw 66). As Elaw's spirit soars above the scene, she feels that she is no longer within the earthly realm, and she sees "bodies of resplendent light" (Elaw 67). Her suggestion that she has briefly encountered heaven seems to invest her with an otherworldly insight that renders her uniquely qualified to act as an intermediary between heaven and earth—and thus as a spiritual authority. She demonstrates this authority in her role as a "praying person."

When Elaw awakens from her trance, she finds herself surrounded by a crowd of weeping people. When she fully recovers, and a prayer meeting begins, she is inspired to offer up public prayer. Implying the success of her effort, she explains, "I was after this very frequently requested to present my petitions to the throne of grace in the public meetings at the camp" (Elaw 67). Her invitations to prayer meetings override the custom of denying women a place of leadership in scheduled services. This unusual privilege helps to establish her authority within the community.

At a later camp meeting, Elaw demonstrates her qualifications to lead when she is divinely charged to travel widely to preach the gospel. As at the previous meeting, she is greatly affected by a stirring sermon. Many others who are also deeply touched by the message crowd into her tent to engage in prayer. As Elaw proceeds to the back of the tent, she believes she feels a hand touch her on the shoulder and that she hears a voice that speaks to her: "Go outside of the tent while I speak with thee" (Elaw 81). Turning around to ascertain where the voice came from, she sees no one, and steps outside. At the door of the tent Elaw feels compelled to exhort the gathering, thus gaining the attention of a large crowd.

As at the 1817 meeting, Elaw is propelled to the forefront as a spiritual leader. But this occasion seems to have even greater significance for her because she gains the acknowledgment of the ministers, who gaze upon her performance with tearful eyes. She links her empowerment to the sermon just preached, which began, "Now then we are ambassadors for Christ. . . . [2 Cor. 5:20]" (Elaw 81). She, too, views herself as an ambassador for Christ. And as such, she believes herself worthy of inclusion in the ranks of the ministry. Elaw, an interstitial subject engaging in an act of improvisation, creates an empowered space within the context of the camp meeting community. Thus officially begins her public ministry, as she hears a voice speak: "Now thou knowest the will of God concerning thee; thou must preach the gospel; and thou must travel far and wide" (Elaw 82).

One is particularly aware of the identity-transforming qualities of location within the context of Elaw's journeys to the southern states. Traversing the Mason-Dixon Line, Elaw makes a transcultural crossing. Though she travels with the assumption that she is privileged with providential guidance and protection, her arrival in the southern territories forcefully reminds her of the multiple significations that an independent black female body invokes in people who encounter her. She is a threat and a curiosity that is not expected to possess a voice, much less a soul or a will of her own. The tension between the subjectivity she has constructed for herself and the object status that people project onto her is evident in the unfolding of an internal battle of wills that she has with a perceived satanic presence while she is addressing a black congregation:

> I had no sooner sat down, than Satan suggested to me with such force, that the slave-holders would speedily capture me, as filled me with fear and terror. I was then in a small town in one of the slave states; and the news of a coloured female preaching to the slaves had already been spread widely throughout the neighbourhood; the novelty of the thing had produced an immense excitement and the people were collecting from every quarter, to gaze at the unexampled prodigy of a coloured female preacher. . . . Being very much alarmed, I removed from my seat to a retired part of the room. (Elaw 91)

The voice of Satan can be read as the resurgence of her own fear, which she seems to have temporarily suppressed in order to summon the courage to address her enslaved brothers and sisters within a threatening context. This fear assails her, forcing her to come to terms with her identity as a black woman located in the midst of a hostile environment. To master her fear requires her to renegotiate her identity by positing an alternative, empowered signification of black woman. As Elaw rallies her strength against Satan, against her own self-doubts and fears, she aligns herself with the power of Christ. More accurately, she becomes Christ figuratively in a manner that reenacts a biblical scene in which Jesus rebukes the defiant disciple, Peter: "I inquired within myself, 'from whence cometh all this fear?' My faith then rallied and my confidence in the Lord returned, and I said, 'get thee behind me Satan, for my Jesus hath made me free'" (Elaw 91).[18] No longer does Elaw allow herself to be read as impotent, as breeder, as dispossessed. Instead, she substitutes these degraded signifieds with those that identify her as powerful, as a radical spiritual mother, as the progeny of a divine heritage.

Elaw survives her momentary identity crisis and emerges as a woman who has confidence in her ability to appeal not only to black slaves but to white slaveholders as well. As her narrative continues, it is clear that she has powerful appeal to people of all races, classes, and genders. For example, in speaking about the positive effects she helps to bring about through her preaching in the city of Alexandria, Virginia, Elaw asserts, "The work of the Holy Spirit was greatly manifested in this city; both high and low, rich and poor, white and coloured, all drank out of the living streams which flowed from the City of our God" (Elaw 96).

Elaw later makes another trip to the slave states on a preaching mission. Her daring might be compared to that of Harriet Tubman, who repeatedly risks her life to return to the brutal scene of slavery to rescue her fellow bondpersons. Tubman's rescues are physical, whereas Elaw's are spiritual. Her crossing of the Mason-Dixon Line is an intentional act of reconnecting with a community of black women and men from which she has been cut off by the laws of slavery.

The Shaker: Rebecca Jackson

Of all the radical spiritual mothers, Rebecca Jackson is unique in finding a permanent community that shared her religious philosophy and worldview and that acknowledged her as its leader. In 1858, Jackson established a predominantly black and female Shaker community in Philadelphia and became known among her followers as "Mother Rebecca." The establishment of this community occurs at the end of a long journey of personal struggle that takes place both outside herself, with those who are threatened by her religious views and power, and inside herself, with internalized racist and sexist oppression. Not only must she resist the patriarchal narratives of husband, brother, and male church authorities who insist that she is parting husbands from wives (due to her belief in celibacy), is "chopping up the churches" (because she refuses to join any of the established denominations), and is crazy (because she engages in rigorous ascetic practices), but she must also fend off internal voices that tell her she is not worthy, as a black woman, to possess the kind of power that she does.

Jackson begins and ends her journey in Philadelphia, coming full circle, and along the way, arriving at increasingly higher levels of consciousness and spiritual power. As a woman whose complex and vivid dreams and visions come to inform every aspect of her life, Jackson is the ultimate interstitial subject. Her dreams and visions render her a border woman who continually crosses the line between the spiritual and temporal worlds. It is at the intersection of these worlds that she creates her own empowered spaces. These spaces include a series of communities ranging from prayer groups in Philadelphia to a predominantly white Shaker commune in Watervliet, New York, and finally to the predominantly black and female Shaker community in Philadelphia.

The Methodist tradition that informed Jackson's early religious experiences provided opportunities for free black women to develop leadership skills within the intimate environment of prayer groups, which were usually held in homes. Beginning in the 1820s and 1830s, "small, enthusiastic Holiness praying groups" formed within Methodism with the aim of fostering members' efforts to attain sanctification.[19] The Holiness movement, according to most sources, seemed to have been dominated by women, and was especially attractive to black women in antebellum America. Black women, who daily faced the realities of racism, benefited psychologically from the sense of assurance that accompanied the experience of sanctification.[20]

The Holiness movement was distinguished by praying bands that were completely or primarily comprised of women; these groups would be an ongoing presence in American black Methodism. Sharing spiritual experiences within these bands led many black Methodist women to consider expanding their preaching beyond the confines of the groups. Within these small, democratic meetings in which women actively engaged, participants found support for the development of their speaking and spiritual gifts. These gatherings probably played an important role in preparing women for public speaking and preaching careers, especially in light of the antagonism or wariness that female religious leaders aroused in some congregations and in individual black church leaders.[21]

Just as Amanda Smith benefited from her membership in a praying band, Jackson's early religious career included her participation in a number of prayer groups throughout Philadelphia that allowed her to gradually develop religious leadership skills. After her sanctification in 1831, she helped to lead a praying band whose members strove together toward spiritual perfection. Jackson describes the manner in which these meetings proceeded:

> The meeting that we held once a week at Sister Mary Peterson's we called the Covenant Meeting, because we covenanted together for a holy life. This meeting we held on Wednesday night. They appointed Mary Peterson and me to lead. We desired to move as we believed the Spirit of God directed us. Sometimes we sat in silent prayer, in reading a portion of scripture, in singing, in rising on our feet and speaking as we believed the spirit gave us utterance. So we had no appointed way. We never knowed [*sic*] what way we were agoing to lead our next. And all the Covenant members had the same liberty to move as they felt. Mary would lead one night, and I the other. That is, we would open the meeting, then they would move in whatever gift of God they believed they had. (Jackson 102)

The leadership skills that Jackson is allowed to exercise in this group differ vastly from the circumscribed roles assigned to her in family life. Although two men, Jackson's husband and Thomas Gibbs, are original members of the group, they nevertheless defer leadership to the women. Despite Jackson's authority, she encourages a flexible structure, which privileges the right of all members to equally express their spiritual gifts as they see fit.

Participation in this praying band helps to fulfill Jackson's desire for a community that recognizes her spiritual authority, but it raises other issues that are problematic. The group's popularity grows immensely, attracting not only new members but also the attention of church leaders who are disturbed by rumors that Jackson is "aholding class meetings and aleading the men" (Jackson 105). Aside from her leadership of men, the radical views she espouses regarding the issue of celibacy are particularly threatening to church authorities, who fear that she may undermine the patriarchal family structure and, thus, male dominance.

Jackson must contend with external resistance, but she also faces opposition from within the group. Since she is perceived as possessing a higher level of spiritual awareness than the other members and has a much more stringent standard for holy living, she often finds herself at odds with less gifted members:

> I cried mightily to God to make me holy. And sometimes when praying and in speaking I would manifest this in meeting, when the effects that followed, were as if I had opened a bottle of cayenne pepper among the people. They would begin to dispute my testimony, by saying they never expected to be holy in this life. . . . They did not expect to be saved by works, but by the righteousness of Christ. To be sanctified was the highest state of grace they had ever heard of and that was enough for them. They said I was hunting for something I did not know what. (Jackson 87)

What Jackson is "hunting" for is a community that shares her ideals on spiritual perfection, including her belief in celibacy. While suffering under a burden of intense criticism and a feeling of isolation that her religious ideals garner, she envisions the community of which she longs to be a part:

> Then my spiritual eyes was opened and I saw in the distance flocks of kids, white as snow, on beautiful green grass. They laid close to the ground. Their forefeet were crossed and their chin rested on their forefeet. They were many miles apart. They all looked like one kid yet I seen them distinct. And when I saw them, it was said to me, "These are my people. These live the life that I have called you to live. And if you are faithful, I will bring you to see them." (Jackson 137)

This allegorical vision foretells her involvement with the white Shakers at Watervliet. Her description of the kids as "white as snow" not only suggests the racial identity of the community that she will join but also seems to reflect an acceptance of whiteness as a signifier of purity. In this case, whiteness probably signifies purity of the heart or soul in connection with the Shakers' favored status as God's true people on earth.

Though Jackson and the other spiritual writers consciously resist racial and sexual stereotypes, they at times reflect the extreme difficulty of completely liberating themselves from particular cultural symbols, such as the equation of whiteness with goodness and blackness with evil. Julia Foote, for example, joyfully declares: "Jesus' blood will wash away all your sin and make you whiter than snow" (Foote 189). Another example of this kind of uncritical acceptance of the cultural values assigned to color is found in Jackson's description of the anguish she experienced during her conversion: "My sins like a mountain reached to the skies, *black* as sack cloth of hair and the heavens was as brass against my prayers and everything above my head was of one solid blackness" (Jackson 72). Also noting these women's equation of whiteness with purity, Richard Douglass-Chin comments: "Indeed, the motif of whiteness as purity is a common one. The fact that the black evangelist women use it suggests to me a consciousness deeply rooted in a white Christian system of symbolism struggling against the obvious conflicts that the adoption of such a system precipitates for black people."[22]

The radical spiritual mothers' acceptance and perpetuation of the cultural values assigned to color seem to speak to the pervasiveness and deeply entrenched nature in American culture of what Toni Morrison calls "Africanism." In *Playing in the Dark,* Morrison defines Africanism as "the denotative and connotative blackness that African peoples have come to signify, as well as the entire range of views, assumptions, readings, and misreadings that accompany Eurocentric learning about these people."[23] In particular, Africanism involves "the fetishizing of color, the transference to blackness of the power of illicit sexuality, chaos, madness, impropriety, anarchy, strangeness, and helpless, hapless desire."[24] The radical spiritual mothers' possession of a complex double-consciousness may help to explain why they, as black women, accept the negative values attached to blackness.

Before Jackson can reach the point of joining the Shakers, she must undergo a process of identity development that takes place within the context of the numerous places that she travels to during her itinerant preaching career. Not only does she envision the kind of community she would like to inhabit, but in 1831 she also envisions the type of person she desires to become:

> [A]ll at once I saw a woman step before me. She was dressed in light drab. Her bonnet was close to her face. Her arms hung down at her side. She walked straight forward. She neither looked nor turned to the right nor left. [Nothing in this world seemed to take her attention.][25] She was about twelve feet from me right in the path before me. And it was spoken in my heart, "This is the way I want you to walk and to dress and when you are as you ought to be, you will look like this woman and be like her." (Jackson 93)

The woman Jackson sees is attired in traditional Shaker dress and is a recurring vision that guides the spiritual writer's identity development.[26] As Jackson continues to grow in her faith, she gets closer in proximity to the woman in her vision, until she at last catches up with her in 1834. At that time, she and her visual guide converge into one woman, symbolically marking the completion of a critical stage in Jackson's identity development. Taken together, the vision of the Shakers ("A Vision in 1831, of God's True People on Earth, Who Live in Christ and Christ in Them")[27] and the vision of the Shaker woman ("My Holy Leader, a Woman") represent the ultimate promise of the union of identity and community.

Jackson breaks away from her family and begins her itinerant preaching career in 1833 at Marcus Hook, Pennsylvania. The scope of her travels is much less extensive than that of Elaw, including tours through New York, Pennsylvania, New Jersey, and the New England states. The kinds of identity-developing experiences that Jackson encounters during her journeys are no less significant, however. One such experience occurs in 1835, as Jackson traveled west of Philadelphia to undertake a preaching tour. During this period in her life, she found herself the target of intense persecution because of her beliefs. AME ministers warned the church trustees not to allow her to speak in the church nor to let anyone open their homes to her to preach. Anyone daring to go to listen to Jackson would be thrown out of the church. One minister in particular rode about on his horse, warning people not to allow her to preach. The only person who dared to open his home to her was a drunken man who did not belong to the church. His house soon overflowed with people eager to hear Jackson speak. Burdened by the weight of persecution, feeling an acute sense of loneliness, and standing before this crowd of expectant listeners, Jackson experiences a revelation that there is a Mother in the deity that coexists with the heavenly Father. She sees this maternal divinity in a vision as she stands before the people. She is awestruck with this knowledge of a divine Mother and is inspired to speak of her discovery to the crowd: "And was I not glad when I found that I had a Mother! And that night She gave me a tongue to tell it! The spirit of weeping was upon me, and it fell on all the assembly. And though they never heard it before, I was made able by Her Holy Spirit of Wisdom to make it so plain that a child could understand it" (Jackson 154). In this passage, Jackson articulates a joyfulness befitting that of a child who has been united with an absent but cherished parent. This heavenly Mother not only inspires joy in Jackson, but She also provides her with a new language, a Mother tongue, with which to address the people.

Jackson's discovery of a female component in the deity not only coincides with the Shaker belief in a Mother/Father God but also reflects an affinity with gnostic beliefs in a maternal deity. Elaine Pagels explains that gnostic texts reveal three primary characterizations for the divine Mother: the Mother as part of an original couple, as Holy Spirit, and as Wisdom. The last characterization aligns most closely with the Shaker conceptualization of the female deity as Holy Mother Wisdom.[28] Moreover, Mary Farrell Bednarowski argues that religious movements that espouse a dual-gender conception of the divine are more likely to support leadership roles for women.[29]

This is an occasion for a conceptual transformation for Jackson that has significant implications for the societal distribution of power, for the belief in the inherent superiority of males that characterizes patriarchal religions serves to legitimate male domination in society at large. To assert the existence of a female God who is equal in importance and power with the male God is potentially threatening to the very foundations of patriarchal culture.[30] This is a moment of conceptual transformation that also marks a dramatic change in the material circumstances of Jackson's life. Doors that had been tightly shut against her are now opened. The minister who had been trying to suppress her voice is stopped by people who are sympathetic to her. Having intended to spend only two weeks on this preaching tour, Jackson ends up traveling for four months, delivering sixty-nine sermons. Jackson, empowered by the knowledge of the divine Mother, is allowed to reinhabit homes (though she is not restricted to this sphere), including church-homes, with her message.

Spiritual maternity plays an important role for Jackson during the period of her persecution in 1835. Her consciousness of a maternal deity is empowering for Jackson both spiritually and materially, but also significant is her embracing of her own spiritual maternity as a radical spiritual mother to shield herself from male aggression. In particular, she is persecuted by three ministers who believe she deserves to suffer a violent death for her preaching: "One said I ought to be stoned to death, one said tarred and feathered and burnt, one said I ought to be put in a hogshead, driven full of spikes, and rolled down a hill" (Jackson 149).[31] Jackson responds to this verbal assault by praying to God to enable her to control her thoughts and feelings toward these men in order to avoid harboring hostility for them and to acknowledge the men's worth despite their cruelty. Jackson reports that she is successful in managing her thoughts, feelings, and interactions with the ministers, due largely to the gentle maternal demeanor she is divinely inspired to adopt toward them: "And I always spoke to them, when I saw them, kindly, and I felt a kind and motherly feeling toward them, for which I both praise and thank God for the gift" (Jackson 149). As a radical spiritual mother who regards the family of God as her spiritual children, Jackson seems to draw upon her spiritual maternity to disarm her attackers.

Up to this point, Jackson has not yet found a community that embodies her earlier vision of God's true people on earth. She first visits a Shaker meeting in the fall of 1836 while on a preaching mission in Albany. When she enters the room in which they gather, Jackson's inner voice utters, "These are my people" (Jackson 139). Their appearance of seeming to be "not of this world, but as if they were living to live forever" (Jackson 139) helps to confirm Jackson's belief that this is indeed the community of which she is destined to become a member. She does not join them immediately, however, because she has not yet completed the itinerant phase of her career that God has assigned her to carry out. It is not until 1847 that she officially unites with the Shakers at Watervliet for the first of two periods of residence.

Jackson was drawn to the Shakers for a number of reasons. She found that their religious and social views closely coincided with her own independently formed beliefs. In particular, she was impressed by their positive regard for celibacy, their denunciation of governments and churches for wrongly appropriating the authority that legitimately belonged to the authentic Christian community, their support of ecstatic experience as a valid aspect of worship, and their belief in the human capacity to receive and reveal divine revelation. The Shakers derived their sense of harmony and unity from their privileged relationship to the sacred. Their policy of admitting blacks as members sharing equal status with whites may have also been a drawing force for Jackson. What may have ultimately led Jackson to join the Shakers was their acknowledgment of her as a true prophet. During a three-day visit at Watervliet in 1843, Jackson displayed her special gifts through experiencing a series of significant visions and by having what seemed to be a seizure, which she perceived to be a bodily manifestation of her special status as a chosen one selected by Holy Mother Wisdom.[32]

Jackson's narrative does not offer a very full account of her life during her first residence at Watervliet (1847–51). Shaker records reveal that she continued her work as a seamstress. This was in keeping with the Shaker practice of dividing labor in a traditional manner according to gender. Jackson also continued her preaching in the context of Sabbath meetings. Her preaching was considered uncommon since this was not an ordinary practice among Shaker sisters except for eldresses. She formed a very close friendship with another black woman, Rebecca Perot, who joined the Shakers at the same time Jackson did. The two women are almost always referred to as a pair ("the two Rebeccas") in Shaker records. They likely lived together throughout this four-year period. Jackson probably also formed close friendships with a number of the white sisters.[33]

The nature of the relationship between Jackson and her companion Rebecca Perot has been the subject of critical discussion. In her introduction to Jackson's narrative, Jean Humez comments, "Perhaps, had she [Jackson] been born in the modern age, she would have been an open lesbian."[34] In her review of *Gifts of Power,* Alice Walker takes exception with this suggestion, arguing, "Though women ministers who worshiped and lived with other women were perceived by the male leaders of the early churches as 'closeted lesbians,' because they followed their own inner voices rather than the 'fathers' of the church, there is nothing in these writings that seems to make Jackson one."[35] Walker further emphasizes that Jackson asserts her "'deadness' to sexuality or 'lust'" and her commitment to a life of celibacy.[36] In a footnote to her speculation about Jackson's sexual orientation, Humez actually comes close to expressing the same sentiments as Walker: "Rebecca Jackson's writings offer very little direct evidence either to support or to contradict the theory that there was an acknowledged sexual component in her relationship with her lifelong disciple and companion, Rebecca Perot. That the love they felt for each other helped make heterosexual relationships unnecessary for either seems very clear, but both also subscribed to an antisexual ideology."[37] In the same footnote, Humez directs the reader to Carroll Smith-Rosenberg's essay on "female homosocial networks" of the nineteenth century as a useful source for thinking about Jackson and Perot's relationship.[38] Evaluating primarily middle-class white women's friendships within an eighteenth- and nineteenth-century American cultural and social context, Smith-Rosenberg asserts that "an abundance of manuscript evidence suggests that eighteenth- and nineteenth-century women routinely formed emotional ties with other women. Such deeply felt, same-sex friendships were casually accepted in American society."[39] Such behavior as kissing, hugging, sleeping together, and ardently expressing one's love for one another were deemed acceptable interactions within women's friendships in a culture[40]

> characterized in large part by rigid gender-role differentiation within the family and within society as a whole, leading to the emotional segregation of women and men. The roles of daughter and mother shade imperceptibly

and ineluctably into each other, while the biological realities of frequent pregnancies, childbirth, nursing, and menopause bound women together in physical and emotional intimacy. It was within just such a social framework . . . that a specifically female world did indeed develop, a world built around a generic and unself-conscious pattern of single-sex or homosocial networks.[41]

Clearly, the rigid gender boundaries that existed for middle-class white women were relaxed for working-class women, whose labor necessarily took them beyond the confines of the domestic sphere; moreover, the events of pregnancy, childbirth, and nursing would not be facts of life for celibate women living in Shaker communities; however, I think it could be argued that the cultural ethos of nineteenth-century America would serve to normalize the intimacy characterizing Jackson and Perot's relationship.

Jackson joined the Shakers during a period in the group's history known as "the Era of Manifestations" or "Mother Ann's Work," which lasted from 1837 through 1847 but continued in diminishing degrees until 1857. It was characterized by the manifestation of ecstatic gifts practiced by a large number of Shakers who functioned as mediums or instruments conveying visions, messages, and rituals believed to represent the spiritual world that humans would ultimately enter after the Resurrection was completed. This was a period of spiritual revival and a time of intensified isolation from the outside world.[42] It was this exaggerated withdrawal from the world and a perceived preoccupation with worldly concerns that Jackson found objectionable during her first residence with the Shakers: "After I came to Watervliet, in the year 1847, and saw how Believers seemed to be gathered to themselves, in praying for themselves and not for the world, which lay in midnight darkness, I wondered how the world was to be saved, if Shakers were the only people of God on the earth, and they seemed to be busy in their own concerns, which were mostly temporal" (Jackson 220). Jackson cannot understand how society can be transformed when the Shakers refuse to become actively involved in it. This is one point of contention between her and the Shaker leaders.

Related to this issue of isolationism was the perceived lack of commitment to addressing the needs of blacks that Jackson detected on the part of the leaders. Ideologically, Shakers were committed to racial equality and abolitionism. But Richard Williams points out that ideals did not always translate into action. Though the Believers were gathered unto themselves, they were not immune to social pressures from the outside world regarding their racial policy. Shakers sometimes compromised their commitment to racial equality to avoid violence. For example, a separate black family (called Blackliet, the Black Family, or the Maple Leaf) headed by a black elder was organized at South Union, Kentucky, in order to appease neighbors who asserted that blacks should be treated as slaves. In another case, Shakers succumbed to pressure from people in the surrounding area by "freezing out" a fellow black Shaker at a brief Shaker experiment in White Oak, Georgia, in 1898.[43]

Perhaps the most fundamental problem that Jackson had with the Shakers was their reluctance to recognize the primacy of her inner voice's authority. Rather than giving unconditional deference to Shaker leaders, Jackson unyieldingly privileged the guidance provided by the divine voice within. This reflects an important quality of radical spiritual mothers: not only do they seek communities that share their beliefs, but they also require communities that will allow them to lead. With a compelling need to exercise spiritual autonomy and a strong commitment to helping to improve the lives of African Americans, Jackson left Watervliet with Rebecca Perot in 1851 to return to Philadelphia, where they undertook missionary work among the black community. Thus, in a letter to a friend, Susan Smith, dated November 12, 1854, Jackson writes:

> After I was gathered home to Zion, I expected to stay forever. But before many days, it was made known to me that I had yet a greater work to do in the world, and I must return to the world. . . . The time given me to stay in Zion, was four years and one day, from the time I went in until I came out. I went in June 2nd, 1847, and was to have come out June 3rd, 1851. But I stayed beyond the time, and came out July [5], 1851, with a sorrowful heart. (Jackson 249)

Here Jackson dismisses any personal reasons for departing Watervliet in 1851, instead attributing her move to divine predestination. This seems to mask her feelings of discontent and alienation that are reflected elsewhere in her writing.

Jackson's separation from Watervliet is not wholly satisfactory to her because the Shaker leaders (in particular Eldress Paulina Bates) refuse to bless her missionary pursuits before she departs. Jean Humez explains that Bates's refusal actually reflected the Shaker leadership policy of not allowing Believers to have excessive contact with the people of "the world," who, from the Shakers' standpoint, harbored aberrant values and engaged in depraved behavior.[44]

Jackson, however, does not feel she can remain in Philadelphia without first returning to Watervliet to resolve her differences with Bates. Jackson's dream life helps her to come to terms with the actions she must take in her waking life to gain Bates's blessing. One dream in particular, which occurs in April 1858, "Dream of Home and Search for Eldress Paulina," is critical to this process of resolution as well as to grappling with repressed feelings of racial tension that she experienced at Watervliet.[45] In this dream, Jackson and Perot have returned to Watervliet and notice that conditions have changed dramatically, particularly in the treatment of black Believers. Observing a large family of African Americans, she says: "I asked why the colored sisters had no caps on, and was told that they did not think it worth while to put caps on them, until they knew whether they would make Believers. I thought mentally how strange it was—it must be because they were colored people. For when I was at home, as soon as any set out, they put caps on them" (Jackson 268). Humez explains that the Shakers probably would not have openly discriminated against blacks, particularly in the New York and New England communities, since this would have undermined their principle of equality. She suggests that Jackson may have felt that the predominantly white community failed to address the needs of blacks regardless of its professed commitment to equality.[46] Looking back at the vision that Jackson had of the Shakers in 1831, one can detect an image of the insight Jackson gains into the true state of affairs at the Watervliet commune. Of the lambs in her vision, she says, "They all looked like one kid yet I seen them distinct" (Jackson 137). Thus, there is an illusion of unity among these people, but as Jackson actually lives among them, she becomes disillusioned. Her ability to "see them distinct" speaks to her realization that racial harmony is not fully achieved. This theme of dissatisfaction with the treatment of blacks continues in the dream when Jackson notices a group of black believers sitting alone in an area strewn with garbage. Again, Humez points to the unlikelihood of this condition since those who observed Shaker communities during the nineteenth century invariably attest to the cleanliness of these organizations. She suggests that the filth in which the black family sits symbolizes Shaker hypocrisy.[47]

In the dream, Jackson does not pause for very long in any particular place because she is anxious to find Eldress Bates. When she finally does locate her, Bates greets Jackson as a mother would a naughty child: "'Here I am! Come along here, you good for nothing child! You have caused me so much trouble!' And she took me in her arms and kissed me, and shook me, and said, 'I'm in a great mind to give you a good whipping, you have caused me so much trouble!'" (Jackson 270). Jackson submits to Bates and expresses sorrow for having caused her so much trouble. She also articulates a deep love for her. Bates's infantilization of Jackson perhaps reveals the latter's discomfort with the idea of having to subjugate the authority of her inner voice to that of the Shaker eldress. The white woman's threat to whip Jackson may suggest that she views Bates with some hostility, as a kind of mistress figure.

The dream closes with Mary Ann Ayers, an eldress at Watervliet, articulating, "Now this people can be gathered all together, and Rebecca Jackson can see to them" (Jackson 270). This declaration provides a dream affirmation of Jackson's fitness to lead blacks in the way of Shakerism in Philadelphia. Jackson actualizes her dream by returning with Perot to Watervliet in 1857 for a final year of residence. During this time, she sees a vision of Holy Mother Wisdom, who affirms Jackson's years of faithfulness, and releases her from the covenant she made with God in 1831 to obey her inner voice completely. This allows her to promise the obedience that Paulina Bates requires of her in order to gain her blessing for her missionary work in Philadelphia. After receiving this blessing, Jackson and Perot again depart in 1858 for Philadelphia to establish a separate black Shaker outfamily. In April 1859, Jackson holds her first meeting as eldress of the new community: "Saturday evening, April 30, 1859. I held my first solemn meeting. We went forth and worshiped God in the dance" (Jackson 280).

Jackson is called Mother Rebecca by her followers in Philadelphia. This title has special significance in the Shaker tradition. As mentioned in chapter 1, Ann Lee is considered to be the spiritual mother of the Shakers since it was through her that its members were reborn into the life of Christ. Jackson, too, is a spiritual mother in relation to her gathering because it is through her that the people are born into the life of Shakerism. Moreover, she is a radical spiritual mother because she radicalizes Shakerism by "digesting, selecting, and transforming, to fit her own experience and her view of black needs, the doctrine explained in Shaker publications that she had acquired during her Watervliet years."[48] Within this group she finds the autonomy that she lacked at the Watervliet commune. Geraldine Duclow describes Jackson's spiritual family as "a racially integrated group of men and women who lived in a totally urban setting."[49] Though its members were unable to all live together, several of the women shared the same house, and all worked outside the home. The whole group would meet and worship together on Sabbaths and during the evenings.[50]

Unlike other Shaker Societies, the Philadelphia outfamily kept no family diaries or daily journals, so what we know about this community has been gleaned from the writings of Shakers who visited the outfamily. Family journals and daybooks contain limited facts about this gathering and glimpses of its members' lives.[51] Following are excerpts from a letter dated January 14, 1872, written by Eldresses Eliza Ann Taylor and Polly Reed to the elders at Groveland, New York. The letter describes the family six months following Jackson's death, and, according to Geraldine Duclow, is the first known reference by the Shakers to the community in Philadelphia:[52]

> It seems that the day of ingathering of souls to Zion (tho' it may be very near at hand,) has not as yet ushered in upon any of our Societies: our spiritual status thro' out seems to be nearly on a level. But we have a little band of very Zealous colored believers in Philadelphia, the proselytes of Rebecca Jackson & Rebecca Perott [*sic*], that perhaps you would be interested to hear something about. The above named sisters once lived at the South Family in this place, & were true & faithful believers, and very much beloved & respected by all who were acquainted with them.[53]

The image that emerges from this passage is of a group of individuals who are strongly committed to their faith, and who have been under the leadership of two highly respected women, Jackson and Perot. Richard Williams thus asserts, "The success of The Philadelphia Out-Family is then directly related to the charismatic leadership of both Rebeccas."[54] It seems that even in the midst of a general leveling off of spiritual fervor among the Shakers, this group demonstrated a high degree of religious zeal.

As Taylor's and Reed's letter continues, one gains insight into the particulars of the family's daily routine:

> Br. [George] Albert [Lomas] went to Philadelphia a few weeks since, & called on Rebecca & the little band gathered together to visit & hold meeting with him. And he says he never was so taken back in his life as he was to witness the sincerity & true devotion of that little company. How they had kept the manners & customs of Believers in their singing & manner of worship, timing with their hands, spreading their handkerchiefs in their laps &c &c. And those who had not a Shaker cap wore something like a night cap, so as to be in uniform. They rise at 5 in the winter & at 1/2 past four in summer & retire as was believers custom when the Rebeccas lived with us. They now number four males & eleven females, & more have received faith & are ready

to unite. . . . Bro. Albert was there saying they had kept up prayer meetings every Sabbath evenings since, & felt that they were uniting with Mother's good children. They hold meetings every Wednesday, Thursday & saturday [*sic*] evening & two meetings on the Sabbath. . . . We are not sure but our colored brethren & sisters will yet step in & take the birthright of some of our white faces who have sold theirs, for a mess of pottage.[55]

The last sentence, though probably meant as an expression of admiration, nevertheless seems to betray some anxiety over the degree of success that the "little band" has achieved. Brother Lomas almost seems "blown away" by what he witnesses. This is a group that not only has kept up traditional Shaker practices but has also learned to improvise (as with the use of nightcaps) to suit their needs.

According to Richard E. Williams, "One of the longest, most detailed accounts of a visit to Philadelphia Family" is provided by Elder Henry C. Blinn, a member of the Canterbury, New Hampshire, Shaker Society.[56] The account is contained in a journal that he kept in 1873 during a trip taken to visit several Shaker communities. This excerpt gives an idea of who the members of the family are. At the time, they are living at 522 South 10th Street:[57]

At 7 o'clock P.M. we again went to the residence of the sisters, as they expected to be at home at this time. We were now introduced to Caroline Marston, an English woman of some 65 or 70 yrs. Caroline is the oldest white woman in the house. Also met Hattie Walton (white) the Jewess. She, although with all of the advantages of the world on her side, in respect to property, education & friends, has connected herself with the little company of Shakers.[58] We engaged in conversation till Sister Rebecca Jackson (colored) came. She is short, thick set and unqualifiedly black. She spoke very pleasantly and readily entered into conversation concerning our gospel relation. Her kindness of heart would soon engage the affections of any christian [*sic*] mind, provided they were not prejudiced against color, a thing which in this house does not seem to be noticed. . . .

Supper ended we all pass into the meeting room and engage in conversation, when we learn that thirteen belong to the family—Rebecca Jackson (B) Maria Nesey (B) Alice Sharp (B) Abagail Brown (B) Amanda Miller (B) Leah Collins (M) Anna Fisher (B) Caroline Marston (W) Hattie Walton (W) Lydia Kimball, Mary Greene (W) Susan Thomas, Frances Valentine.[59]

Blinn confuses Rebecca Perot with Rebecca Jackson, who had died two years earlier. Not only does Perot take over Jackson's position after her death, but she also adopts her name, thus becoming Rebecca Jackson Jr.[60] As Williams asserts, this letter helps to bring the group to life. Blinn's identification of most of the women by race gives us even further insight into the makeup of the family.

Rebecca Jackson died of a stroke on May 24, 1871, at Lebanon.[61] Perot, taking over the leadership of the group, remained in Philadelphia until 1896, when she returned to Watervliet. She died there in 1901 at the age of eighty-three.[62] The Philadelphia family continued to exist at least until 1909, but the manner in which the group endured is not known.[63]

In searching for communities of faith, radical spiritual mothers found themselves both at and on crossroads. Upon experiencing sanctification and accepting the divine call to travel and preach the gospel, these women stood poised upon the horizon of new lives that greatly diverged from the well-defined and circumscribed realities with which they had become so familiar. And because they engaged in Christian missions, the roads they were obliged to travel may literally be regarded as crossroads. With the exception of Rebecca Jackson, all of the radical spiritual mothers engaged in a problematic search for lasting communities that validated their spiritual gifts and allowed them to function as leaders. Because Jackson chose to become involved in an urban setting and to be actively engaged with the world around her, even she could not completely escape the realities of the deeply entrenched racism, sexism, and classism of her culture. Perhaps it is the process itself that must above all be valued, the process of seeking, of moving, and of shaking up those who could not or would not share in the empowering visions of the radical spiritual mothers. In the end, it is these visions that we, as a community of readers, must be responsible for preserving and honoring.

5

MOTHERS OUTRAGED AND RADICAL

Sexuality and Subjectivity in the Nineteenth-Century Narratives of Enslaved and Free Black Women

The lives of the radical spiritual mothers were intimately connected with those of enslaved black women. Not only do their narratives reveal similar concerns, such as desires for literacy and freedom, but the degraded status of slave women bore directly upon the ways in which radical spiritual mothers were perceived and treated. Moreover, the physical and sexual abuse suffered by enslaved black women likely played a significant role in motivating the radical spiritual mothers to seek control over their bodies and their sexuality by leading celibate lives upon the deaths of their husbands or, in the case of Rebecca Jackson, within marriage. In this chapter, I analyze the treatment of sexuality and the body as it occurs in the spiritual autobiographies and in the emancipatory narratives of Harriet Jacobs, Mary Prince, and Sojourner Truth. In doing so, I argue that the pursuits of physical and spiritual freedom in which the radical spiritual mothers engage are largely defined by an awareness of their connectedness with the plight of enslaved black women.

The lives of enslaved women and the radical spiritual mothers were connected ideologically through a system of negative images and stereotypes that were imposed upon black women by the antebellum white patriarchy. One of the most widespread and damaging myths focused on black women's sexuality. Deborah Gray White labels the sexually promiscuous behavior wrongly attributed to black women as that typical of a Jezebel: "One of the most prevalent images of black women in antebellum America was of a person governed almost entirely by her libido, a Jezebel character. In every way Jezebel was the counterimage of the mid-nineteenth-century ideal of the Victorian lady. She did not lead men and children to God; piety was foreign to her. She saw no advantage in prudery, indeed domesticity paled in importance before matters of the flesh."[1] White explains that the myth of black female sensuality originated with Englishmen's voyages to Africa to acquire slaves. These men misinterpreted the semi-nudity adopted by Africans to suit the tropical climate as licentiousness. They also misunderstood African cultural traditions and thus pointed to polygamy as evidence of unbridled sexual desire and to traditional dancing as orgiastic.[2] The character of black women was assailed in European travel accounts, which contained shallow analyses of life in Africa. Crude jokes about "[N]egro wenches" were common by the nineteenth century, and both Europeans and northerners accepted the assumptions on which they were based. Southerners commonly held that black women were lewd and invited the sexual attention of white men. Any resistance that they may have shown was regarded as pretense.[3] Though the radical spiritual mothers were free women, they were nevertheless perceived in the same manner as their enslaved sisters.[4]

Neither group met the standards governing proper female behavior established by the cult of true womanhood. Chattel slavery's expropriation of enslaved women's reproductive labor, its denial of a protected private sphere, and its insistence upon women's hard labor outside the home were all factors disqualifying slave women from the definition of "woman." Similarly, radical spiritual mothers failed to meet these standards because of their active participation in the public sphere, the physical and sexual autonomy that they demanded in order to carry out their missions, and the direct challenges they posed to the patriarchal authority of husbands, male family members, and church leaders. The exclusion of enslaved women and radical spiritual mothers from the category of "woman" and the negativity associated with their sexuality led both groups to engage in similar projects of "reconstructing womanhood" in order to assert more complex definitions of "woman" that reflected their unique experiences.[5]

Textual representations of sexuality and the body were central to the slave women's and radical spiritual mothers' refigurations of the definition of woman. The dominant theme of Harriet Jacobs's narrative is the sexual oppression of slave women. The author seeks to politicize this issue by revealing the painful truth of her own sexual history, which includes unrelenting sexual harassment by her master, Dr. James Norcom (Dr. Flint),[6] and her decision to take a white lover, Samuel Tredwell Sawyer (Mr. Sands), as an act of revenge against Norcom and as an attempt to exercise a degree of control over her own sexuality. Jacobs conceives two children from the relationship, Joseph (Benjamin) and Louisa Matilda (Ellen), who become the motivating forces for her escape from slavery. Jacobs holds up her own life as an illustration of the kinds of abuses that slave women had to endure on a daily basis. She wants her readers to be apprised of the circumstances informing the desperate choices she felt compelled to make for the sake of her own survival and that of her children.

According to Sharon Block, James Norcom's sexual coercion of Harriet Jacobs was an ongoing process in which master and slave not only struggled for control over Jacobs's body but also fought for the power to publicly interpret those sexual acts.[7] Jacobs claims this power of interpretation through the publication of her narrative, which has had a far-reaching impact: "Writing and publishing her story, she had created herself as a representative woman, shaping her past from a private tale of shame of a 'slave girl' into a public testimony against a tyrannical system."[8]

Harriet Jacobs, prevented by the conditions of slavery from living up to the standards of sexual purity demanded by the cult of true womanhood, gestures toward an alternative standard by which slave women might be judged: "Still, in looking back, calmly, on the events of my life, I feel that the slave woman ought not to be judged by the same standard as others" (Jacobs 56). The tiny garret in her grandmother's house—a space she is forced to inhabit for seven years while negotiating the freedom of her children and awaiting her own opportunity for escape—may be regarded as a metaphor for the confining domestic ideology to which she tries so diligently to mold herself. The small, awkward-shaped space that stifles light and air functions as a distorted domestic sphere in which Jacobs manages to sew, read, write, and strategize ways to achieve freedom for her children and herself. But neither the garret nor the domestic ideology that it symbolizes was designed for her. Together they leave her physically and spiritually crippled. It is only when she emerges from the "prison" of the garret that she begins to rethink her relationship to this ideology and to imagine its transformation to incorporate her experiences. The tiny "loophole" that she bores into the wall of her hiding place—allowing her to frequently see passersby, including her children and Dr. Norcom—provides her with an angle of vision that prefigures the mature perceptions that she has on her own life and on the condition of slave women more broadly, after attaining freedom in the North.

Like Jacobs, the radical spiritual mothers proposed an alternative standard of judgment for themselves as women divinely charged to become spiritual leaders. Prior to sanctification, they, too, felt compelled to live up to the standards of the cult of true womanhood by performing traditional roles within the home and by recognizing the authority of their husbands. But as they came to understand the plan that God had for their lives, they felt justified in stepping out of these traditional roles and placing God's authority above that of men. They began to judge themselves, and to expect others to judge them, according to their faithfulness as God's servants.

Harriet Jacobs wished to be recognized as a devoted mother who struggles for the freedom and safety of her children. It is through her identity as a slave mother that she hopes to galvanize the support of northern white women. And it is within the context of this maternal identity that she wages her fiercest battles against sexual degradation. Joanne Braxton explains that until recently, the criteria used to define the genre of the emancipatory narrative have been based mainly upon the experiences of male slaves. As embodied in Frederick Douglass's 1845 narrative, the heroic, articulate male who comes to recognize the ways that struggle, literacy, and freedom are connected has been the archetype for this genre. Braxton thus argues for a more expansive and balanced understanding of these narratives by considering the ways in which enslaved women "shape[d] their experience into a different kind of literary language."[9] She suggests a counterpart to the paradigm of the heroic male: an equally heroic and articulate female archetype, which she calls the "outraged mother," and which is exemplified by Harriet Jacobs. Of this archetype, Braxton explains, "She is a mother because motherhood was virtually unavoidable under slavery; she is outraged because of the intimacy of her oppression."[10] In Jacobs's own words, the outraged mother "may be an ignorant creature, degraded by the system that has brutalized her from childhood; but she has a mother's instincts, and is capable of feeling a mother's agonies" (Jacobs 16). As important as freedom is to her, she sacrifices opportunities to escape without her children. Braxton adds, "Implied in all her actions and fueling her heroic ones is abuse of her people and her person."[11]

Sexual abuse, then, is a primary factor in determining the behavior of the outraged mother. The ways that she "manage[s] the aggressive sexuality of white masters"[12] is central to her creation of an empowered subjectivity that challenges the object status of concubine and breeder that her owner attempts to force upon her. The object status of the slave and her efforts to resist this status has, I believe, a profound effect upon the psyche and behavior of radical spiritual mothers, who had direct contact with women who experienced slavery. Joined as these two groups of women are by prevailing racist and sexist ideology and by a culture of resistance to this ideology (the culture of dissemblance), there is evidence in the narratives of the radical spiritual mothers to suggest a conscious awareness and refiguration of the physical degradation of slave women, as well as parallels with slave women's acts of resistance to this degradation. Thus, outraged motherhood helps to shape the development of radical spiritual motherhood.

Joanne Braxton identifies the 1831 narrative of Mary Prince as a precursor to that of Harriet Jacobs, citing similarities in themes and narrative strategies:

> Not only does *Mary Prince* prefigure the later *Incidents* in its criticism of sexual liaisons forced on slave women but also in specific uses of language. *Incidents* and *Mary Prince* employ similar modes of verbal discourse. There are clear uses of "sass" and invective as verbal weapons. . . . Also, within the narrative strategy of *Mary Prince,* there seems to be a tendency, found later in *Incidents,* to alternate between confrontations with the reader and concealment of certain details considered to be "too horrible" to report. The authenticating documents appended to the text support the idea that *Mary Prince* was considered "shocking" in its day.[13]

Representations of Sexuality and the Body in the Narrative of Mary Prince

In November 1828, Mary Prince arrived at the Anti-Slavery Society in Aldermanbury, England, in search of assistance after having departed the home of her last owners, Mr. and Mrs. John A. Wood. The Bermuda-born slave was faced with the difficult choice of remaining free in England without her husband or returning to him in Antigua, where she had been a slave for many years. To return would surely mean resuming a life of brutality to which she was daily subjected. It was Thomas Pringle, then secretary of the Anti-Slavery Society, who took a particular interest in her case and played an active role in trying to attain her freedom. To record Prince's narrative, Pringle enlisted the help of a close friend, Susanna Moodie, a well-known writer of prose, short fiction, and poetry. It is through the collaborative interactions of Prince, Pringle, and Moodie that her authority and discursive subjectivity are constructed.

Representations of Prince's body are central to her construction of subjectivity and authority. As an ex-slave, she is expected to textually display her physical wounds to the public in order to evoke the outrage necessary to challenge the slave system. But she is not merely a passive victim. The narrator engages in a type of "body language" that posits the corporeal as a catalyst for a transformation of consciousness leading to self-affirmation and agency. In the early stages of the narrative, Prince represents herself as a helpless victim who is subject to the brutal whims of her owners. She is sold away from her family and is frequently stripped and beaten by sadistic masters and mistresses: "To strip me naked–to hang me up by the wrists and lay my flesh open with the cow-skin, was an ordinary punishment for even a slight offence."[14] As the narrative progresses and she passes into the hands of another cruel master, the severe abuse continues, but Prince displays a growing sense of outrage that leads her to fight back with her tongue:

> He [Mr. D ——] had an ugly fashion of stripping himself quite naked, and ordering me then to wash him in a tub of water. This was worse to me than all the licks. Sometimes when he called me to wash him I would not come, my eyes were so full of shame. He would then come to beat me. One time I had plates and knives in my hand, and I dropped both plates and knives, and some of the plates were broken. He struck me so severely for this, that at last I defended myself, for I thought it was high time to do so. I then told him I would not live longer with him, for he was a very indecent man–very spiteful, and too indecent; with no shame for his servants, no shame for his own flesh. (Prince 202–203)

In this passage, Prince equates the exposed body of her master with the worst kind of physical punishment. He represents for her the naked aggression of chattel slavery, which if left unchecked could destroy the tenuous grasp she has on her bodily and psychological integrity. When his body threatens to cross the line of morality she has drawn for herself, she must verbally defend herself. The modesty that Prince represents herself as exhibiting in response to her master's sexual forwardness also reflects an awareness of her audience, which was comprised of men and women for whom decorum was important. Following this incident, she is hired to work elsewhere and is eventually sold. She thus succeeds in exercising her agency to extricate herself from an unbearable situation and preserves her integrity.

Toward the end of her narrative, Prince has been sold to another master and mistress and, in addition to suffering the usual physical abuse, finds herself stricken with rheumatism. Her owners take her with them from Antigua, where she has gotten married, to England, where she is expected to continue her role as housekeeper. The cold climate as well as the laborious chore of washing clothes intensifies her rheumatism, making it impossible to keep up with her work. Her owners threaten to throw her out of the house if she does not do as she is commanded. Following the fourth such threat, Prince reluctantly leaves, after giving what I think is the most important speech in the text because it is the most self-affirming. After packing her clothes in a trunk and enlisting the help of a man to carry it away, she commands:

> Stop, before you take up this trunk, and hear what I have to say before these people. I am going out of this house, as I was ordered; but I have done no wrong at all to my owners, neither here nor in the West Indies. I always worked very hard to please them, both by night and day; but there was no giving satisfaction, for my mistress could never be satisfied with reasonable service. I told my mistress I was sick, and yet she has ordered me out of doors. This is the fourth time; and now I am going out. (Prince 211–212)

As Prince's body progressively weakens through relentless brutalization, she evinces a concomitant growth in self-determination and assertion of voice. Her ultimate act of self-empowerment is to take up the position of autobiographical narrator. The narrative ends with Prince claiming her right to speak with authority about the cruel realities of slavery: "This is slavery. I tell it, to let English people know the truth" (Prince 215). With Pringle's and Moodie's assistance, Prince rhetorically reverses the power relationship between master and slave; she discursively exposes, verbally thrashes, and courageously holds up her former owners for public condemnation.

Though there is a sexual element to much of the abuse that Prince suffered, the narrator is nevertheless silent on the more explicit forms of sexual abuse. She does not mention any instances in which she or any other slave woman is raped. Even if she personally had not suffered such treatment, she certainly would have been aware of other slave women who did. It is quite possible that Susanna Moodie, as her primary mediator and as a woman aware of the importance of observing conventions of decorum, may have censored any such disclosures. It would be thirty more years before Jacobs and her white female editor, Lydia Maria Child, find the courage to collaborate in forging a discourse for treating the volatile issue of the sexual abuse of slave women. It is also possible that Pringle may have suppressed any sexually explicit references. He certainly was quite adamant about deleting a portion of a letter from John Wood in which the slave master describes the depravity of Prince during an alleged quarrel with another woman. Pringle asserts that the circumstance is "too indecent to appear in a publication likely to be perused by females" (Prince 220). Of course, there is also the possibility that Prince herself suppressed information of a sexual nature to help preserve some dignity for herself and other women.

A desire to preserve her dignity is probably what led her to suppress a premarital relationship she was said to have had with a white man, which is revealed in the supplement attached to her narrative (227, 232). The only reason that the relationship is mentioned at all is because John Wood has accused Prince of immorality. In response to this accusation, Joseph Phillips, a resident of Antigua, and Rev. J. Curtin , a minister in England who had lived in Antigua, both mention Prince's relationship with a Captain ——, but neither man views it as a serious fault in an enslaved black woman. Phillips points out the commonness of these kinds of connections in slave colonies. Curtin dismisses it by saying that Prince always dressed becomingly when she attended his chapel and that she seemed to be trusted by her owners. Part of Wood's anger toward Prince may stem from the fact that she *chose* to be intimate with Captain ——. Like Jacobs and other slave women who exercised their agency in forming relationships contrary to the wishes of their masters, Prince had to be punished.

But Prince's nondisclosure may in fact be a more radical strategy. It could be an instance of "withholding her body" sexually from the public for the purpose of critiquing the prevailing images of black women as sexually aggressive and morally degraded.[15] Such an act would represent a productive use of silence, a voiceless "talking back" that parallels the verbal resistance she includes in her narrative. In the context of the histories of subjectivity described by Sidonie Smith, discussed in chapter 2, Prince is a doubly embodied subject. She brings to her text a history of bodies that do not belong to their inhabitants and that legally cannot be raped. But what she cannot control physically, she can control to a certain degree rhetorically by withholding her body from the scrutinizing gaze of the public. Beside the image of helpless victim, she juxtaposes a picture of a woman who grows in self-determination, self-sufficiency, and moral responsibility. She portrays her body as an industrious one that does not wish to reap the fruits of idleness but that strains to earn the money to buy her own freedom—in an honest fashion. Even after she leaves her owners in England she projects an image of industriousness: "I did not like to be idle. I would rather work for my living than get it for nothing. They [the Anti-Slavery Society] were very good to give me a supply, but I felt shame at being obliged to apply for relief whilst I had strength to work" (Prince 213). The body that she portrays in this manner is one that *she* controls and that is productive for her own benefit.

Maternity and Sexuality in the Narrative of Sojourner Truth

The transformation from outraged motherhood to radical spiritual motherhood is embodied in the life of Sojourner Truth, who boldly walked away from slavery and into the role of itinerant preacher. After attaining her freedom, she insisted upon defining herself on her own terms, taking on the identities of preacher, abolitionist, and women's rights activist.

Born as Isabella about 1797 in Ulster County, New York, she and her parents, Elizabeth and James, belonged first to the Hardenbergh family, who spoke Dutch. Her mother most likely had ten or twelve children, but most of them were sold away; Isabella was the second-youngest. She and her parents passed to the ownership of Charles Hardenbergh when the elder Johannes Hardenbergh died in 1799. When she was about nine years old, Isabella's parents were freed upon the death of their second owner, but Isabella and her younger brother were sold to John Neely, with whom she remained for one or two years. This was a particularly difficult time in her life because she spoke only Dutch, but her owners spoke English. She was frequently whipped for misunderstanding orders given to her.[16]

Isabella was eventually sold to the Schryvers, who were "crude," but who usually treated her fairly well. In 1810, at about age thirteen, she again changed hands, this time being bought by John Dumont. Dumont valued Isabella for her industriousness, but his wife frequently complained about her work. After having been denied marriage to Robert, a slave from a neighboring plantation, Isabella eventually married Tom, one of Dumont's slaves. She bore five children: Diana, Peter, Elizabeth, Sophia, and James, who died as a child.[17]

A 1799 law in New York State providing for the gradual abolition of slavery would have freed Isabella and her husband on July 4, 1827. Because of her hard work, Dumont promised to free the couple a year earlier and also to provide them with their own log cabin. When July 4, 1826, arrived, however, her master reneged on the promise, stating that Isabella was not entitled to her freedom because an injury to her hand had prevented her from performing the usual volume of work. Isabella, indignant over the injustice, decided to take her baby, Sophia, and walk to freedom. She explained, "I thought it was mean to run away, but I could walk away."[18] With infant in hand, Isabella walked several miles, stopping first at the home of Quaker Levi Roe and then at the residence of Isaac and Maria Van Wagenen. The couple took her in, allowed her to work for them, and bought her freedom from Dumont, who soon came look-ing for her.[19]

When Isabella's actions are examined within the context of outraged moth-erhood, one becomes aware that she does not neatly fit the model. As ex-plained, the outraged mother sacrifices opportunities to escape bondage with-out her children. Isabella, however, chooses to walk off with only one child. Why does she leave the rest of her children (and her husband) behind? In her narrative, she explains that her husband had made an earlier attempt to es-cape slavery when a former wife had been sold away from him. He ran away to New York City but was eventually captured and returned to Dumont. He therefore was not willing to risk the dangers of another escape. Isabella also felt that Thomas could look after the remaining children in slavery, particularly since her meager wages would not allow her to support them all (Truth 47, 64). Moreover, Carleton Mabee speculates that she may have been aware on some level that her taking all of the children would have exacerbated the illegality of her taking only one child and would have also increased the financial loss for her master.[20] He further points out that Isabella had been deprived of forming the natural bonds that a mother forges with her children because she was re-quired to devote so much of her time to working and caring for her mistress's children.[21] Mabee thus quotes a speech in which she says, "'I did not know how dear to me was my posterity, I was so beclouded and crushed.' If I had known it would have been 'more than de mine could bear. . . . I'se been robbed of all my affection for my husband and for my children.'"[22]

As Braxton indicates, Isabella does, however, exhibit some of the character-istics of outraged motherhood through her tenacious pursuit of her son Peter, who had been illegally sold into slavery just a few months before she walked to freedom.[23] In her narrative, it is explained that New York State emancipa-tion laws prohibited the removal of slaves from the state to prevent the circum-vention of the release of slaves at the appointed time. Dumont, however, sold Peter to the neighboring Gidney family, who in turn sold the boy to a relative, Mr. Fowler. Fowler then took Peter as his slave to Alabama (Truth 30).[24] When Isabella hears of the sale of her son while she is living with the Van Wagenens, she walks alone to the home of her former owners and confronts Mrs. Dumont. The woman, appalled that Isabella dared to show so much concern for her child, replies: "*Ugh!* a *fine* fuss to make about a little *nigger*! Why haven't you as many of 'em left as you can see to, and take care of?" (Truth 31). Indignant, Isabella expresses her strong determination to have her son returned: "*I'll have my child again. . . .* Oh my God! I know'd I'd have him agin. I was sure God would help me to get him. Why, I felt so *tall within*—I felt as if the *power of a nation* was with me!" (Truth 31). Isabella's comment is suggestive of the kind of consciousness exhibited by the radical spiritual mothers, whose actions are fueled by a vision of society ruled by principles of justice. Like Lee, Elaw, Foote, Smith, and Jackson, Isabella places her faith in the power of divine authority to overcome human opposition. After a tiresome process of legal procedures, she does eventually prevail, getting Peter back with the aid of people who are sympathetic to her circumstances.

Sojourner Truth's ideas about motherhood were shaped by slavery, by lessons learned from her own mother, and by her relationship with God. With an early lack of consciousness, Truth embraced her role as breeder while she was enslaved: "In process of time, Isabella found herself the mother of five children, and she rejoiced in being permitted to be the instrument of increasing the property of the oppressors!" (Truth 24). For Truth's amanuensis, abolitionist Olive Gilbert, such willingness to cooperate with the economic agenda of a slave owner is inconceivable: "Think, dear reader, without a blush, if you can, for one moment, of a *mother* thus willingly, and with *pride,* laying her own children, the 'flesh of her flesh,' on the altar of slavery—a sacrifice to the bloody Moloch! But we must remember that beings capable of such sacrifices are not mothers; they are only 'things,' 'chattels,' 'property.'" (Truth 24–25). Gilbert can only reconcile Truth's mind-set by concluding that at this point in her life, she—by definition, "chattel"—was not fully human and therefore not capable of living up to conventional ideals of maternity. Gilbert reassures her readers that since this time of early ignorance, Truth has evolved in humanity and maternity: "But since that time, the subject of this narrative has made some advances from a state of chattelism towards that of a woman and a mother; and she now looks back upon her thoughts and feelings there, in her state of ignorance and degradation, as one does on the dark imagery of a fitful dream" (Truth 25).

The anxiety that Gilbert expresses over Truth's early attitudes about motherhood within the context of slavery reflects the dynamics of the creation process of the ex-slave's narrative. Jean Humez describes this text, and others like it, as a "mediated" or "facilitated" autobiography that was created through the collaborative process of a literate amanuensis interviewing a nonliterate subject in order to produce her life history. However, Truth was not a passive participant in this process; she makes her presence known throughout the text, asserting her views and values on motherhood, slavery, and spirituality.

The result is a double-voiced narrative in which two strong-willed women with often-competing perspectives and agendas collaborate to represent and make meaning out of the ex-slave's life experiences.[25]

Truth is particularly assertive in expressing her views about motherhood. In fact, as Humez points out, the longest direct quotation of words evidently spoken by Truth is one that reflects her assessment of her role as a mother. She does not accept blame for the way her children's lives have unfolded; neither does she blame slavery as the sole determiner of her behavior as a mother. Instead, she believes that, given the circumstances, she has done an acceptable job as a mother.[26] "'Oh,' she says, 'how little did I know myself of the best way to instruct and counsel them! Yet I did the best I then knew, when with them. I took them to the religious meetings; I talked to, and prayed for and with them; when they did wrong, I scolded at and whipped them'" (Truth 56).

Truth credits her mother with instilling in her the importance of honesty, even to the point of allowing her children to go hungry rather than steal needed food from her master: "In obedience to her mother's instructions, she had educated herself to such a sense of honesty, that, when she became a mother, she would sometimes whip her child when it cried to her for bread, rather than give it a piece secretly, lest it should learn to take what was not its own!" (Truth 21).[27] Truth's adherence to this strict code of honesty with her children is presented with ambivalence in the narrative. On the one hand, Gilbert asserts that "Isabella glories in the fact that she was faithful and true to her master; she says, 'It made me true to my God'—meaning, that it helped to form in her a character that loved truth, and hated a lie, and had saved her from the bitter pains and fears that are sure to follow in the wake of insincerity and hypocrisy" (Truth 21–22). On the other hand, Truth is shown to be deeply regretful of her actions: "I have already alluded to her care not to teach her children to steal, by her example; and she says, with groanings that cannot be written, 'The Lord only knows how many times I let my children go hungry, rather than take secretly the bread I liked not to ask for'" (Truth 25). Truth's desire to develop a strong moral character and to view her faithfulness to an earthly master as training for her steadfastness to a heavenly master seems to be at odds with her understanding of her maternal obligation to provide life-sustaining support for her children.

This dilemma seems to be reconciled in large part through Truth's transition from outraged mother to radical spiritual mother; her adoption of the identity of radical spiritual mother provides the psychic space within which to release her obligations as biological mother in order to serve her spiritual children as an itinerant preacher called by God. Her renunciation of her former name, "Isabella," and her adoption of the name "Sojourner Truth" in 1843 marks this symbolic transformation from outraged motherhood to radical spiritual motherhood. As the name suggests, and as she explains in her narrative, Truth feels a spiritual calling to engage in a life of travel, specifically to journey east from New York City to preach. After a number of disappointments in New York, which she came to view as a city of evil, she felt it necessary to depart and begin a new life dedicated to spreading spiritual enlightenment (Truth 78–80). Harriet Beecher Stowe later reported Truth's explanation of the manner in which she acquired this name:

> My name was Isabella; but when I left the house of bondage, I left everything behind. I wa'n't goin' to keep nothin' of Egypt on me, an' so I went to the Lord an' asked him to give me a new name. And the Lord gave me Sojourner, because I was to travel up an' down the land, showin' the people their sins, an' bein' a sign unto them. Afterwards I told the Lord I wanted another name, 'cause everybody else had two names; and the Lord gave me Truth, because I was to declare the truth to the people.[28]

Truth's assuming a new identity and pursuing the life of an itinerant preacher mark a significant turning point in her life; however, I believe that it was her action of distancing herself from her son and allowing him to mature by living with the consequences of his own behavior that helped provide important mental preparation for this transition from biological to spiritual maternity.

When she and her son, Peter, had been free for about a year, they went to live in New York City. Here, Truth found employment as a servant, and her son, who succumbed to bad influences in the city, frequently found himself in trouble, shunning school and abusing the privileges granted him by his employer. Truth often bailed him out of these difficulties, but when the boy showed no signs of reforming, she at last allowed him to suffer the consequences of his actions. She stood firm, allowing Peter to remain in jail when he again got into trouble; however, he was rescued by a black barber whose name he had been assuming (Peter Williams). Upon his release from jail, Peter kept his promise to Mr. Williams to leave New York aboard a ship that sailed in 1839, something that Truth had previously failed to convince Peter to do, in order to get him away from the city's bad influences (Truth 56–59).

Truth received several letters from her son during his voyages, letters containing wording that seems calculated to evoke sympathy in her, such as: "I am your only son, that is so far from your home, in the wide, briny ocean" (Truth 59), and "[I]f I ever should return home safe, I will tell you all my troubles and hardships" (Truth 59). According to Peter, his mother never responded to any of his letters (Truth 60); however, her maternal instincts seem to be strong: "Since the date of the last letter, Isabella has heard no tidings from her long-absent son, though ardently does her mother's heart long for such tidings, as her thoughts follow him around the world, in his perilous vocation, saying within herself—'He is good now, I have no doubt; I feel sure that he has persevered, and kept the resolve he made before he left home;—he seemed so different before he went, so determined to do better'" (Truth 61). Truth's lack of correspondence with her son may be a strategy of tough love to help straighten him out, but perhaps it also serves as the beginning of an emotional and psychological segue into the next phase of her in life: in order to be a radical spiritual mother, she cannot be bound by the cares of her own family, but rather she must learn to embrace the wider spiritual family that she will adopt, nurture, and guide in the new role that God has in store for her.

After Truth adopts the identity of radical spiritual mother, spiritual maternity is privileged over biological maternity. She thus begins her travels as an itinerant preacher and lecturer without informing her children of her leaving, fearing that they might hinder her mission: "She determined on leaving; but these determinations and convictions she kept close locked in her own breast, knowing that if her children and friends were aware of it, they would make such an ado about it as would render it very unpleasant, if not distressing to all parties" (Truth 79–80). Humez also notes the distance that Truth places between herself and her children at this point in her life, describing Truth as "a middle-aged woman who had turned her face from a former phase of life (which included two marriages and maternity) to an entirely new one—whether her adult offspring were ready for this change or not."[29]

As a radical spiritual mother, Truth acquires an extended spiritual family to whom she ministers and a Mouth Almighty with which she powerfully conveys wisdom that influences this family. This is evident on many occasions, but is especially clear during a camp meeting in Windsor Locks, Connecticut, at which she learns more about Millerite doctrines—"the 'Second Advent' doctrines; or, the immediate personal appearance of Jesus Christ" (Truth 88). Demonstrating her characteristic habit of carefully gathering as much information as possible on a subject before arriving at her own judgments, Truth concludes that the crowd is "laboring under a delusion" (Truth 89). In a compelling voice, she thus addresses the people to allay their anxiety:

> "Hear! hear!" When the people had gathered around her, as they were in a state to listen to any thing new, she addressed them as "children," and asked them why they made such a "To-do;—are you not commanded to 'watch and pray?' You are neither watching nor praying." And she bade them, with the tones of a kind mother, retire to their tents, and there watch and pray, without noise or tumult, for the Lord would not come to such a scene of confusion. (Truth 89)

The bearing that Truth assumes and the language with which she addresses this gathering shows that she has drawn upon a familiar role as biological mother to carry out her spiritual role as God's instrument; she relates to the crowd as a mother who has her "children's" well-being at heart. The crowd acknowledges her reasoning and obeys her admonishment to retire to their tents.

The crowd at the camp meeting is receptive to Truth's guidance as a wise and chiding "mother"; however, she evokes a more unsettling maternal persona in 1858 at an antislavery meeting in Silver Lake, Indiana, when she responds to men present who claim she is not really a woman because of her strong, authoritative voice. The men therefore demand that she prove her sexual identity by showing her breast to some of the women present. Without shame, Truth reveals her breast to the whole assemblage:

> Sojourner told them that her breasts had suckled many a white babe, to the exclusion of her own offspring; that some of those white babies had grown to man's estate; that, although they had sucked her colored breasts, they were, in her estimation, far more manly than they (her persecutors) appeared to be; and she quietly asked them, as she disrobed her bosom, if they, too, wished to suck![30]

In this symbolic maternal act and accompanying speech, Truth emasculates and infantilizes the men and condemns slavery as an institution that undermines the mother-child bond by expropriating the practice of nursing.[31] Moreover, she implicitly critiques conventional notions of white feminine decorum through her public exposure of body and voice.[32] Further, on this occasion, Truth is not only an outraged mother from whom the intimate act of nursing had been ex-propriated for her owners' use, but she is also an outrageous mother who is not afraid to use suggestive body language and her Mouth Almighty to challenge aggressive individual and institutionalized patriarchal power.

Though Truth may act boldly in various maternal roles, she is much more reticent regarding the issue of sexual abuse in slavery. Unlike Jacobs, whose struggle to maintain her sexual integrity is foregrounded in her narrative and is central to her construction of an empowered subjectivity, Truth suppresses dis-cussion of her own sexual trials. According to Painter, she was sexually abused as a child in slavery by her mistress, Sally Dumont, whom she loathed.[33] A veiled reference to this abuse is made in the narrative:

> From this source [Mrs. Dumont] arose a long series of trials in the life of our heroine, which we must pass over in silence; some, from motives of deli-cacy, and others, because the relation of them might inflict undeserved pain on some now living, whom Isabel remembers only with esteem and love; therefore, the reader will not be surprised if our narrative appear somewhat tame at this point, and may rest assured that it is not for want of facts, as the most thrilling incidents of this portion of her life are from various motives suppressed. (Truth 18)

This abuse is also implied in commentary later in the narrative:

> There are some hard things that crossed Isabella's life while in slavery, that she has no desire to publish, for various reasons. First, because the parties from whose hands she suffered them have rendered up their account to a higher tribunal, and their innocent friends alone are living, to have their feel-ings injured by the recital; secondly, because they are not all for the public ear, from their very nature; thirdly, and not least, because, she says, were she to tell all that happened to her as a slave—all that she knows is "God's truth"—it would seem to others, especially the uninitiated, so unaccount-able, so unreasonable, and what is usually called so unnatural, (though it may be questioned whether people do not always act naturally,) they would not easily believe it. "Why, no!" she says, "they'd call me a liar! they would, indeed! and I do not wish to say any thing to destroy my own character for veracity, though what I say is strictly true." (Truth 63–64)

Though Gilbert says that Truth wishes to protect those who are innocent from the emotional backlash of exposing the abuse suffered by the ex-slave, it seems to me that the issues of "delicacy" and credibility are most salient surrounding the desire for secrecy regarding Truth's sexual victimization. Washington explains that sexuality was considered to be a "delicate" or "indelicate" subject by nineteenth-century men and women.[34] She thus argues that it was Gilbert who censored material of a sexual nature, due to her conventional values and Truth's inability to write for herself. Humez, however, asserts that it was Truth herself who insisted upon suppressing such details, based on evidence throughout the narrative suggesting that Truth played an active role in helping to determine the content and structure of the narrative as part of the collaborative process of producing the text.[35] Both scholars make valid arguments, but Humez is particularly convincing in suggesting ways in which Truth exerted some control in the creation of her narrative. For example, in response to the first passage above that alludes to the cruelty of Truth's mistress, Humez comments: "This passage strongly suggests to me that Gilbert, the Garrisonian abolitionist, wanting to expose slavery's cruelties for an audience of whites who were ignorant of them, was urging Truth to tell more stories that would 'thrill' her white northern antislavery readers with virtuous indignation. Meanwhile Truth, just as staunchly, was refusing to do so."[36]

If Truth was, in fact, the one who censored this sensitive material, then she, like Mary Prince, may have been strategically withholding her body from the narrative to demonstrate her agency in textual production and to further her own agenda of creating a dignified persona whom readers could admire. For Jacobs, presenting her body as the object of sexual aggression, as well as her heroic efforts to thwart this aggression, is a strategy for establishing the strength and dignity of her character. For Truth, however, creating an image of herself as one who is morally upright and credible meant purging her text of a body that has been victimized sexually.

One might ask, however, why Truth would carefully withhold her body from the narrative and then shamelessly put it on display for men and women alike during the breast-baring incident at the 1858 antislavery meeting in Indiana. Again, the issue is credibility. As her chosen name suggests, the former slave had a vested interest in establishing herself as an irreproachable teller of truth. And in the breast-baring incident, it was necessary for her to assert the truth of her sexual identity. Thus, she accepted the challenge to back up her "manlike" voice with her female body in order to establish this truth: "In vindication of her truthfulness, she told them that she would show her breast to the whole congregation."[37] Further, Truth was very aware of her audience, which included many proslavery members.[38] Demonstrating her audience-oriented subjectivity, and invoking the "calculated theatricality" attributed to this kind of subjectivity, she thus performs in a manner calculated to effectively silence her detractors.[39]

Though baring her breast "entrained everything connected with sexuality without her naming it,"[40] the castigating maternal persona that Truth evokes, with her emphasis on nursing and her harsh criticism of her male persecutors, undercuts the sexual impact. She in fact uses maternity as a weapon against her tormentors. The persona that Truth adopts is quite different from the gentle maternal persona that Rebecca Jackson assumes when interacting with the three ministers who want her dead.[41] For Jackson, maternity is a shield against male aggression; for Truth, it is a sword.

The Influence of Outraged Motherhood upon Radical Spiritual Motherhood in the Narratives of Zilpha Elaw, Julia Foote, and Rebecca Jackson

The discussions of Sojourner Truth's and Mary Prince's texts are useful for arguing for reading practices that consciously explore the silences that often surround the issue of sexuality in the narratives of black women. In looking for connections between outraged motherhood and radical spiritual motherhood in Zilpha Elaw's autobiography, it is also necessary to look beneath the surface for sexual influences that are not fully articulated. Early in her text, the author explains, "At twelve years of age I was bereaved of my mother, who died in childbirth of her twenty-second child, all of whom, with the exception of three, died in infancy" (Elaw 53). Though there is no mention of her mother's ever having experienced slavery, the image of the breeder forced to regularly reproduce property for her master most likely influenced Elaw's consciousness on some level. The arduousness of giving birth to twenty-two children, the trauma of losing most of these children, and the ultimate horror of death resulting from this difficult cycle must surely have had a profound effect upon the author. Elaw herself had only one child. It is plausible that the effect of the image of the breeder upon her psyche may have caused her to limit her own reproduction and may also have influenced her decision to remain unmarried and celibate after the death of her husband. Elaw's trips to the southern states brought her face to face with the deplorable conditions of enslaved women. She experiences the anxiety of traveling alone in this dangerous territory, knowing that at any moment she could be abducted and sold into slavery. Her crossing of the Mason-Dixon Line thus initiates a dangerous blurring of the boundaries of radical spiritual motherhood and outraged motherhood. As shown in chapter 4, it is her belief in providential protection and her ability to renegotiate her identity in the midst of crises that allows her to maintain the integrity of this boundary.

In chapter 2, I discussed some of the ways in which Julia Foote's relationship with her mother helps to shape her identity as a radical spiritual mother. I wish to go further with this idea to suggest ways in which her mother's experiences as an outraged mother are refigured in Foote's text. It is characteristic of the outraged mother to fiercely resist sexual degradation and physical abuse by using wit, cunning, and verbal warfare as a kind of female trickster. One particularly important weapon of self-defense she utilizes is "sass," or talking back. Braxton illustrates how Jacobs uses this tactic in her narrative:

> The first time that Flint hits Linda [pseudonym for Jacobs], she hits back, not with her fists, but with sass: "You have stuck me for answering you honestly. How I despise you." When he threatens to send her to jail, she responds, "As for the jail, there would be more peace for me there than there is here" (*Incidents* 39, 40). . . . Sass preserves the slave girl's self-esteem and increases the psychological distance between herself and the master.[42]

Though Foote does not provide the details of the way that her mother resisted her master's sexual advances, it is not unrealistic to speculate that she fought back with her tongue. She had no problem speaking her mind to her mistress to expose the indecent behavior of her master. One could imagine her engaging in a linguistic duel of wits. However she resisted, she was brutally whipped for her actions. In chapter 2, I suggested that Foote attempted to rewrite this tragic scene by chopping up a rawhide with which she herself was whipped as a girl. I believe that she also refigures her mother's abuse ritualistically, in the form of sermons. Though the radical spiritual mothers frequently describe the powerful effects that their preaching has upon their audiences, they rarely share the texts of their sermons. In an unusual move, Foote includes the text of only one sermon, near the end of her narrative.[43] It is drawn from Micah 4:13 and is delivered at the request of an influential man in Detroit who is concerned about the condition of his soul.[44] Foote calls this sermon "A 'Threshing' Sermon," and I quote from it here:

> 710 B.C. corn was threshed among the Orientals by means of oxen or horses, which were driven round an area filled with loose sheaves. By their continued tramping the corn was separated from the straw. That this might be done the more effectually, the text promised an addition to the natural horny substance on the feet of these animals, by making the horn iron and the hoof brass.
>
> Corn is not threshed in this manner by us, but by means of flails, so that I feel I am doing no injury to the sentiment of the text by changing a few of the terms into which are the most familiar to us now. The passage portrays the Gospel times, though in a more restricted sense it applies to the preachers of the word. Yet it has a direct reference to all God's people, who were and are commanded to arise and thresh. Glory to Jesus! now is this prophecy fulfilled—Joel ii. 28 and 29. . . . [45]
>
> There are many instances of the successful application of the Gospel flail, by which means the devil is threshed out of sinners. With the help of God, I am resolved, O sinner, to try what effect the smart strokes of this threshing instrument will produce on thy unhumbled soul. This is called the sword of the Spirit, and is in reality the word of God. Such a weapon may seem contemptible in the eyes of the natural man; yet, when it is powerfully wielded, the consequences are invariably potent and salutary. Bless God! the Revelator says: "They overcame by the blood of the Lamb and by the word of their testimony; and they loved not their lives unto the death" [Rev. 12:11]. (Foote 222–23)

Foote's sermon is a stylized version of "sass" that indicts all oppressive power structures, especially chattel slavery, and asserts the right and responsibility of God's chosen people (Foote included) to seek out and destroy these structures. In the spiritual context, power dynamics are reversed, and the weak, divinely strengthened, "beat in many pieces" the strong who oppress them. The symbolic weapon of castigation and destruction is that of the flail, a kind of whip. What a psychological boon it is for Foote to be able to figuratively snatch the whip from her mother's tormentor and apply it in kind. The author cites Revelation 12:11; the revelation is that when the mother's blood, shed by the whip of her master, is reclaimed through the narrative testimony of the daughter, both women, slave and free, find redemption.

For Rebecca Jackson, the links between outraged motherhood and radical spiritual motherhood are explicitly established in her characterization of her marriage as "bondage."[46] After she is sanctified during a prayer meeting in 1831, she laments: "I then saw for the first time what the sin of the fall of man was, and I thought if I had all the earth, I would give it, to be a single woman. How to return home to my husband again I knowed not" (Jackson 76–77). From this moment on, she seeks to lead a celibate life. She can no longer reconcile her evolving life of faith with her role as a wife in the full sense of the term. She is not able, however, to immediately achieve her goal of sexual abstinence. She must first demonstrate to herself and to her husband that she can master her own body through a rigorous routine of ascetic practices, for she realizes that along with self-control comes power. When Jackson returns home from the prayer meeting, her husband is visibly displeased. She passes by him quickly and continues to praise God for her newfound blessing. But as she does so, she initiates a process of bodily negotiation by demonstrating before Samuel her intentions to reclaim herself from his control:

> My husband went down cellar, got wood, made a fire, left the door open, put the coffee pot on top of the stove. So in my march appraising God, I went from the cellar door to the stove and when I would get to the stove I would lay my hands on the stove and then turn to the cellar with my eyes shut all the while. These two things caused my husband to believe that it was more than nature. He expected every time I laid my hands on the stove to see the skin come off on the stove, and when I went to the cellar door, to see me fall down the cellar. He said it seemed as though I was turned right around. Sometimes I went to the cellar leaping, sometimes in a swift march, and often on the very sill, and the coffee aboiling on the top while my hands was on the stove. He had not power to touch me, and when I was permitted to open my eyes, I saw him sitting on a chair with his two hands under his chin and ashaking like a person under a heavy fit of ague. (Jackson 77)

Jackson's march from cellar to stove symbolically reenacts the daily routine that she engages in as a woman responsible for running the household.[47] The drudgery of this routine assumes a new meaning as it is transformed into an act of praise, not unlike her visionary rewriting of the task of cooking in "Dream of the Cakes." As Jackson gains control over her body, Samuel simultaneously loses command of his, as he is given to a fit of shaking. But more importantly, he "had not the power to touch [her]." Jackson is thus laying the groundwork for her liberation from his sexual dominance.

Jackson's secret place of prayer is the garret: "Then I returned home, went up to the chair in the garret. For this had always been my place of prayer since here I found mercy. And I never go out on any account but first I go to this, my place of prayer" (Jackson 82). Like a kindred sister of Jacobs, who utilizes *her* garret to gain new insights into her master's actions in order to escape his dominance, Jackson also takes advantage of her upper room to garner divine guidance that ultimately enables her to elude her husband's control. Moreover, Jacobs's confinement in the garret enacts a kind of ascetic practice: as her body progressively weakens from extreme heat, cold, and disuse, she gains the power to manipulate her master and to ultimately attain freedom.

Jackson continues her regimen of asceticism. On top of working long, hard hours both inside and outside the home and holding nightly prayer meetings in various parts of Philadelphia, she also takes very little food or sleep. This schedule and the physical weakness that ensues draw complaints from both husband and brother, who believe she is ruining her health. Her brother Joseph charges: "Thee is adestroying thy constitution. Thee works hard all day and rounds one half of the night,[48] and eats nothing, till thee is worn away to anatomy.[49] Thee don't look like thyself. Thee sets all day, talks to nobody. Thee will go out of thy mind" (Jackson 86). Joseph Cox is quite right. His sister is going out of her mind—out of her old mind and into a new one that is capable of comprehending the kinds of limitations that have been placed upon her as a woman living within her family, community, and broader culture. Joseph's declaration that she does not look like herself is also correct, particularly when it is read as "You don't *perceive* things the way you used to." Jackson's angle of vision has been irrevocably altered through the experience of sanctification. No longer does she view herself as subordinate to the authority of men, as she makes clear in the assertion, "I had started to go to the promised land and I wanted husband, brother, and all the world to go with me, but my mind was made up to stop for none" (Jackson 87).

The final break from her husband's dominance can be achieved only when Jackson has reached a certain level of literacy—visionary literacy.[50] The manner in which she achieves literacy of the written word is dramatic and allows her to escape the "editorial tyranny" of her brother.[51] As is true in the emancipatory narrative genre, Jackson also draws explicit links between literacy and freedom, but it is her ability to read her dreams in particular that is central to attaining sexual liberation. In 1836, Jackson has a dream while she is forty miles west of Philadelphia, on an itinerant preaching tour. Through the dream and the subsequent actions she takes as result of it, she draws directly upon the outraged mother paradigm by symbolically refiguring certain racial and gender power relations that are characteristic of the master/slave relationship. In this dream, which she calls "A Dream of Three Books and a Holy One," Jackson comes home from preaching and is met by her husband:

> I thought I came home, and as I came near the house, Samuel came out of the back door, which opened on the east side. He came around on the south side, and met me on the west side, which was where our front door was. And the way he came, was no passage, for a house stood there. And as he came he said, "Here she is now," as if he was aspeaking to somebody in the house. And he turned right around and went back. And when he got to the door, he turned his face to me, as I followed him, and he handed me into the house. (Jackson 146)

Jackson has this dream on January 1. In her chapter entitled "The Slaves' New Year's Day," Harriet Jacobs explains that the first of the year is the time when slaves are hired out for the coming year. This is an occasion of great anxiety for slaves since they have no way of knowing whether they will come under the control of a kind master or a cruel one: "At the appointed hour the grounds are thronged with men, women, and children, waiting like criminals, to hear their doom pronounced. The slave is sure to know who is the most humane, or cruel master, within forty miles of him" (Jacobs 15). On this particular New Year's Day, Jackson experiences a symbolic exchange of masters: she is given by her husband to a benevolent white man, who promises to educate her in every avenue of spiritual knowledge that she needs to know:

> A white man took me by my right hand and led me on the north side of the room, where sat a square table. On it lay a book open. And he said to me, "Thou shall be instructed in this book, from Genesis to Revelations." And then he took me on the west side, where stood a table. And it looked like the first. And said, "Yea, thou shall be instructed from the beginning of

creation to the end of time." And then he took me on the east side of the room also, where stood a table and book like the two first, and said, "I will instruct thee—yea, thou shall be instructed from the beginning of all things to the end of all things. Yea, thou shall be well instructed. I will instruct." (Jackson 146)

In a reversal of the normal policy of denying slaves instruction, the white "master" has vowed to provide his charge with a thorough education. Moreover, this white man is stripped of all threatening qualities. Indeed, he is almost feminized as Jackson describes the softness of his hands: "When this man took me by the hand, his hand was soft like down" (Jackson 146). The man has the appearance of a Shaker and probably prefigures her later joining of the white Shaker commune at Watervliet.

At the end of January, Jackson actualizes her dream by dissolving her marriage. She titles this section of her narrative "My Release from Bondage":

> Shortly after this dream I came home. I was commanded to tell Samuel I had served him many years, and had tried to please him, but I could not. "And now from this day and forever, I shall never strive again. But I shall serve God with all my heart, soul, mind, and strength and devote my body to the Lord and Him only. And when I have done it, He will be pleased." This was in the latter part of the month that I had the dream of the three books. It was January 31, 1836. (Jackson 147)

Like Jacobs, who insists upon a measure of control over her own body by establishing a sexual relationship with Samuel Tredwell Sawyer (Mr. Sands), Jackson also demands the right to determine with whom she will share her body. Using language that is suggestive of a woman speaking about her lover, she dedicates her body and soul to God, whom she knows will take great pleasure in her actions. Like Dr. James Norcom (Dr. Flint), who refuses to give up his ownership of Jacobs without a fight, Samuel Jackson is also loath to relinquish control. After she renounces their relationship, he pursues her violently in an effort to kill her. Jackson explains that she is able to elude him through the gift of foresight, which enables her to know what he will do even before he knows himself. After Samuel exhausts all methods of catching her, he finally confesses his evilness, begs her forgiveness, and promises never to trouble her again. Jackson, through the medium of her spiritual beliefs and the power with which she is invested through them, successfully reclaims control of her sexuality and body and asserts the validity of the alternative subjectivity she has constructed for herself.

The radical spiritual mothers, aware of the ownership and degradation of black women's bodies through the experiences of the outraged mothers, contended for control over their own bodies. Foote did this by refusing to be whipped by her employer as a child and through the preaching of sermons that challenged the institution of slavery; Jackson claimed corporeal control through her ascetic practices and by renouncing sexual relations with her husband. Foote and Jackson had no children, and Elaw had just one child; though we are not given any details about why these women had limited or no reproduction, they perhaps on some level were affected by their knowledge of the lack of control over reproduction suffered by their enslaved sisters. Ultimately, the radical spiritual mothers used spiritual justification for corporeal agency: their bodies belonged to God—not men—and it was God alone who invested them with bodily integrity and mobility to be used for His spiritual purposes.

6

PAULI MURRAY
Modern-Day Radical Spiritual Mother

Once I admitted the call of total commitment to service in the church, it seemed
that I had been pointed in this direction all my life and that my experiences were
merely preparation for this calling.

Pauli Murray, *Autobiography*

Pauli Murray strongly believed her life's journey was destined to culminate
in the experience of Episcopal priesthood. As the full title of her autobiography suggests, Murray's identity was marvelously multifaceted. And as Eleanor Holmes Norton contemplates Murray's life and legacy in the introduction
to the text, it becomes clear that Murray embodied the same improvisational
nature that distinguished the lives of the radical spiritual mothers: "It is not
simply what Pauli became and overcame as poet, lawyer, writer, teacher, and
priest, it is her purposeful creation of a life full of adventures in achievement
that fascinates, inspires, and teaches."[1] Like the radical spiritual mothers, Mur
ray boldly and creatively made herself up as she went along her life's journey.
Moreover, Murray's energy, sense of purpose, and constant motion link her
to her nineteenth-century spiritual foremothers; she was indeed both a mover
and a shaker: "Pauli was always insatiable and restless for more life and more
challenges. She never put down roots for long. She was like a mountain climber
whose stamina increases with each new climb. Energized by her own achievements she was always in search of new peaks."[2]

It is significant that the chapter from which the above epigraph is taken is
titled "Full Circle." This final chapter of her autobiography ends by describing the irony of the circumstances surrounding Murray's first experience celebrating the Holy Eucharist as a newly ordained Episcopal priest. The event
takes place in North Carolina, in the same chapel in which her enslaved grandmother had been baptized, and Murray stands at a lectern engraved with the
name of the woman who owned her grandmother. Historically and spiritually,

Murray *has* come full circle as she presides in this ironic milieu, standing before an interracial congregation on the weekend of Abraham Lincoln's birthday. Or perhaps more accurately, she has traveled in a spiral, returning to familiar ground, yet resting on a higher plane of consciousness that is both personal and collective. Murray herself articulates much more eloquently the state at which she had arrived:

> All the strands of my life had come together. Descendant of slave and of slave owner, I had already been called poet, lawyer, teacher, and friend. Now I was empowered to minister the sacrament of One in whom there is no north or south, no black or white, no male or female—only the spirit of love and reconciliation drawing us all toward the goal of human wholeness. (Murray 435)

The image that Murray depicts here is one of a rich tapestry that is beautiful in its inclusiveness, wholeness, and openness to divinely inspired human possibility.

In *my* final chapter, I also attempt to bring the reader full circle by exploring the ways in which a thoroughly modern African American woman embodies and celebrates the spiritual and cultural tradition of the radical spiritual mothers, thus demonstrating the continued relevance of their lives and writing. By tracing Pauli Murray's personal evolution into a spiritual leader, I show that she is indeed a modern-day radical spiritual mother. Specifically, I examine the ways in which her civil rights activism and secular feminism inform the theology of liberation and religious feminism that she espouses as a priest; I explore key moments in Murray's text that reveal significant spiritual development, noting the ways that her narrative both fulfills and eludes the classification of spiritual autobiography; and I analyze selected sermons preached by Murray that reflect her feminist views on women's preaching and her support of liberation theology.

Pauli Murray was born on November 20, 1910, as Anna Pauline Murray, in Baltimore, Maryland, and was the fourth of six children of William Henry Murray and Agnes Georgianna Fitzgerald Murray. Her parents were a middle-class couple of mixed ethnic heritage, including African, European, and Native American ancestries. Murray's father was a public school teacher and principal; her mother was a nurse, a graduate of Hampton Institute. In 1914, when Murray was three years old, her mother died of a brain hemorrhage. When her father was unable to take care of his children due to mental illness resulting from typhoid fever, Murray was adopted by her mother's oldest sister, Pauline Fitzgerald Dame, who brought her to Durham, North Carolina, to live. Her father was later murdered, in 1923, by a guard at Crownsville State Hospital, where he had been committed.

Murray received her primary and secondary education in Durham's public schools. She graduated in 1926 from Hillside High School and spent a year at New York City's Richmond Hill High School to prepare to meet the entrance requirements at Hunter College, which she entered in 1928. Despite contending with the economic difficulties of the Great Depression and coping with the emotional strain of a short and troubled marriage, Murray received her A.B. degree in 1933 from Hunter College.

Murray sought to enter law school at the segregated University of North Carolina at Chapel Hill in 1938; however, her attempts to integrate the school were thwarted. She instead attended Howard University Law School, where she graduated with an LL.B. degree in 1944, first in her class and the only woman among her classmates. Murray applied to Harvard Law School that same year in hopes of pursuing a master's degree; however, she was not accepted because women were not admitted. She then spent a year at the University of California at Berkeley's Boalt Hall of Law, where she in 1945 took the LL.M. degree. Murray went on to become the first African American to earn a doctorate in juridical science at Yale University Law School in 1965.

Murray traces her civil rights activism to her birth by associating the date of her own birth with that of the NAACP and the National Urban League, which were founded in 1909 and 1910, respectively. While a law student at Howard University, Murray helped to organize and participated in sit-ins to desegregate restaurants in downtown Washington, D.C. The nonviolent resistance strategies that she and her fellow classmates used in the early 1940s prefigured the sit-ins that took place on a mass scale in the 1960s in the southern and border states. She was also arrested in Virginia after challenging the state segregation law for buses during interstate travel.

Some of Murray's other achievements include cofounding the National Organization for Women in 1966; teaching as a senior lecturer at the Ghana School of Law in Accra from 1960 to 1961, where she initiated a course on constitutional and administrative law; serving as vice president of Benedict College in Columbia, South Carolina, in 1967; and working as a professor of law at Brandeis University in Waltham, Massachusetts, from 1968 to 1973. As a writer and poet, Murray authored *States' Laws on Race and Color* (1951), *Proud Shoes: The Story of an American Family* (1956), *Dark Testament and Other Poems* (1970), and many articles and monographs.[3]

The death of Pauli Murray's mother and her subsequent adoption by her aunt Pauline Fitzgerald Dame, for whom she was named, were major factors in determining the course of Murray's life as one committed to social justice and societal transformation. Her roots in the segregated world of Durham, North Carolina, helped shape her understanding of race and its impact upon her psyche and developing identity; the racial dynamics created through segregation and the discriminatory practices of Jim Crow cultivated an early consciousness of the need to resist unjust treatment (Murray 31–39).

Of all the occurrences that helped to shape Murray's early social consciousness and set the course for a lifelong commitment to human rights, perhaps none was more significant than the violent death of her father when Pauli was twelve years old. William Henry Murray was an intelligent and accomplished man who felt driven to constantly better his education and to achieve excellence in his career as a teacher and principal in order to combat by personal example the prevailing racial ideologies that asserted the inferiority of African Americans. William was struck with typhoid fever several years before Pauli's birth; his condition was exacerbated by encephalitis. Although he eventually recovered physically from the illness, his mental state was permanently affected; he suffered from bouts of depression and violent behavior that eventually led to his being committed to Crownsville State Hospital. While institutionalized, he was beaten to death by a white hospital guard in what was believed to be a racially motivated attack. This experience affected Murray profoundly, not only for the deep grief and anger with which it left her but also for the ways in which it helped her to relate to others who are suffering, a quality that would be instrumental to her later ministry, and for the ways it helped to foster a commitment to nonviolent resistance (Murray 8–10, 12, 55–57):

> The more lasting effect on me was a vulnerability to human sorrow, especially when it was the result of human violence. I totally identified with the children of John F. Kennedy, Robert F. Kennedy, and Martin Luther King, Jr. And while I could not always suppress the violent thoughts that raged inside me, I would nevertheless dedicate my life to seeking alternatives to physical violence and would wrestle continually with the problem of transforming psychic violence into creative energy. (Murray 57–58)

Murray would have the opportunity to develop her philosophy of non-violent direct action for civil rights as a law student at Howard University by participating in student-led sit-ins in segregated restaurants in Washington, D.C., in 1943 and 1944. During World War II, Washington, D.C., symbolically served as the capital of the Allied nations waging war against the Axis powers. As such, the city's support for war objectives such as the Four Freedoms led black activists to regard it as a logical venue in which to pursue their struggle for equality.[4] The discrepancy between the nation's war rhetoric and its tolerance of discriminatory practices was starkly represented in its own capital (Murray 200).

Tension was heightened surrounding the issue of segregation in Washington by growing evidence that African American men were being mistreated in the military. Further, there was increasing resentment among students who had never faced segregated public facilities before coming to Washington, students who refused to accept Jim Crow as a permanent lifestyle. The event that touched off student civil rights protests was the arrest of three female students who refused to pay the full price when they were overcharged for hot chocolate at a local store. The women were later released, but the incident angered many students. Having knowledge of Ghandian techniques of nonviolent resistance, Murray joined other law students in adapting these methods to fight segregation in restaurants in the nation's capital (Murray 362, 385).

Besides having a distinguished career as a civil rights activist struggling for racial equality, Murray also embraced feminism in her efforts to combat sexism, which she regarded as the "twin evil" of racism, and which she referred to as "Jane Crow." Three decades before helping to found the National Organization for Women, Murray was cultivating a budding feminism as a student at Hunter College. While attending Hunter, she lived and worked at the YWCA in Harlem, where she came to know a variety of women who were professionals and leaders associated with the organization, women she regarded as role models. In particular, she linked these women of strength and independence with those who would become active three decades later in the feminist movement: "None of these women would have called themselves feminists in the 1930s, but they were strong, independent personalities who, because of their concerted efforts to rise above the limitations of race and sex and to help younger women do the same, shared a sisterhood that foreshadowed the revival of the feminist movement in the 1960s" (Murray 75).

Murray's secular feminism carried over to her concerns for attaining women's equality within the Episcopal Church, of which she had been a member since childhood. Her critiques of ecclesiastical sexism clearly link her with the struggles of the radical spiritual mothers. Of this link, Jean Humez asserts: "In connecting her story of inner transformation through spiritual experience with a politicized critique of the male-dominated churches, she contributes to a surprisingly long tradition of such stories by Afro-American women preacher/ autobiographers."[5] Murray was well aware, however, that the struggle for women's rights within a religious context was characterized by a unique set of challenges:

> Inevitably, my growing feminist consciousness led me to do battle with the Episcopal Church over the submerged position of women in our denomination. Challenging inequalities in religious life was much more difficult than challenging similar inequities in the secular world, because church practices were often bound up with questions of fundamental faith, insulating them from attack. An aura of immutability surrounded the exclusion of women from the clergy, reinforced by a theology which held that an exclusively male priesthood was ordained by almighty God. Other privileges enjoyed by males–lay participation in the liturgy and governance of the church– carried the weight of centuries of custom. (Murray 369)

Murray's critique of sexism within the church took many forms. Her initial protest was sparked one Sunday in 1966 during the celebration of the Holy Eucharist at Saint Mark's Church in New York; the traditional exclusion of women from assisting in this solemn ritual was particularly troublesome to Murray on this day and underscored for her the inequities based on gender that existed in the opportunities for participation in church activities. Murray's anger led her to eloquently voice her concerns in a letter to the church rector and vestry, effectively drawing parallels between gender and racial discrimination:

> I could not take Communion this morning because . . . I was rebellious and resentful and had a grievance against my brothers in the Church.
>
> Throughout the services, I kept asking myself: Why is not one of the candle bearers a little girl? Why cannot the crucifer be a girl or woman? Why cannot the vestmented lay reader be a woman of the church? Why cannot women and men, boys and girls, participate equally in every phase of Church activity?

If, as I believe, it is a privilege to assist the priest in the solemn Eucharist, to hold the candles for the reading of the Gospel, to be the lay reader at the formal churchwide 10:30 service, why is this privilege not accorded to all members without regard to sex? Suppose only white people did these things? Or only Negroes? Or only Puerto Ricans? We would see immediately that the Church is guilty of grave discrimination. There is no difference between discrimination because of race and discrimination because of sex. I believe . . . that if one is wrong, the other is wrong. (Murray 371)

Murray's letter sparked discussions within her church regarding expanded roles for women and led to lasting connections with other women in positions of authority with whom she shared the letter. In speaking out, she recognized that the secular women's movement in fact overlapped with efforts made by women in religious settings to achieve greater equality: "In some respects the women's movement was also an ecumenical religious movement, and the term 'sisterhood' had religious as well as political meaning" (Murray 372).

Perhaps Murray's strongest expression of religious feminism was her push for women's right to ordination in the Episcopal Church. By 1970, organized efforts to attain women's ordination were intensifying. In the spring of that year, Murray joined a group of forty-five Episcopal women for a conference at Graymoor Monastery in New York State for the purpose of articulating the goals of Episcopal women. The result was the adoption of a resolution demanding the "equality of women in every aspect of the life of the church, including admission to all levels of the clergy" (Murray 418). The conference at Graymoor Monastery paved the way for the Episcopal Women's Caucus, which was an important force in garnering support for women's ordination (Murray 418).

That same year, Murray was appointed to the Commission on Ordained and Licensed Ministries to examine the subject of women's ministries and to report their findings. After discovering in the Constitution and Canons of the Episcopal Church that women were not in fact officially barred by the document's language from ordination, the commission determined that all that was required to confirm women's eligibility for ordination was approval at the upcoming General Convention of the Episcopal Church in 1970 (Murray 418–19).

The delegates of the General Convention did not follow the recommendation of the Commission on Ordained and Licensed Ministries to approve women's ordination at all levels; however, General Convention delegates did allow the ordination of women to the diaconate, which was the lowest level of the clergy. Angered over what Murray perceived to be a deliberate attempt to confine women to a subordinate position within the clergy, she protested by refusing to attend church: "Like many other women on the periphery of organized religion, I began to question the authority of a traditional faith which continued to treat half of its members as less than fully human" (Murray 419). It would not be until the General Convention of 1976 in Minneapolis that the ordination of women at all levels of the clergy would be approved (Murray 432).

Murray's narrative of her life experiences is not a spiritual autobiography in the strictest sense; yet at its core, it really is. The genre of spiritual autobiography involves the subject's close examination of his or her life, recording his or her personal journey of spiritual development in order to arrive at an understanding of his or her place and fate within God's plan.[6] This in fact is the fundamental project in which Pauli Murray engages. Above all else, she portrays a spiritual journey, beginning in the segregated South, where her earliest understandings of race and identity are established, and traveling through a myriad of experiences, all of which contribute to her learning and help her to come to an awareness that "my experiences were merely preparation for this calling" (Murray 427).

Jean Humez also notices qualities about Murray's autobiography that led her to place it within the tradition of African American women's spiritual autobiography:

> In *Song in a Weary Throat,*[7] we are made aware of an intense religious sense of the meaning of events which goes beyond the merely rational, and sometimes seems in conflict with the control sought by the narrating voice. Events are felt to have been mysteriously ordered and given meaning by divine power: They are "providential," or "miraculous," or they "foreshadow," "forebode," and "forecast" later events. Because of this sense of providential pattern, and because of the intensity with which the book explores difficult emotional realities, *Song in a Weary Throat* can usefully be seen as a contribution to a "tradition" of women's spiritual awakening stories, particularly strong in Afro-American women's history, which is presently under construction by literary critics and historians.[8]

Though there is no single defining moment during which Murray is dramatically sanctified, as is the case for the radical spiritual mothers, I would

argue that she is instead gradually sanctified over time through her life experiences, experiences that reveal an abiding commitment to social justice and
human wholeness. The ways in which Murray adapts the genre of spiritual
autobiography to articulate her own extraordinary experiences suggests that
the improvisational nature of her subjectivity had some impact on the formal
elements of her text as well.

The moments in Murray's autobiography where she explicitly foregrounds
the spiritual elements of her experiences are often in reference to friendships
shared with other women. Just as Zilpha Elaw's narrative depicts the ways that
communities of women serve as vital contexts for her spiritual development,
so does Murray's text reveal similar depictions. For example, regarding the
women at the YWCA whom she admired as a college student for their feminist
attributes, Murray explains, "There was also a spiritual dimension in these associations which contributed to my growth" (Murray 75).

Murray illustrates this spiritual dimension by describing an interaction she
had one night while working as an elevator operator at the YWCA. On this
night, a woman whom she did not know entered the elevator and presented her
with a beautifully decorated comb, explaining that she had just lost her temper; whenever this happened, she insisted on "do[ing] penance" by sacrificing
something of value to her by giving it to someone else. The astonished Murray
never had the opportunity to talk with the woman again, but her magnanimous
gesture left a lasting impression upon her that she would never forget (Murray 75). Perhaps the most significant spiritual bond that she shared with another woman is that which existed between herself and Irene "Renee" Barlow,
a woman she met while working in New York at the large law firm Paul, Weiss,
Rifkind, Wharton and Garrison:

> An underlying spiritual dimension which had been present from the outset
> gave our relationship a special quality I had not found in other friends of
> my own age. In our first conversation outside the office we recognized in
> each other a religious commitment which a natural reserve prevented us
> from revealing to other business associates. . . . Our discovery that we were
> both worshiping Episcopalians was the beginning of a spiritual bond which
> found its first expression during Lent that spring, when we used our lunch
> hours to attend the Wednesday services at Saint Bartholomew's Church on
> Park Avenue a few blocks from the office. The bond deepened over the six-
> teen years I knew and worked with Renee within the Episcopal Church. It

helped to reinforce our faith as we struggled in the 1960s to express the full personhood of women in our religious communion and felt the pain, and often the rage, of rejection at the deepest levels of our being. (Murray 316–17)

Murray was particularly drawn to Barlow, the office manager/personnel director at the law firm, for the humanizing spirit she brought to the work environment. This spirit was cultivated as a child growing up in poverty. Having been clad in worn, hand-me-down clothes, having experienced repeated evictions from her home along with her mother and four sisters due to poverty, and having been ridiculed for her ethnic difference, this English-born woman understood what it meant to be set apart. The sensitivity toward people that she cultivated as a result led her to become a quiet but diligent advocate for civil rights. Of this remarkable woman, Murray further reflects, "As I came to know Renee, our association lifted me beyond my narrow parochial concerns to a broader understanding of the human condition" (Murray 315).

Not only does Barlow help Murray to expand her vision, but she also helps her to sharpen it in regards to her ministerial calling. Murray is enabled to perceive this calling through caring for her dear friend as she dies from cancer. In 1967, Barlow was struck with breast cancer; she underwent a radical mastectomy and nearly died from serious complications from the surgery. She survived, but five years later, she developed a brain tumor. As the person invested with her power of attorney, Murray faced the daunting responsibility of authorizing radical medical treatments on her friend's behalf in efforts to prolong her life. The awareness of the life-and-death power that she possessed over another human life was overwhelming for her, especially in light of the fact that she lacked experience in dealing with a patient so gravely ill. After a temporary period of recovery, Barlow's health declined as the tumor spread throughout her brain (Murray 421–23). As she kept vigil over her dying friend, the distraught Murray engaged in an inner battle that is reminiscent of Amanda Smith's struggle to subdue her own will to that of God as she watched the life of her beloved son, Will, slip away:

For several days I lived in a state of split consciousness. Part of me functioned as a lawyer, organizing Renee's business files and papers in preparation for the administration of her estate by the law firm for which she then worked. The other part of me carried on a dialogue with God, alternately praying, "Thy will be done," and arguing angrily, "It isn't fair, Lord." (Murray 423)

Murray receives some unexpected help in this unfolding battle of wills from a longtime friend and doctor, Gerry Burton, whose own sister was fighting terminal cancer. Burton explained to Murray that "each person who is ill has a lifeline and clinging to that lifeline could go on indefinitely. She thought that I might be Renee's lifeline, and that I had to decide whether I could let her linger in the condition she was now in. Only I could decide that question" (Murray 424). That night as Murray watched her friend in visible discomfort, she knew that she must release this lifeline: "'Take her, God, I can't bear to see her suffer this way.' No priest was available, so I stood by her bed reading the Twenty-third Psalm, and when I finished I kissed her goodbye and said, 'Rest'" (Murray 424). Barlow died the next morning.

As a final act of honoring her dear friend, Murray organized a memorial service. Reflecting back on the role she had played during Barlow's final hours and the support she had given to Barlow's family during the memorial service and funeral, Murray realized that the groundwork for her future ministry was being laid. As if to confirm this calling, Rev. Thomas Pike, who officiated at the memorial service, commented:

> "You may not have realized it, but you have been acting as an enabler, a function of a deacon in our church. Have you ever thought of ordination?" Late that afternoon as I drove back to Boston thinking of Tom Pike's words, an exquisite sunset of gold, blue, pink, and aqua filled the western sky. It was as if Renee's spirit was smiling in approval as she bade me farewell. (Murray 425)

Irene Barlow's struggle with death and her symbolic postmortem affirmation of Murray's calling through the vivid colors gracing the evening sky recollects the occasion on which Elaw's sister, on her deathbed, relays the divine message that Elaw is destined to preach the gospel. It was not easy for Elaw to accept this message, and neither was it for Murray. Elaw and the other radical spiritual mothers found it difficult to reconcile their God-ordained roles with the negative views society held of them as black women; similarly, Murray had to grapple with her own doubts that she was too old and was unworthy of accepting such a noble calling. The death of Irene Barlow occasions a period of reflection upon this inner conflict:

> For the second time in my life I had been called upon to *be with* a devout Christian whom I loved in the crisis of death and to minister in ways I asso-

ciated only with the ordained clergy.[9] As I reflected upon these experiences, the thought of ordination became unavoidable. Yet the notion of a "call" was so astounding when it burst into my consciousness that I went about in a daze, unable to eat or sleep as I struggled against it. (Murray 426)

Murray further adds, with a consciousness akin to that which Amanda Smith seemed to possess upon the death of her son: "It had taken a cataclysm, watching my friend in an abyss of suffering, to force my submission and obedience to Divine Will. Now that Will seemed to be leading me into the unknown, on a journey that demanded utmost faith and trust" (Murray 426). Assessing her life in the light of this revelation, she further adds the words with which I began this chapter: "Once I admitted the call of total commitment to service in the church, it seemed that I had been pointed in this direction all my life and that my experiences were merely preparation for this calling" (Murray 426–27).

When Murray later became a priest, she cultivated "a special ministry to the ill and dying."[10] In doing so, she, like the radical spiritual mothers, was a kind of interstitial subject positioned between the temporal and spiritual worlds, one who helped to facilitate peoples' passage into eternity. In trying to come to terms with the impending death of Irene Barlow, Murray in fact imagined death in metaphors of liminality: "Why should one fear what is as natural as birth, or what is, perhaps, merely crossing a threshold? . . . I began to think of the experience of death as a transition in which a person may swing back and forth between two states of being, not quite out of this world and not quite into the next" (Murray 424). And as if to connect with the maternal tropes upon which her spiritual foremothers drew, she also imagines death as a mother: "Suppose death is a 'loving mother' waiting to enfold us in a protective embrace rather than the 'grim reaper' that haunted my childhood" (Murray 424).

At the time of Irene Barlow's death, Murray was the Louis Stulberg Professor of Law and Politics in the American Studies Department at Brandeis University. Having accepted the authenticity of her calling to the ministry, she resigned this tenured position, moved to New York, and enrolled in the General Theological Seminary in the fall of 1973; she earned a master of divinity in 1976 in preparation for her ordination (Murray 417, 427).

Murray's ordination on January 8, 1977 at the National Cathedral in Washington, D.C., made her the first African American woman and the second African American to be ordained an Episcopal priest.[11] With an image of light and brilliant color paralleling that which emanated from the beautiful sunset witnessed by Murray upon the death of Irene Barlow, her ordination seems to receive divine sanction:

> I was the last of the six to be consecrated, and was told later that just as Bishop Creighton placed his hands upon my forehead, the sun broke through the clouds outside and sent shafts of rainbow-colored light down through the stained-glass windows. The shimmering beams of light were so striking that members of the congregation gasped. When I learned about it later, I took it as the sign of God's will I had prayed for. (Murray 435)

Murray went on to serve as pastor for Baltimore's Church of the Holy Nativity and Washington, D.C.'s Church of the Atonement.[12] In her service as priest she has been described as engaging in an "extended ministry" because she held several interim positions in Baltimore, Washington, D.C., and Pittsburgh.[13] She is also said to have been the priest of a "floating parish" in Alexandria, Virginia, for homebound and hospitalized people. Forced to retire in 1982 because Episcopal Church law stipulated that priests retire at age seventy-two, she nevertheless remained active in these temporary positions. Moreover, Murray was very popular as a lecturer and minister, addressing black and white congregations across denominations.[14] It thus seems that Episcopal Church law and Murray's own personal appeal to people from all walks of life combined to foster a pattern of itinerancy not unlike that engaged in by the radical spiritual mothers. Further, Murray, in crossing multiple occupational and conceptual boundaries throughout her life, might be said to have engaged in a kind of intellectual itinerancy. Pauli Murray's physical and intellectual mobility establish her as a migratory subject in the full sense of the term.

Murray's proclivity to physical mobility was evident even as a child; she recalls her aunt Pauline describing her as "an unusually happy baby and a very cheerful small child, always in perpetual motion even . . . when sleeping" (Murray 3). This childish restlessness carried into her adult life, as is evident from Eleanor Holmes Norton's introduction: "Pauli was always insatiable and restless for more life and more challenges. She never put down roots for long. She was like a mountain climber whose stamina increases with each new climb. Energized by her own achievements she was always in search of new peaks."[15]

The migratory subject's rejection of subjugation and ideological confinement is evident in Murray's civil rights and feminist activism as well as in her espousal of liberation theology as a priest, which will be further examined in this chapter. And as mentioned, Murray's "purposeful creation of a life full of adventures in achievement,"[16] and the slippery manner in which her narrative both fulfills and eludes the genre of spiritual autobiography, demonstrates the improvisational qualities inherent in the migratory subject.

Murray's improvisational nature and her rejection of subjugation and ideological confinement were not only sources of strength but also sources of inner conflict as she strove to define herself on her own terms in regard to her gender and sexuality. According to Doreen Drury, Murray was homosexual, but she refused to identify herself as such because she "was deeply troubled by the fact that her same sex desires were characterized as 'abnormal' by dominant discourses of the times and in particular, that they violated Black middle-class norms of respectability."[17] Middle-class African American values stressed the importance of heterosexuality and the establishment of nuclear families. Murray thus felt that homosexuality was at odds with her aspirations to become a respected leader for African Americans.[18] Another factor possibly influencing her rejection of a homosexual identity was her family history. Because three family members had been hospitalized for psychological problems, Murray had a long-standing fear of insanity.[19] Murray knew that "discourses on homosexuals often attributed same-sex attraction to a weakness of the mind and morals."[20] So severe were Murray's inner conflicts with regard to her gender and sexuality that she suffered physical and emotional breakdowns leading to treatment at psychiatric hospitals in 1937, 1940, and 1943.[21]

Influenced by medical and popular literature of her time, Murray tried to make sense of her inner turmoil by conceiving of herself as a "pseudo-hermaphrodite," or an intersexed individual possessing both female and male sex organs. Conceptualizing herself as such permitted Murray to regard her sexual attraction to women and her "masculine self-presentation" as normal in light of this condition, and she would be spared from having to adjust to living as a conventional heterosexual woman. Moreover, she would be able to attribute her inner struggles to a physiological cause, rather than to one that was psychological, which she rejected.[22]

What Murray really wanted was to become a heterosexual male because she believed that this identity would garner her respectability and would bestow upon her many privileges, such as "the right to love whom she loved, the right to appear as she chose in the world, and the right to career choices she wanted to make, given, of course, the constraints of race bias."[23] One must be aware, however, that Murray had a very particular kind of masculinity in mind that she wanted to embody:

> [S]he never stated that she wanted to be "a man." Like many other butch lesbians or mannish women in the 1930s and '40s, Murray sought access to male prerogatives, but ultimately identified as someone more than and different from "not woman." She saw herself as better than a man in many ways and as embodying the best of what she thought women were looking for in a partner.[24]

Thus, the gender identity that Murray sought to create for herself eluded the binary categories of man and woman; it seems that she wanted to cultivate a kind of interstitial subjectivity that was liberating in allowing her to fulfill her desires and aspirations. Furthermore, Murray's self-affirming act of renaming herself in her early twenties from Anna Pauline to the "gender-ambivalent" "Pauli" seems to reflect this insistence upon embodying a more complex identity.[25]

In order to bring about this unique vision of herself, Murray engaged in a decade-long pursuit from 1937 to 1947 of doctors who would be willing to use medical science to locate internal male sex glands or to subject her to experimental male hormone treatments. However, despite Murray's persistence in trying to effect this transformation, gynecological surgery in 1947 verified that she did not possess any male sex organs. After the surgery, Murray seems to have relinquished her efforts to become a male.[26]

Pauli Murray's Mouth Almighty

Unfortunately, Pauli Murray died before she was able to carry out her plan to write a book specifically detailing her life in the ministry.[27] However, we are fortunate to have access to some of her published sermons.[28] As Murray's voice became sanctified throughout a life dedicated to speaking out passionately for social justice, she, like the radical spiritual mothers, acquired a Mouth Almighty. Her sermons reflect the power of this God-emboldened voice. In the remainder of this chapter, I examine two of these sermons: "Women Seeking Admission to Holy Orders—As Crucifers Carrying the Cross" and "Salvation and Liberation."

"Women Seeking Admission to Holy Orders—As Crucifers Carrying the Cross" was Murray's "'Inaugural' sermon," preached on March 3, 1974, as a postulant seeking holy orders in the Episcopal Church.[29] In the course of her sermon, Murray poses the poignant question, "Why is it that at this particular moment in the history of our church and of other faiths women are beginning to rise up and seek the ordained priesthood with such determined insistence?"[30] She begins to answer the question by drawing a parallel between the cultural crisis occurring in ancient Israel during the eighth and seventh centuries B.C. and the one which she believed characterized American culture in 1974. With critical insight, she asserts that during both historical periods, there existed

> a comparatively advanced civilization[,] militarized dominion over weaker peoples, governmental intrigues, political assassinations, exploitations of the poor by the rich, neglect of the weak and defenseless, dishonesty and deceit in the marketplace, bribery and corruption of public officials and of the administration of justice, the drive for affluent living, carousing, and lavishment in food and drink, the jockeying for supremacy by the international great powers—and above all, the apostasy of the chosen people—the falling away from God. In the 8th Century B.C., the people gave lip service to Yahweh and took for granted that as the *elect,* God's chosen people, they would be saved. In the United States of the late 20th Century, we have relied upon our military strength, our bountiful natural resources, our "America First" mentality and our historical ethos of "Manifest Destiny."[31]

Murray follows her critical assessment, which has strong resonance in the twenty-first century, with an assertion that women, as people who have historically been among the oppressed, have a prophetic role to play in indicting their fellow countrymen for their transgressions, calling for their repentance, and communicating a message of hope for their redemption:

> And we are now in a deep and pervasive national crisis not unlike the crisis the 8th Century prophets and their successors foresaw in their own era. In such periods of human crisis, God has called forth prophets who will not be silenced, who will not be coopted by the established hierarchies whether they be clerical or secular. The role of these prophets is to call the people to repentance, to return to the God of salvation. Their message is two-fold. They speak of the awful judgment of God's anger and the infinite tenderness and mercy of God's love. They proclaim that the gloom which attends the devastation will be followed by salvation and joy and the rebuilding on the part of those who remain faithful to God.
>
> I believe that today God has chosen his messengers to warn of God's

judgment upon a sinful and rebellious people and simultaneously to bring
a gospel of hope and joy to those who will listen and have faith. I believe
that God is choosing these messengers from the ranks of the dispossessed,
the oppressed, and from those who have listened to his Word and are open
to feel deeply the sorrow of the human condition. And I believe that many
women of all ages are answering that call because they have suffered and
endured and are particularly vulnerable to human sorrow and need.[32]

Murray's assertion that women in growing numbers are answering the call
to play a prophetic role within their culture links them to the radical spiritual
mothers, as they, too, entreated those in positions of power and authority to
repent of the sins of sexism and racism. Murray's observation that women of
all ages are heeding this call doubtless refers to their varied physical ages, particularly in light of Murray's own advanced age in pursuing the priesthood;
however, one can also read this as an acknowledgment of women's ministerial
work throughout all historical ages, thus indirectly recognizing the work of the
radical spiritual mothers. Further, Murray insists that for those whom God calls
to service as ministers, their obedience really is beyond their control: "We dare
to answer this call because, in a very real sense, we have no choice in the matter. God has spoken to us through an event or through a series of events which
point us in one direction—toward full time service of God."[33] In their insistence
upon the right to obey a higher authority than that of humans, these contemporary preaching women evince the same sense of urgency and inevitability as
the radical spiritual mothers.

The necessity for marginalized and oppressed peoples to speak liberating
truths in efforts to make Christianity a more active force for social justice and
societal change is the theme of "Salvation and Liberation." This sermon was
delivered on April 1, 1979, at Philadelphia's Unitarian Society of Germantown
in light of the various liberation theologies that were being developed beginning in the 1960s in Europe, Latin America, and the United States as oppressed
groups began demanding that traditional Christian theology be reconceptualized to reflect their experiences and perspectives and that it play a central role
in helping to critique and eliminate oppressive structures and practices.[34]

In describing the characteristics of liberation theologies, Murray explains:

They are concerned with the relation of faith to social change and are ori-
ented toward the transformation of the world in history, the "shared efforts

[of men and women] to abolish the current unjust situation and to build a different society, freer and more human," as Gustavo Gutierrez, the Latin American theologian puts it;[35] or in Ruether's words "an overthrowing of this false world which has been created out of man's self-alienation, and a restoration of the world to its proper destiny as the 'place where God's will is done on earth, as it is in heaven.'"[36] This restoration refers to the physical environment as well as social organization.[37]

Liberation theologies' goals of transforming the world to bring about an earthly realm that approximates the Kingdom of God mirror the ideals of the social gospel espoused by the radical spiritual mothers. Just as the social gospel stressed the importance of not only rooting out individual sin but also engaging in "social sanctification" to eradicate institutional sin such as slavery and racism, liberation theologies strive to effect change on a broad scale:

Sin also acquires a different meaning in this perspective, and is seen to include corporate or social evil as well as individual transgression. This view attempts to correct tendencies within the traditional Church to concentrate upon sin as an individual, private, or merely interior reality necessitating a "spiritual" redemption while ignoring the presence of sin in institutional structures which alienate and oppress people and prevent their communion with God and with one another.[38]

In addition, liberation theologies are concerned with bringing about concrete change in the present world, rather than merely focusing on perfection in the next life:

Russell speaks of the "broadening of the understanding of individual salvation in the afterlife to include the beginnings of salvation in the lives of men and women in society. . . . Emphasis is placed upon the longed-for eternal life as a quality of existence in the *here and now*." Salvation is stressed, not as an escape into "heaven" but rather "the power and the possibility of transforming the world, restoring creation and seeking to overcome suffering.[39] Gutierrez, a Roman Catholic, speaks of the growth of the Kingdom of God as "a process which occurs historically *in* liberation, insofar as liberation means a greater fulfillment of man. . . . Without liberating historical events, there would be no growth of the Kingdom."[40]

Pauli Murray, as a modern-day radical spiritual mother, embodies the spirit, vision, God-emboldened voice, mobility, and improvisational nature of her nineteenth-century foremothers. Moreover, her strivings for equality and social justice on individual and societal levels further link her to the lives and texts of the radical spiritual mothers. Murray and the radical spiritual mothers also faced periods of doubt and inner conflict as they struggled to come to terms with their callings, with Murray grappling with the additional challenge of trying to reconcile her sexual identity. These women's strengths, flaws, and divine sense of purpose help to establish them as significant figures in the tradition of women's preaching in America.

CODA

Jarena Lee, Zilpha Elaw, Julia Foote, Amanda Berry Smith, Rebecca Jackson, and Pauli Murray can all be considered a part of what Marilyn Richardson describes as "a black female tradition of activism founded on a commitment to religious faith, human rights, and women's struggles."[1] Another notable member of this tradition of "religious social activism" is Harriet Tubman.[2] The radical spiritual mothers posited authentic, powerful alternative models of womanhood as they carried out the important work for which they had been divinely appointed. And like Tubman, once attaining their own liberation, they heeded the calling to shepherd others along in their individual pursuits of freedom. Desires for personal freedom were incorporated into womanist theologies of liberation that held the potential to effect human liberation on a broad scale.

The radical spiritual mothers made difficult choices in pursuing the paths to which they believed they were divinely led. Some might argue that they were merely sacralizing their desires for an unconventional way of life. To "break up housekeeping" in order to travel and preach the gospel was, to their fiercest critics, potentially threatening to the established order of patriarchal authority. But did these women really have a choice? Jarena Lee's descent into a "state of general disability" when she tried to repress her spiritual gifts while she was married seems to suggest that they were truly preaching for their lives.[3]

C. Eric Lincoln and Lawrence Mamiya suggest that other noted women in the tradition of religious social activism, such as Maria Stewart, Anna Julia Cooper, and Mary McCleod Bethune, sublimated their potential to become religious leaders through their involvement in teaching and political activism, and that had the option been available, they would have become ordained clergy.[4] Lincoln and Mamiya name Sojourner Truth as one who took such a sublimated path. But for Truth and the radical spiritual mothers, human ordination seemed to be of little consequence. They were preachers in their own right.

The radical spiritual mothers were bold in their acts of self-improvisation, rejecting the accepted norms of female behavior and literally making themselves up as they went along on their travels. Not only did they improvise on their own subjectivities, but they also made creative use of the form of spiritual autobiography. By documenting the realities of their experiences with interlocking systems of racial, sexual, and class oppression, the radical spiritual mothers expanded and complicated the possibilities for representing the nuances of human struggle for spiritual and physical liberation. Sojourner Truth and Harriet Tubman went even further to transform the genre, as Joanne Braxton explains:

> By questioning what they [Sojourner Truth and Harriet Tubman] saw as illegitimate authority, they established a "wild zone," or space of difference, from which to wage rebellion against an intemperate, sexist, and slaveholding society; they believed that God was on their side and that they acted on divine authority. Taken altogether, these narrators might be said to "radicalize" the form of spiritual autobiography and re-create it as a tool for temporal liberation. With such "power with God," they wielded an almost superhuman influence over the world around them as they sought to restructure that world in their own image.[5]

To "restructure the world in their own image," to "set the world right side up," to help bring God's kingdom to earth are all expressions of the formidable project of which the radical spiritual mothers courageously envisioned being an integral part.[6] Their legacy of spiritual fortitude and social justice is one from which black women continue to draw strength and inspiration. Perhaps what Lee, Elaw, Foote, Smith, Jackson, and Murray ultimately contribute through their womanist narratives of vision and empowerment is a textual witness to the indefatigability of the human spirit when charged with a sense of calling of the highest order.

NOTES

INTRODUCTION

1. Primary texts include: Rebecca Jackson, *Gifts of Power: The Writings of Rebecca Jackson, Black Visionary, Shaker Eldress,* ed. Jean McMahon Humez (Amherst: University of Massachusetts Press, 1981); Amanda Smith, *An Autobiography: The Story of the Lord's Dealings with Mrs. Amanda Smith the Colored Evangelist* (1893; New York: Oxford University Press, 1988); Jarena Lee, *The Life and Religious Experience of Jarena Lee, A Coloured Lady, Giving an Account of Her Call to Preach the Gospel. Revised and Corrected from the Original Manuscript, Written By Herself* (1836); Zilpha Elaw, *Memoirs of the Life, Religious Experience, Ministerial Travels and Labours of Mrs. Zilpha Elaw, An American Female of Colour; Together with Some Account of the Great Religious Revivals in America [Written by Herself]* (1846); and Julia A. J. Foote, *A Brand Plucked from the Fire: An Autobiographical Sketch by Mrs. Julia A. J. Foote* (1879). The narratives of Lee, Elaw, and Foote are republished in *Sisters of the Spirit: Three Black Women's Autobiographies of the Nineteenth Century,* ed. William L. Andrews (Bloomington: Indiana University Press, 1986). All references to these narratives will come from this edition. Hereafter primary texts will be cited parenthetically.

2. In place of the term "slave narrative," I use "emancipatory narrative," which I borrow from Eleanor Traylor. Traylor argues that the term "slave narrative" alludes to the narrator's past in bondage but does not account for the freedom that he or she desires and ultimately achieves, whereas "emancipatory narrative" suggests both the subject's past bondage and his or her quest for freedom. Moreover, I think the term also suggests that the act of telling one's own story is in itself liberating—on an emotional, psychological, and spiritual level. There is actually a dynamic tension between slavery and freedom that exists whenever a former slave tells his or her story, a tension that is eloquently described by Jennifer Fleischner in *Mastering Slavery: Memory, Family, and Identity in Women's Slave Narratives* (New York: New York University Press, 1996):

> All narratives of traumatic experiences recounted after the events raise questions about liberation and enslavement as they relate to the act of telling. Finding a measure of linguistic relief in telling, narrators sought to liberate themselves from their memories. . . .
> In recounting the events of her life, [Kate] Drumgoold, like other narrators, asserts her humanity as a desire and capacity (through writing, which had often been forbidden to slaves) to free herself from bad memories by transforming them into a positive gain. Yet, as a "*slave* narrator"—retaining being a slave as a unifying metaphor in her narrative life—she also enacts another autobiographical rite: the repetition (in the sense of reenacting, not retelling) of memory. The tensions between liberation and enslavement are implicit in all narratives. (135)

See also Eleanor W. Traylor, "Naming the UnNamed: African American Criticism and African American Letters," *Black Books Bulletin: WordsWork* 16, no. 1–2 (1993–94): 68, 71, 73, 74.

3. Joanne M. Braxton, *Black Women Writing Autobiography: A Tradition within a Tradition* (Philadelphia: Temple University Press, 1989).

4. See Jean M. Humez, "In Search of Harriet Tubman's Spiritual Autobiography," in *This Far by Faith: Readings in African-American Women's Religious Biography,* ed. Judith Weisenfeld and Richard Newman (New York: Routledge, 1996); and Jean M. Humez, "Reading *The Narrative of Sojourner Truth* as a Collaborative Text," *Frontiers: A Journal of Women's Studies* 16, no. 1 (1996).

5. Joycelyn Moody, *Sentimental Confessions: Spiritual Narratives of Nineteenth-Century African American Women* (Athens: University of Georgia Press, 2001), x.

6. Ibid., 17.

7. Darlene Clark Hine, *Hine Sight: Black Women and the Re-Construction of American History* (Brooklyn: Carlson, 1994), 47, quoted in Moody, *Sentimental Confessions,* 162.

8. Richard J. Douglass-Chin, *Preacher Woman Sings the Blues: The Autobiographies of Nineteenth-Century African American Evangelists* (Columbia: University of Missouri Press, 2001).

9. Ibid., 3.

10. This definition of sanctification is from Harald Lindström, *Wesley and Sanctification* (London: Epworth, 1950), quoted in Andrews, *Sisters of the Spirit,* 15.

11. Rebecca Jackson insisted upon celibacy *within* her marriage.

12. "Migratory subjectivity": Carole Boyce Davies, *Black Women, Writing and Identity: Migrations of the Subject* (London: Routledge, 1994).

13. Angelo Costanzo, *Surprizing Narrative: Olaudah Equiano and the Beginnings of Black Autobiography* (New York: Greenwood, 1987), 49, 50; Daniel B. Shea Jr., *Spiritual Autobiography in Early America* (Princeton, N.J.: Princeton University Press, 1968), xi; Andrews, *Sisters of the Spirit,* 10, 11.

14. Costanzo, *Surprizing Narrative,* 28.

15. Shea, *Spiritual Autobiography,* 209.

16. Costanzo, *Surprizing Narrative,* 113.

17. Shea, *Spiritual Autobiography,* 119.

18. Ibid., 47.

19. Linda H. Peterson, "Gender and Autobiographical Form: The Case of the Spiritual Autobiography," in *Studies in Autobiography,* ed. James Olney (New York: Oxford University Press, 1988), 213–14.

20. Costanzo, *Surprizing Narrative,* 11–13.

21. Shea, *Spiritual Autobiography,* 14–15.

22. Virginia Lieson Brereton, *From Sin to Salvation: Stories of Women's Conversions, 1800 to the Present* (Bloomington: Indiana University Press, 1991), 38.

23. Ibid.

24. Ibid.

25. William L. Andrews, *To Tell a Free Story: The First Century of Afro-American Autobiography, 1760–1865* (Urbana: University of Illinois Press, 1986), 7.

26. Nellie Y. McKay, "Nineteenth-Century Black Women's Spiritual Autobiographies: Religious Faith and Self-Empowerment," in *Perspectives on American Methodism: Interpretive Essays,* ed. Russell E. Richey, Kenneth E. Rowe, and Jean Miller Schmidt (Nashville: Kingswood/Abingdon, 1993), 181.

27. Ibid., 191.

28. Christian Smith, *The Emergence of Liberation Theology: Radical Religion and Social Movement Theory* (Chicago: University of Chicago Press, 1991), 27.

29. Pauli Murray, "Black Theology and Feminist Theology: A Comparative View," in *Black Theology: A Documentary History*, ed. James H. Cone and Gayraud S. Wilmore, 2nd ed., vol. 1, *1966–1979* (Maryknoll, N.Y.: Orbis, 1993), 304–6.

30. Letty M. Russell, *Human Liberation in a Feminist Perspective—A Theology* (Philadelphia: Westminster, 1974), 63, 64.

31. Ibid., 67.

32. Jacqueline Grant, "Womanist Theology: Black Women's Experience as a Source for Doing Theology, with Special Reference to Christology," *Journal of the Interdenominational Theological Center* 13 (1986): 201.

33. Jacqueline Grant, "Black Theology and the Black Woman," in *Black Theology,* ed. Cone and Wilmore, 1:334.

34. Grant, "Womanist Theology" 210.

35. Alice Walker, *In Search of Our Mothers' Gardens* (San Diego: Harcourt, 1983), 231–43.

CHAPTER ONE

1. My sources for this biographical sketch are: Lee, *The Life and Religious Experience;* Lee, *Religious Experience and Journal of Mrs. Jarena Lee, Giving an Account of Her Call to Preach the Gospel* (1849), republished in *Spiritual Narratives,* ed. Susan Houchins (New York: Oxford University Press, 1988); William L. Andrews, introduction to *Sisters of the Spirit: Three Black Women's Autobiographies of the Nineteenth Century,* ed. Andrews (Bloomington: Indiana University Press, 1986), 4–6; Jualynne Dodson, "Nineteenth-Century A.M.E. Preaching Women: Cutting Edge of Women's Inclusion in Church Polity" in *Women in New Worlds,* ed. Hilah F. Thomas and Rosemary Skinner Keller (Nashville: Abingdon, 1981), 278; and Maxine Sample, "Jarena Lee (1783–?)," in *African American Autobiographers: A Sourcebook,* ed. Emmanuel S. Nelson (Westport, Ct.: Greenwood Press, 2002), 231–32.

2. My sources for this biographical sketch are: Elaw, *Memoirs of the Life;* and Andrews, introduction to *Sisters of the Spirit,* 6–9.

3. My sources for this biographical sketch are: Foote, *A Brand Plucked from the Fire;* Andrews, introduction to *Sisters of the Spirit,* 9–10; Sample, "Julia A. J. Foote (1823–1900)," in *African American Autobiographers,* ed. Nelson, 138–39; and Bettye Collier-Thomas, ed., *Daughters of Thunder: Black Women Preachers and Their Sermons, 1850–1979* (San Francisco: Jossey-Bass, 1998), 287 n. 34.

4. My sources for this biographical sketch are: Amanda Smith, *An Autobiography: The Story of the Lord's Dealings with Mrs. Amanda Smith the Colored Evangelist* (1893; New York: Oxford University Press, 1988); Collier-Thomas, *Daughters of Thunder,* 48–52; and Adrienne M. Israel, *Amanda Berry Smith: From Washerwoman to Evangelist,* Studies in Evangelism Series 16 (Lanham, Md.: Scarecrow, 1998), 42.

5. My sources for this biographical sketch are Jackson; Jean Humez, "Jackson, Rebecca Cox (1795–1871)," in *Black Women in America: An Historical Encyclopedia,* vol. 1, ed. Darlene Clark Hine, Elsa Barkley Brown, and Rosalyn Terborg-Penn (Brooklyn: Carlson, 1993), 626–27; and

Richard E. Williams, *Called and Chosen: The Story of Mother Rebecca Jackson and the Philadelphia Shakers,* ATLA Monograph Series 17 (Metuchen, N.J.: Scarecrow, 1981), 128.

6. Leon F. Litwack, *North of Slavery: The Negro in the Free States, 1790–1860* (Chicago: University of Chicago Press, 1961), 153–54.

7. Ibid., 155; Sharon Harley, "Northern Black Female Workers: Jacksonian Era," in *The Afro-American Woman: Struggles and Images,* ed. Sharon Harley and Rosalyn Terborg-Penn (Port Washington, N.Y.: Kennikat, 1978), 11–12.

8. Tera W. Hunter, *To 'Joy My Freedom: Southern Black Women's Lives and Labors after the Civil War* (Cambridge, Mass.: Harvard University Press, 1997), 57.

9. Ibid., 57, 62.

10. Litwack, *North of Slavery,* 155–57.

11. David R. Roediger, *The Wages of Whiteness: Race and the Making of the American Working Class* (London: Verso, 1991), 13, 14.

12. Litwack, *North of Slavery,* 162, 165, 166.

13. Roediger, *The Wages of Whiteness,* 134, 136.

14. Litwack, *North of Slavery,* 168.

15. Ibid., 169.

16. Ibid., 179.

17. Ibid., 175, 178.

18. Sharon Harley, "When Your Work Is Not Who You Are: The Development of a Working-Class Consciousness among Afro-American Women," in *"We Specialize in the Wholly Impossible": A Reader in Black Women's History,* ed. Darlene Clark Hine, Wilma King, and Linda Reed (Brooklyn: Carlson, 1995), 27.

19. Ibid., 27–29.

20. Ibid., 30.

21. Ibid., 32.

22. Shirley J. Yee, *Black Women Abolitionists: A Study in Activism, 1828–1860* (Knoxville: University of Tennessee Press, 1992), 74–76; Judith Weisenfeld, *African American Women and Christian Activism: New York's Black YWCA, 1905–1945* (Cambridge, Mass.: Harvard University Press, 1997), 14; Gwen Athene Tarbox, *The Clubwomen's Daughters: Collectivist Impulses in Progressive-Era Girls' Fiction* (New York: Garland, 2000), 18; Anne M. Boylan, "Benevolence and Antislavery Activity among African American Women in New York and Boston, 1820–1840," in *The Abolitionist Sisterhood: Women's Political Culture in Antebellum America,* ed. Jean Fagan Yellin and John C. Van Horne (Ithaca, N.Y.: Cornell University Press, 1994), 121.

23. Yee, *Black Women Abolitionists,* 77–78.

24. Ibid., 81–84.

25. Boylan, "Benevolence and Antislavery Activity," 122.

26. Ibid., 127–28, 133.

27. Yee, *Black Women Abolitionists,* 87–88.

28. Regarding the use of petitions as an abolitionist tactic, Yee explains: "Male and female abolitionists of both races had frequently used the petition as a way to protest slavery and race discrimination in the 'nominally free states.' They flooded Congress and their state legislatures with antislavery petitions throughout the antebellum period, demanding the end of slavery and race discrimination in the District of Columbia and the United States" (ibid., 128). In regard to

the significance of such a tactic for white women and blacks, who lacked other legal avenues of political expression, Yee adds, "For disenfranchised groups—but not, of course, for white men, who had the right to vote—the petition was the only legal means to make their voices heard and seek changes in the law" (ibid.).

29. Ibid., 87; Jean R. Soderlund, "Priorities and Power: The Philadelphia Female Anti-Slavery Society," in *The Abolitionist Sisterhood,* ed. Yellin and Van Horne, 80–88.

30. *Liberator,* November 17, 1832, 183, quoted in Yee, *Black Women Abolitionists,* 88.

31. Yee, *Black Women Abolitionists,* 136–37.

32. Ibid., 137.

33. Ibid.

34. Ibid., 141.

35. Eleanor Flexner and Ellen Fitzpatrick, *Century of Struggle: The Woman's Rights Movement in the United States,* enlarged ed. (Cambridge, Mass.: Belknap Press of the Harvard University Press, 1996), 99–107; Lori D. Ginzberg, *Women and the Work of Benevolence: Morality, Politics, and Class in the Nineteenth-Century United States* (New Haven, Conn.: Yale University Press, 1990), 133–73.

36. Ginzberg, *Women and the Work of Benevolence,* 134; Flexner and Fitzpatrick, *Century of Struggle,* 101.

37. Ginzberg, *Women and the Work of Benevolence,* 133, 134.

38. Flexner and Fitzpatrick, *Century of Struggle,* 102.

39. Ibid., 102–5.

40. Ginzberg, *Women and the Work of Benevolence,* 136.

41. Ibid., 137. Note that the "National Women's Loyal League" is the name that Ginzberg uses to identify the league organized by Anthony, Stanton, and other women in 1863 to pledge support to the government; Flexner and Fitzpatrick call it the "National Woman's Loyal League."

42. Ginzberg, *Women and the Work of Benevolence,* 137–39.

43. Yee, *Black Women Abolitionists,* 149; Frances Smith Foster, "Harper, Frances Ellen Watkins (1825–1911)," in *Black Women in America,* ed. Hine, Brown, and Terborg-Penn, 534.

44. Elsa Barkley Brown, "Negotiating and Transforming the Public Sphere: African American Political Life in the Transition from Slavery to Freedom," *Public Culture: Bulletin of the Project for Transnational Studies* 7 (1994): 108, 109, 122, 123.

45. Ibid., 124.

46. Ibid, 115, 116.

47. Ibid., 138–41, 142, 144.

48. Yee, *Black Women Abolitionists,* 153.

49. I am using "the black church" as "an umbrella term for historically black denominations," as defined by Judith Weisenfeld in *This Far by Faith,* ed. Weisenfeld and Newman, 3. I use the term with an awareness of its problematic nature for, as Weisenfeld cogently argues: "[T]he tendency to speak of 'the' black church serves to erase a host of complexities inherent in the grouping of these churches in the late nineteenth century. Although we may speak of commonalities of approach to political engagement, agreement on certain theological issues, and the common desire to build religious community that takes seriously both culture and race, no such entity as 'the' black church truly exists" (Weisenfeld, *African American Women,* 15).

50. Evelyn Brooks Higginbotham, *Righteous Discontent: The Women's Movement in the Black Baptist Church, 1880–1920* (Cambridge, Mass.: Harvard University Press, 1993), 5. On the black church's significant role as a site for the cultivation of African Americans' organizational and leadership skills and as a setting for political struggle and community development, see Weisenfeld, *African American Women,* 15; and Hunter, *To 'Joy My Freedom,* 69.

51. Higginbotham, *Righteous Discontent,* 7, 10.

52. Ibid., 10.

53. Catherine A. Brekus, *Strangers & Pilgrims: Female Preaching in America, 1740–1845* (Chapel Hill: University of North Carolina Press, 1998) 3, 5, 6, 7. For a listing of these preaching women, see the appendix on 343–46: "Female Preachers and Exhorters in America, 1740–1845."

54. Ibid., 13.

55. Ibid., 14.

56. Ibid., 14, 15. Brekus describes republican motherhood as follows: "Even though women did not claim the right to exercise any political authority as autonomous individuals—such a notion was unthinkable to most women in Revolutionary America—they insisted they could shape the future of the republic by raising virtuous citizens. As mothers, wives, and sisters, they held the fate of the republic in their hands" (ibid., 148).

57. Ibid., 8.

58. Ibid., 15.

59. Marjorie Proctor-Smith, *Women in Shaker Community and Worship: A Feminist Analysis of the Uses of Religious Symbolism,* Studies in Women and Religion Series 16 (Lewiston, N.Y.: Edwin Mellen, 1985), 98–99.

60. Sacred dancing ("laboring") became an integral part of Shaker worship services as a form of religious expression. This dancing began as individual, spontaneous displays of ecstatic expression but later evolved into collective, ritualized, and choreographed performances, such as the "Square Order Shuffle," "Back Manner," "Skipping Manner," and circular dance (see Jean Humez, ed., *Mother's First-Born Daughters: Early Shaker Writings on Women and Religion* [Bloomington: Indiana University Press, 1993], xviii, xxiii, 69, 72; Stephen J. Stein, *The Shaker Experience in America: A History of the United Society of Believers* [New Haven, Conn.: Yale University Press, 1992], 48; Deborah E. Burns, *Shaker Cities of Peace, Love, and Union: A History of the Hancock Bishopric* [Hanover, N.H.: University Press of New England, 1993], 43, 49).

61. Proctor-Smith, *Women in Shaker Community,* 140.

62. Ibid., 140, 141.

63. Jackson, *Gifts of Power,* ed. Humez, 27, 28.

64. Rosemary Skinner Keller, "Creating a Sphere for Women: The Methodist Episcopal Church, 1869–1906," in *Perspectives on American Methodism,* ed. Richey, Rowe, and Schmidt, 332; C. Eric Lincoln and Lawrence H. Mamiya, *The Black Church in the African American Experience* (Durham, N.C.: Duke University Press, 1999), 275.

65. Collier-Thomas, *Daughters of Thunder,* 18. Though there was no provision in the Discipline for the licensing of women as local preachers, some women were nevertheless granted licenses, the first of whom was Margaret Van Cott in 1869. At the 1880 Conference, however, all such licenses were revoked (see Keller, "Creating a Sphere for Women," 332, 334, 335).

66. Oliver's real name was Anna Snowden; however, she changed it in order to avoid embarrassing her distinguished family, who were mortified by her decision to pursue theological stud-

ies with the intent of becoming a minister (see Kenneth E. Rowe, "The Ordination of Women: Round One; Anna Oliver and the General Conference of 1880," in *Perspectives on American Methodism,* ed. Richey, Rowe, and Schmidt, 298).

67. Undated clipping in President William F. Warren Papers, Boston University Library, quoted in Jeanette E. Newhall, "There Were Giants in Those Days; Pioneer Women and Boston University," *Nexus* 7, no. 1 (1963): 121, quoted in Rowe, "The Ordination of Women," 299.

68. Ibid., 298–99, 303.

69. Ibid., 301.

70. Anna Oliver, *Test Case on the Ordination of Women* (New York: William N. Jennings, printer, 1880), 3, 5, 6, quoted in Rowe, "The Ordination of Women," 303–4.

71. Rowe, "The Ordination of Women," 304.

72. Ibid., 307, 308.

73. Rosemary Skinner Keller, "Creating a Sphere for Women," 332–35.

74. Ibid., 341, 339, 341.

75. Even as local preachers, they were not allowed to pastor churches (see Collier-Thomas, *Daughters of Thunder,* 26).

76. Ibid., 26–27, 32; Lincoln and Mamiya, *The Black Church,* 278.

77. Jean M. Humez, "'My Spirit Eye': Some Functions of Spiritual and Visionary Experience in the Lives of Five Black Women Preachers, 1810–1880," in *Women and the Structure of Society: Selected Research from the Fifth Berkshire Conference on the History of Women,* ed. Barbara J. Harris and JoAnn K. McNamara (Durham, N.C.: Duke University Press, 1984), 130, 138, 140.

78. Lee 7–15; Dodson, "Nineteenth-Century A.M.E. Preaching Women," 277–78; Sample, "Jarena Lee (1783–?)," 232.

79. "Sophie Murray" and "Elizabeth Cole," in Joseph Thompson, *Bethel Gleanings* (Philadelphia: Robert L. Holland, 1881), 34–37, quoted in Dodson, "Nineteenth-Century A.M.E. Preaching Women," 279; "Rachel Evans," in Alexander W. Wayman, *Cyclopaedia of African Methodism* (Baltimore: Methodist Episcopal Book Depository, 1882), 57; James A. Handy, *Scraps of African Methodist Episcopal History* (Philadelphia: A.M.E. Book Concern, n.d.), 345, quoted in Dodson, "Nineteenth-Century A.M.E. Preaching Women," 279; "Harriet Felson Taylor," in John Francis Cook, "Outstanding Members of the First Church—September 1, 1840," manuscript, p. 2, box 1 (ca. 1841), Cook Family Papers, Moorland Spingarn Research Center, Howard University, Washington, D.C., quoted in Dodson, "Nineteenth-Century A.M.E. Preaching Women," 279; "Zilpha Elaw," in Zilpha Elaw, *Memoirs of the Life, Religious Experience, Ministerial Travels and Labours of Mrs. Zilpha Elaw: An American Female of Colour* (London, 1846), 62, quoted in Dodson, "Nineteenth-Century A.M.E. Preaching Women," 279; the date in brackets was inserted by Dodson.

80. Dodson, "Nineteenth-Century A.M.E. Preaching Women," 280–81.

81. Ibid., 282.

82. Joseph Morgan, *Morgan's History of the New Jersey Conference of the A.M.E. Church from 1872 to 1887* (Camden, N.J.: S. Chew, 1887) 45, quoted in Dodson, "Nineteenth-Century A.M.E. Preaching Women," 284.

83. Dodson, "Nineteenth-Century A.M.E. Preaching Women," 285–87.

84. Ibid., 288–89; Dodson, introduction to Amanda Smith, *An Autobiography,* xxxvi, xxxvii.

85. Lincoln and Mamiya, *The Black Church,* 58; Collier-Thomas, *Daughters of Thunder,* 22.

86. According to Barbara Welter, the "cult of true womanhood" was a set of ideals governing the behavior of middle-class white women. In order to be considered a "true woman," one must manifest the four cardinal virtues of piety, purity, submissiveness, and domesticity. Ideally, a woman should be weak, timid, and clingingly dependent. To accept the roles of wife and mother was a woman's sacred duty; within these roles she was to be a source of comfort and a beacon of morality for her family and for American culture at large. Faithfully adhering to the ideals of the cult of true womanhood supposedly assured women the respect and protection of men, as well as power within the confines of their homes (see "The Cult of True Womanhood: 1800–1860," in Barbara Welter, *Dimity Convictions: The American Woman in the Nineteenth Century* [Athens: Ohio University Press, 1976)], 21–41).

87. Joseph G. Mannard, "Maternity . . . of the Spirit: Nuns and Domesticity in Antebellum America," in *History of Women in the United States: Historical Articles on Women's Lives and Activities,* ed. Nancy F. Cott, vol. 13 (Munich: K. G. Saur, 1993), 74 n. 1, 75, 79, 80, 83.

88. Ibid., 85, 87.

89. Ibid., 91.

90. Ibid., 92–93.

91. Mary Ewens, "The Leadership of Nuns in Immigrant Catholicism," in *Women and Religion in America,* ed. Rosemary Radford Ruether and Rosemary Skinner Keller, vol.1 (San Francisco: Harper & Row, 1981), 106–7.

92. Cyprian Davis, *The History of Black Catholics in the United States* (New York: Crossroad, 1990), 99–101; Theresa A. Rector, "Black Nuns as Educators," *Journal of Negro Education* 51, no. 3 (1982): 240, 241, 244.

93. Rector, "Black Nuns as Educators," 245; Davis, *The History of Black Catholics,* 105; Sister Audrey Marie Detiege, *Henriette Delille, Free Woman of Color* (New Orleans: Sisters of the Holy Family, 1976), 22, quoted in Rector, "Black Nuns as Educators, 245, 246.

94. Rector, "Black Nuns as Educators," 246; Davis, *The History of Black Catholics,* 107.

95. Melvin E. Dieter, *The Holiness Revival of the Nineteenth Century* (Metuchen, N.J.: Scarecrow, 1980), 1, 4; Melvin E. Dieter, ed., *The Nineteenth-Century Holiness Movement,* Great Holiness Classics Series 4 (Kansas City, Mo.: Beacon Hill, 1998), 23.

96. Dieter, *The Holiness Revival* 26, 27, 33; Charles Edwin Jones, *Perfectionist Persuasion: The Holiness Movement and American Methodism, 1867–1936,* ATLA Monograph Series 5 (Metuchen, N.J.: Scarecrow, 1974), 2; Nancy Hardesty, Lucille Sider Dayton, and Donald W. Dayton, "Women in the Holiness Movement: Feminism in the Evangelical Tradition," in *Women of Spirit: Female Leadership in the Jewish and Christian Traditions,* ed. Rosemary Ruether and Eleanor McLaughlin (New York: Simon & Schuster, 1979), 226.

97. Dieter, *The Holiness Revival,* 27, 29; Hardesty, L. Dayton, and D. Dayton, "Women in the Holiness Movement," 226; Jones, *Perfectionist Persuasion,* 2, 5.

98. Dieter, *The Holiness Revival,* 35–36; Hardesty, L. Dayton, and D. Dayton, "Women in the Holiness Movement," 242–44.

99. Hardesty, L. Dayton, and D. Dayton, "Women in the Holiness Movement," 246, 247.

100. Ibid., 247.

101. Vinson Synan, *The Holiness-Pentecostal Tradition: Charismatic Movements in the Twentieth Century* (Grand Rapids, Mich.: Eerdmans, 1997), 45–46.

102. Ibid., 47.

103. Ibid., 46; Ted A. Campbell, *Methodist Doctrine: The Essentials* (Nashville: Abingdon, 1999), 60; William Edward Boardman, *He That Overcometh, or a Conquering Gospel* (Boston, 1869), 232, quoted in Timothy L. Smith, *Revivalism and Social Reform in Mid-Nineteenth-Century America* (New York: Abingdon, 1957), 234.

104. Mary Agnes Dougherty, "The Social Gospel According to Phoebe: Methodist Deaconesses in the Metropolis, 1885–1918," in *Perspectives on American Methodism,* ed. Richey, Rowe, and Schmidt, 356–57.

105. Ibid., 358.

106. Ibid., 359.

107. Ibid., 361–62.

108. Ibid., 362–63.

109. Ibid., 364–65.

110. Ann Braude, *Radical Spirits: Spiritualism and Women's Rights in Nineteenth-Century America,* 2nd ed. (Bloomington: Indiana University Press, 2001), xix, 2, 4.

111. Ibid., 6, 7.

112. Ibid., 82–85.

113. Ibid., 28, 29; 205 n. 5.

CHAPTER TWO

1. Shirley J. Yee, *Black Women Abolitionists: A Study in Activism, 1828–1860* (Knoxville: University of Tennessee Press, 1992), 41–44, 51, 54, 58, 59.

2. Evelyn Brooks Higginbotham, *Righteous Discontent: The Women's Movement in the Black Baptist Church, 1880–1920* (Cambridge, Mass.: Harvard University Press, 1993), 8, 47, 187.

3. Ibid., 187.

4. Deborah Gray White, *Too Heavy a Load: Black Women in Defense of Themselves, 1894–1994* (New York: Norton, 1999), 22, 24, 52–55, 69, 70.

5. Glenn Hendler, *Public Sentiments: Structures of Feeling in Nineteenth-Century American Literature* (Chapel Hill: University of North Carolina Press, 2001) 210; see also 23, 145–83.

6. Richard J. Douglass-Chin, *Preacher Woman Sings the Blues: The Autobiographies of Nineteenth-Century African American Evangelists* (Columbia: University of Missouri Press, 2001), 11.

7. Ibid.

8. See my discussions of this in chapters 2 and 3.

9. Sidonie Smith, *Subjectivity, Identity, and the Body: Women's Autobiographical Practices in the Twentieth Century* (Bloomington: Indiana University Press, 1993), 5–17.

10. Carole Boyce Davies, *Black Women, Writing and Identity: Migrations of the Subject* (London: Routledge, 1994), 4.

11. Davies further describes the ways in which migration has been a fundamental part of human experience: "There have been internal and external migrations, voluntary and forced because of radical changes in climate, wars, natural disasters, oppression, radical breaks for change, in search of food, better conditions, land and other circumstances throughout the history of human life on the planet (ibid., 167 n. 9).

12. Ibid., 36, 37.

13. Gloria Anzaldúa, *Borderlands/La Frontera: The New Mestiza* (San Francisco: Spinsters/Aunt Lute, 1987).

14. Davies, *Black Women, Writing and Identity,* 15–16.

15. Ibid., 4.

16. Joycelyn K. Moody, "Ripping Away the Veil of Slavery: Literacy, Communal Love, and Self-Esteem in Three Slave Women's Narratives," *Black American Literature Forum* 24, no. 4 (1990): 646, quoted in Kimberly Rae Connor, *Conversions and Visions in the Writings of African-American Women* (Knoxville: University of Tennessee Press, 1994), 15.

17. William Andrews, *To Tell a Free Story: The First Century of Afro-American Autobiography, 1760–1865* (Urbana: University of Illinois Press, 1986), 177–78.

18. For a discussion of Daniel Payne's role in setting the educational standards for AME ministers, and his conflicts with Jarena Lee on this issue, see David W. Wills, "Womanhood and Domesticity in the A.M.E. Tradition: The Influence of Daniel Alexander Payne," in *Black Apostles at Home and Abroad: Afro-Americans and the Christian Mission from the Revolution to Reconstruction,* ed. Wills and Richard Newman (Boston: G. K. Hall, 1982), 136–39.

19. Dorothy Sterling, ed., *We Are Your Sisters: Black Women in the Nineteenth Century* (New York: Norton, 1984), 85, 92, 215.

20. Nancy A. Hardesty and Adrienne Israel, "Amanda Berry Smith: A 'Downright, Outright Christian,'" in *Spirituality and Social Responsibility: Vocational Vision of Women in the United Methodist Tradition,* ed. Rosemary Skinner Keller (Nashville: Abingdon, 1993), 63. Besides economic necessity, the strains of an unhappy marriage were also a factor in the couple's living arrangement. Regarding this marital discord, see Adrienne M. Israel, *Amanda Berry Smith: From Washerwoman to Evangelist,* Studies in Evangelism 16 (Lanham, Md.: Scarecrow, 1998), 24, 41, 50.

21. In doing research for her dissertation on the Shaker personal narrative, Sarah Diane Sasson studied the original manuscript of Jackson's narrative and found it very difficult to read due to Jackson's use of phonetic spelling and her deficiencies in punctuation. It was Alonzo Giles Hollister (1830–1911), Shaker author of theological essays and copyist of numerous Shaker manuscripts, who copied and edited Jackson's narrative to make it more legible (see Sarah Diane Sasson, "The Shaker Personal Narrative: Studies in a Nineteenth-Century Autobiographical Tradition" [Ph.D. diss., University of North Carolina, 1980], 21, 22).

22. I am drawing upon Antonio Gramsci's conception of the organic intellectual (see *Selections from the Prison Notebooks of Antonio Gramsci* [New York: International, 1971], 5–23 passim). For a brief discussion of the Christian intellectual as organic intellectual, see Cornel West, *Prophetic Fragments* (Grand Rapids, Mich.: Eerdmans, 1988), 271–72.

23. Rebecca Jackson, *Gifts of Power: The Writings of Rebecca Jackson, Black Visionary, Shaker Eldress,* ed. Jean McMahon Humez (Amherst: University of Massachusetts Press, 1981), 11, 13, 15.

24. Ibid., 15.

25. Cyprian Davis, *The History of Black Catholics in the United States* (New York: Crossroad, 1990), 101.

26. Ibid., 100. Davis further explains, "It is also possible that the Association of the Holy Slavery of the Mother of God is related to the devotion preached by St. Louis-Marie Grignion de Montfort (1673–1716), a French priest who stressed handing over to Mary the disposition of one's merits and graces. The metaphor used was that of slavery. De Montfort's teaching was not the first to use the term 'holy slavery,' but his form of the devotion became the most popular and best known" (Ibid.).

27. Hardesty and Israel, "Amanda Berry Smith," 69.

28. Ibid., 69–70.

29. Ibid., 70.

30. W. E. B. Du Bois, *The Souls of Black Folk: Essays and Sketches* (1903), Fisk Diamond Jubilee ed. (Nashville: Fisk University Press, 1979), 3.

31. See William L. Andrews, Frances Smith Foster, and Trudier Harris, eds., *The Oxford Companion to African American Literature* (New York: Oxford University Press, 1997), 483.

32. Darlene Clark Hine, *Hine Sight: Black Women and the Reconstruction of American History* (Brooklyn: Carlson, 1994), 42, 43.

33. Ibid., 37.

34. Ibid., 44.

35. Ibid., 46–47.

36. Ibid., 43.

37. Frances Smith Foster, *Witnessing Slavery: The Development of Ante-bellum Slave Narratives,* 2nd ed. (Madison: University of Wisconsin Press, 1994), xxix–xli.

38. Jane Tompkins, *Sensational Designs: The Cultural Work of American Fiction, 1790–1860* (New York: Oxford University Press, 1985), 151.

39. See chapters 3 and 4, for example, for discussions of the ways that Lee and Elaw link domesticity with the power and publicity of their evolving roles as itinerant preachers.

40. He is afraid that people will think she is driven to ascetic practices by a guilty conscience (see Jackson, *Gifts of Power,* ed. Humez, 18).

41. Sarah Diane Sasson provides a similar reading of Jackson in the role of Christ: "Here Mother Rebecca once again sees her life in the pattern of the life of Christ. Like Christ feeding the multitude with a few loaves and fishes, Mother Rebecca with three tablespoons of batter feeds all who come to her. Like Him, she also nourishes those who follow her" (Sasson, "The Shaker Personal Narrative," 265). See Matthew 14:13–21 for the story of Jesus's feeding of the multitude.

42. For the story of Eve's temptation, see Genesis 3:1–7.

43. The brackets were placed in the text by Humez to indicate that Jackson's copyist and editor, Alonzo Hollister, edited this material, and therefore the diction and syntax are likely different from Jackson's (Jackson, *Gifts of Power,* ed. Humez, 67).

44. Commenting on the white racial identity of the people in Jackson's dream, Humez states: "This dream account apparently aims to justify the fact that RJ's early congregations were often white or predominantly white. It may reflect her retrospective uneasiness with the fact that the Shakers, 'God's true people on earth,' were predominantly white" (ibid., 99 n. 39).

45. Ibid., 30–31.

46. Both Thomas and Perot are black and become members of the Shaker community in Philadelphia. Rebecca Perot joined the Watervliet Shakers at the same time as Jackson, and the two women developed a very close friendship. Humez confirms Thomas's racial identity in her "Glossary of Proper Names," ibid., 360.

47. Humez comments: "Suggests that in her dream she is 'housekeeping' somewhere near Seventh and Spruce. Jackson probably lived in or frequently visited this neighborhood, prior to joining the Shakers" (ibid., 219 n. 30).

48. H. L. Eades, "Duality in Godhead," *Shaker* 1, no. 2 (1871): 15, quoted in Robley Edward Whitson, ed., *The Shakers: Two Centuries of Spiritual Reflection* (New York: Paulist, 1983), 254. Ann

Lee, known as Mother Ann, is regarded as the spiritual mother of the Shakers since she is the person through whom the Shakers experienced rebirth into the life of Christ. Born in England, Lee was the principal founder of the Shakers in America.

49. Whitson, *The Shakers,* 33.

50. Jackson recorded what she had prayed for the day before on February 14: "I earnestly prayed to God that He would give me something the next day, that would encourage me in His holy work, as that is my birthday" (Jackson, *Gifts of Power,* ed. Humez, 218).

51. Mary's Magnificat can be found in Luke 1:46–55.

52. In *The American Heritage College Dictionary,* 3rd ed. (Boston: Houghton Mifflin, 1993), "manger" is defined as "[a] trough or an *open box* holding feed for livestock" (824; my emphasis).

53. Luke 1:48 (New International Version).

54. Ibid.

55. In *Black Feminist Thought: Knowledge, Consciousness, and the Politics of Empowerment* (New York: Routledge, 1991), Patricia Hill Collins identifies four stereotypes derived from the experience of slavery that have been applied to black women for the purpose of their social, economic, and political subordination: "mammy," "matriarch," "welfare mother," and "Jezebel." Regarding the "mammy" stereotype, Collins explains: "Created to justify the economic exploitation of house slaves and sustained to explain Black women's long-standing restriction to domestic service, the mammy image represents the normative yardstick used to evaluate all Black women's behavior. By loving, nurturing, and caring for her white children and 'family' better than her own, the mammy symbolizes the dominant group's perceptions of the ideal Black female relationship to elite white male power. Even though she may be well loved and may wield considerable authority in her white 'family,' the mammy still knows her 'place' as obedient servant. She has accepted her subordination" (71).

56. William Andrews notes the telling similarity between Foote's language and that used by Chief Justice Roger B. Taney in the Dred Scott decision of 1857, in which Taney asserted that blacks "had no rights which the white man was bound to respect." Andrews believes that Foote brilliantly links the sexism that she experiences at the hands of black male church officials with the political racism that all blacks faced in American society (see Andrews, *Sisters of the Spirit,* 20).

57. The biblical reference to Jesus in the Garden of Gethsemane is Matthew 26:39: "Going a little farther, he fell with his face to the ground and prayed, 'My Father, if it is possible, may this cup be taken from me. Yet not as I will, but as you will'" (New International Version). See also Mark 14:35.

58. Smith's willingness to sacrifice the life of her beloved child to prove her faithfulness is reminiscent of the Hebrew patriarch Abraham's willingness to kill his only son, Isaac, for the same purpose (see Genesis 22).

59. Israel, *Amanda Berry Smith,* 39, 50.

60. Ibid., 40.

61. Two of the children are away at this time (Jackson, *Gifts of Power,* ed. Humez, 82).

62. The bracketed material was inserted by Humez.

63. Regarding these songs, Humez explains, "Possibly these are the 'spiritual songs' favored by the 'sanctified sisters' within the A.M.E. church of the early nineteenth century but disapproved of by many of the regular clergy" (Jackson, *Gifts of Power,* ed. Humez, 133 n. 12).

CHAPTER THREE

1. In using the term "sanctification," I am specifically referring to the doctrine of "entire sanctification," on which I will further elaborate.

2. In Zora Neale Hurston's *Their Eyes Were Watching God,* a novel vividly portraying a southern black woman's journey to selfhood and personal fulfillment, protagonist Janie Woods disparagingly refers to members of the black town of Eatonville, Florida, as "Mouth-Almighty." She does this because the collective mouth of her hometown is full of gossip about her following her return home after burying her third husband. I am, however, redefining this term to positively refer to the God-emboldened mouths of the radical spiritual mothers following sanctification. Through the power of God, these women gain the ability to speak freely in any situation when divinely inspired to do so. Regarding Hurston's use of the term, see *Their Eyes Were Watching God* (New York: Harper & Row, 1998), 5.

3. Other names by which entire sanctification is known include "Christian perfection," "Christian holiness," "scriptural holiness," "perfect love," "second blessing," "heart purity," "the baptism of the Holy Spirit," "the deeper life," and "the rest of faith" (see Melvin Dieter, ed., *The Nineteenth-Century Holiness Movement,* vol. 4 (Kansas City, Mo.: Beacon Hill, 1998), 18.

4. Harald Lindström, *Wesley and Sanctification* (Wilmore, Ky.: Asbury, 1981), 131.

5. Ibid., 131, 148.

6. Ibid., 145.

7. Dieter, "The Wesleyan Perspective," in *Five Views on Sanctification,* ed. Stanley N. Gundry (Grand Rapids, Mich.: Zondervan, 1987),14.

8. Ibid., 14.

9. Lindström, *Wesley and Sanctification,* 113.

10. *The American Heritage College Dictionary,* 3rd ed. (Boston: Houghton Mifflin, 1993), 589.

11. Dieter, "The Wesleyan Perspective" 16.

12. Ted A. Campbell, *Methodist Doctrine: The Essentials* (Nashville: Abingdon, 1999), 55.

13. Lindström, *Wesley and Sanctification,* 113–14.

14. Ibid., 84, 116.

15. Ibid., 116–18.

16. Dieter, *The Nineteenth-Century Holiness Movement,* 18.

17. Lindström, *Wesley and Sanctification,* 118; Dieter, "The Wesleyan Perspective," 18–19; Dieter, *The Nineteenth-Century Holiness Movement,* 18.

18. Dieter, *The Nineteenth-Century Holiness Movement,* 18.

19. Dieter, "The Wesleyan Perspective," 30.

20. Virginia Lieson Brereton, *From Sin to Salvation: Stories of Women's Conversions, 1800 to the Present* (Bloomington: Indiana University Press, 1991), 6.

21. Amanda Smith, *An Autobiography: The Story of the Lord's Dealings with Mrs. Amanda Smith the Colored Evangelist* (1893; New York: Oxford University Press, 1988), 54; Adrienne M. Israel, *Amanda Berry Smith: From Washerwoman to Evangelist* (Lanham, Md.: Scarecrow, 1998), 42.

22. John S. Inskip was one of the key organizers of the National Camp Meeting Association for the Promotion of Holiness, which became central to the Holiness movement following the Civil War. The organization grew out of the first successful interdenominational camp meeting held on a national scale, which took place in 1867 in Vineland, New Jersey. Subsequent

national camp meetings were sponsored by the NCMA, a regular facet of which was exploring the ways that the Holy Spirit powerfully manifested itself in the lives of believers during conversion, but particularly during the experience of sanctification (see J. Lawrence Brasher, *The Sanctified South: John Lakin Brasher and the Holiness Movement* [Urbana: University of Illinois Press, 1994], 30). In addition, Inskip was one of the many people who encouraged Smith to write her autobiography.

23. The New International Version reads: "and to put on the new self, created to be like God in true righteousness and holiness."

24. See the chapter entitled "The Oppositional Gaze: Black Female Spectators" in bell hooks's *Black Looks: Race and Representation* (Boston: South End, 1992), 115–31.

25. This phrase is from Ralph Ellison's *Shadow and Act* (New York: Random House, 1964), 45.

26. Diane H. Lobody, "'That Language Might Be Given Me': Women's Experience in Early Methodism," in *Perspectives on American Methodism: Interpretive Essays,* ed. Russell E. Richey, Kenneth E. Rowe, and Jean Miller Schmidt (Nashville: Kingswood/Abingdon, 1993), 133.

27. Ibid., 134, 136.

28. Richard Allen and Jacob Tapisco, *The Doctrines and Discipline of the African Methodist Episcopal Church* (Philadelphia: Allen & Tapisco, 1817), 105.

29. Ibid., 105–6.

30. These four pillars include preaching, testifying, singing, and praying (see Cheryl Townsend Gilkes, *If It Wasn't for the Women: Black Women's Experience and Womanist Culture in Church and Community* [Maryknoll, N.Y.: Orbis, 2001], 125).

31. Ibid., 137.

32. Allen and Tapisco, *Doctrines and Discipline,* 106–7.

33. Ibid., 107.

34. Revised Standard Version.

35. This interpretation was suggested by Harryette Mullen, who stated that Foote's bathing counteracts the washing with salt water that her mother received (Mullen, lecture in the fall 1990 course "Slave Narratives and the Production of Afro-American Literature," Cornell University).

36. Isaiah 54:1, New International Version.

37. Richard J. Douglass-Chin, *Preacher Woman Sings the Blues: The Autobiographies of Nineteenth-Century African American Evangelists* (Columbia: University of Missouri Press, 2001), 126.

38. Ibid.

39. In a note, William Andrews explains: "Lee alludes to 2 Cor. 12:2–4, although it was not Paul but an unnamed acquaintance of Paul who was 'caught up to the third heaven'" (see Andrews, *Sisters of the Spirit,* 238 n. 5).

40. When Jeremiah is called by the Lord to prophesy to the people of Judah, he resists, insisting that he lacks the talent for speaking. God replies by assuring him that He has put words into his mouth (see Jeremiah 1:9). William Andrews notes that "Lee's commissioning experience echoes that of several biblical prophets and missionaries. See Jer. 1:9; Exod. 4:1, 12; and Luke 21:15" (Andrews, *Sisters of the Spirit,* 238 n. 6).

41. Ibid., 18.

42. As mentioned in chapter 1, "house-church" is the term used to characterize the home in which Phoebe Palmer held her popular "Tuesday Meeting for the Promotion of Holiness."

It also seems appropriate to apply this term to the homes in which the radical spiritual mothers exercised their preaching gifts.

43. Lindström, *Wesley and Sanctification,* quoted in Andrews, *Sisters of the Spirit,* 15.

44. George Dixon Greer, "A Psychological Study of Sanctification as a *Second* Work of Divine Grace" (Ph.D. diss., Drew University, 1936), 172.

CHAPTER FOUR

Epigraph: In a footnote, William Andrews explains, "According to Paul the Apostle, Demas forsook him and the Christian ministry because of his love of 'the present world.' 2 Tim. 4:10" (see William L. Andrews, *Sisters of the Spirit: Three Black Women's Autobiographies of the Nineteenth Century* [Bloomington: Indiana University Press, 1986], 241 n. 26).

1. In developing the idea of the envisioned communities of the radical spiritual mothers, I am echoing the title of Benedict Anderson's *Imagined Communities: Reflections on the Origin and Spread of Nationalism* (London: Verso, 1991).

2. I borrow this term from William Andrews (see Andrews, *Sisters of the Spirit,* 20).

3. While I am specifically focusing on black Christian women, I do not mean to suggest that Christianity is the only avenue by which one can arrive at a radical consciousness or posit a radical egalitarianism.

4. "Care-in-relationship": Bebb Wheeler Stone, "Celebrating Embodied Care: Women and Economic Justice," in *Reformed Faith and Economics,* ed. Robert Stivers (Lanham, Md.: University Press of America, 1989), 172.

5. Kimberly Rae Connor, *Conversions and Visions in the Writings of African-American Women* (Knoxville: University of Tennessee Press, 1994), 5.

6. See chapter 2, "The Power of Self-Definition," in Patricia Hill Collins's *Black Feminist Thought: Knowledge, Consciousness, and the Politics of Empowerment* (New York: Routledge, 1991), 91–114.

7. See chapter 2 for my discussion of migratory subjectivity.

8. Jarena Lee, *Religious Experience and Journal of Mrs. Jarena Lee, Giving an Account of Her Call to Preach the Gospel* (Philadelphia: printed for the author, 1849); reprinted in *Spiritual Narratives,* ed. Susan Houchins (New York: Oxford University Press, 1988), 88.

9. Joycelyn Moody, *Sentimental Confessions: Spiritual Narratives of Nineteenth-Century African American Women* (Athens: University of Georgia Press, 2001), 74.

10. The temptation to which Elaw refers is the strong conviction that Hannah temporarily experiences during her illness that she is condemned to go to hell despite having lived an exemplary Christian life.

11. Moody, *Sentimental Confessions,* 75.

12. Dickson D. Bruce Jr., *And They All Sang Hallelujah: Plain-Folk Camp-Meeting Religion, 1800–1845* (Knoxville: University of Tennessee Press, 1974), 4, 5.

13. Toni Morrison, *Beloved* (New York: Plume, 1987), 87.

14. See Judylyn S. Ryan's "Spirituality and/as Ideology in Black Women's Literature: The Preaching of Maria W. Stewart and Baby Suggs, Holy" for a discussion of Baby Suggs as a character that reflects African cosmological elements, such as the interconnectedness of cultural and

spiritual identity, the use of spirituality as epistemology, and the recognition of ancestors as a vital, guiding presence within communal life. Her essay appears in *Women Preachers and Prophets through Two Millennia of Christianity,* ed. Beverly Mayne Kienzle and Pamela J. Walker (Berkeley and Los Angeles: University of California Press, 1998).

15. Bruce, *And They All Sang Hallelujah,* 72, 73.

16. Ibid., 75, 76.

17. Ibid., 86, 87.

18. See Matthew 16:21–23 for the scene between Jesus and Peter.

19. Rebecca Jackson, *Gifts of Power: The Writings of Rebecca Jackson, Black Visionary, Shaker Eldress,* ed. Jean McMahon Humez (Amherst: University of Massachusetts Press, 1981), 5.

20. Ibid.

21. Ibid., 6.

22. Richard J. Douglass-Chin, *Preacher Woman Sings the Blues: The Autobiographies of Nineteenth-Century African American Evangelists* (Columbia: University of Missouri Press, 2001), 150.

23. Toni Morrison, *Playing in the Dark: Whiteness and the Literary Imagination* (Cambridge, Mass.: Harvard University Press, 1992), 6–7.

24. Ibid., 80–81.

25. Humez has placed in brackets material edited by Alonzo Hollister that probably differs in syntax and diction from Jackson's original language (see "A Note on the Text," in Jackson, *Gifts of Power,* ed. Humez, 67).

26. In an 1850 vision, it is revealed to Jackson that this woman is Mother Lucy Wright, an early Shaker leader.

27. Though Jackson states that this vision occurred in 1831, Jean Humez believes that she did not write her account of it until after the winter of 1843, when she made an extended visit to Watervliet. The confidence that Jackson expresses in her commitment to the Shakers suggests a later date to Humez (see Jackson, *Gifts of Power,* ed. Humez, 137 n. 19).

28. See chapter 3 of Pagels's *The Gnostic Gospels* (New York: Vintage, 1989).

29. Specifically, Bednarowski has identified four factors that tend to promote women's equality and leadership positions for women: "1. a perception of the divine that deemphasized the masculine either by means of a bisexual divinity or an impersonal, nonanthropomorphic divine principle; 2. a tempering or denial of the doctrine of the Fall; 3. a denial of the need for a traditional ordained clergy; 4. a view of marriage that did not stress the married state and motherhood as the proper sphere for woman and her only means of fulfillment." Groups embodying these assumptions have usually been marginal religious movements and include the Shakers, Christian Scientists, Theosophists, and Spiritualists (see Mary Farrell Bednarowski, "Outside the Mainstream: Women's Religion and Women Religious Leaders in Nineteenth-Century America," *Journal of the American Academy of Religion* 48, no. 2 (1980): 209.

30. Again, the connection with gnosticism is instructive. Pagels has found a correlation between the belief in a maternal god and sociopolitical equality for women. Gnostic groups such as the Valentinians accorded equal status to men and women, with women holding such roles as traveling evangelists, priests, prophets, teachers, healers, and possibly bishops. However, by the year 200 A.D., all gnostic texts had been purged from the canonical writings of orthodox Christians, thus eliminating most images of God as feminine (see Pagels, *The Gnostic Gospels,* 57, 60).

31. Regarding this incident, Humez explains: "This verbal attack by three 'Methodist' ministers (at least two of them A.M.E.) probably occurred in 1835. . . . It is also possible that she refers here to a series of incidents that took place over ten years, roughly from 1833 when she began to travel to 1843 when she made a commitment to the Shakers" (see Jackson, *Gifts of Power*, ed. Humez, 149 n. 38).

32. Ibid., 26, 27.

33. Ibid., 28.

34. Ibid., 9.

35. Alice Walker, *In Search of Our Mothers' Gardens* (San Diego: Harcourt, 1983), 80.

36. Ibid., 80, 81.

37. Jackson, *Gifts of Power*, ed. Humez, 9 n. 10.

38. Carroll Smith-Rosenberg, "The Female World of Love and Ritual: Relations between Women in Nineteenth-Century America," *Signs: A Journal of Women and Culture and Society* 1, no. 1 (1975): 1–29.

39. Ibid., 1.

40. Ibid., 2, 7, 10, 21, 22.

41. Ibid., 9.

42. Robley Edward Whitson, ed., *The Shakers: Two Centuries of Spiritual Reflection* (New York: Paulist, 1983), 19; Jackson, *Gifts of Power*, ed. Humez, 31.

43. Richard E. Williams, *Called and Chosen: The Story of Mother Rebecca Jackson and the Philadelphia Shakers* (Metuchen, N.J.: Scarecrow, 1981), 146.

44. Jackson, *Gifts of Power*, ed. Humez, 31, 32.

45. The inner conflict that Jackson experiences is reflective of the "double-consciousness" she possesses as an African American.

46. Jackson, *Gifts of Power*, ed. Humez, 268 n. 51.

47. Ibid., 269 n. 55.

48. Ibid., 37.

49. Geraldine Duclow, "The Shaker Family of Philadelphia," *Shaker Messenger* 13, no. 3 (1991): 5. Though the family included blacks and whites, males and females, it was nevertheless predominantly black and female.

50. Ibid.

51. Williams, *Called and Chosen,* 109.

52. Duclow, "The Shaker Family of Philadelphia," 6; Williams, *Called and Chosen,* 115. Note that Williams dates the letter January 14, 1872, while Duclow dates it January 4, 1872.

53. Eliza Anne Taylor and Polly Reed to Elders at Groveland, New York, January 14, 1872, Watervliet, New York, quoted in Williams, *Called and Chosen,* 115.

54. Williams, *Called and Chosen,* 107.

55. Ibid., 116; the names in brackets were inserted by Williams.

56. Ibid., 116–17.

57. Ibid., 117.

58. One of the notations in "Daybook of the Second Family" (quoted ibid., 112) reads:

July, Monday 28, (1873)
Elds. Paulina Bates and Sister Alvira Conklin early to Albany after a Juish [sic] Sister

Hatty Wallden [Hattie Walton] and got home late with her seemingly half dead. She fled from Philadelphia to escape marriage.

Hattie Walton's name in brackets was added by Williams.

59. Henry Blinn, "Notes by the Way, While on a Journey to the State of Kentucky in the Year 1873" (Canterbury, N.H., 1873), quoted in Williams, *Called and Chosen,* 118, 121.

60. Williams, *Called and Chosen,* 52, 107, 123. Duclow further explains: "Some confusion has arisen from the fact that Perot also called herself Rebecca Jackson. This was not only after Rebecca Jackson's death, as we had thought, but before as well. I discovered that Perot used the name Jackson in the 1870 census records, several months before Jackson died. Sometimes for clarification Perot is called Rebecca Jackson, Junior" (Duclow, "The Shaker Family of Philadelphia," 6).

61. Richard Williams believed this meant Lebanon, Pennsylvania, but Geraldine Duclow now thinks that it refers to Philadelphia's Lebanon Cemetery, an eleven-acre plot established by a group of African Americans in 1849 (see Williams, *Called and Chosen,* 106; and Duclow, "The Shaker Family of Philadelphia," 6).

62. Williams, *Called and Chosen,* 107, 128; Duclow, "The Shaker Family of Philadelphia," 7.

63. Williams, *Called and Chosen,* 128.

CHAPTER FIVE

1. Deborah Gray White, *Ar'n't I a Woman?: Female Slaves in the Plantation South,* rev. ed. (New York: Norton, 1999), 28–29.

2. Winthrop D. Jordan, *White over Black: American Attitudes toward the Negro, 1550–1812* (Chapel Hill: University of North Carolina Press, 1968), 1–43, quoted in White, *Ar'n't I a Woman?* 29.

3. White, *Ar'n't I a Woman?* 29, 30.

4. Because mobility is so central to the identity of the radical spiritual mother, she must, by definition, be a free woman.

5. I borrow the phrase "reconstructing womanhood" from the title of Hazel V. Carby's *Reconstructing Womanhood: The Emergence of the Afro-American Woman Novelist* (New York: Oxford University Press, 1987).

6. In her narrative, not only does Jacobs assume the pseudonym Linda Brent, but she also disguises the names of many other people as well. She explains this approach as follows: "I have concealed the names of places, and given persons fictitious names. I have no motive for secrecy on my own account, but deemed it kind and considerate towards others to pursue this course" (Jacobs 1). Regarding Jacobs's intentions for using the pseudonym "Linda Brent," Jean Fagan Yellin further explains: "Harriet Jacobs had become 'Linda Brent,' but not to hide behind a pseudonym or to disappear under a fictitious name. As 'Linda' she had empowered herself to write about a life that as 'Harriet,' she could neither speak nor write" (see Yellin, *Harriet Jacobs: A Life* [New York: Basic Civitas Books, 2004], 144).

7. Sharon Block, "Lines of Color, Sex, and Service: Comparative Sexual Coercion in Early America," in *Sex, Love, Race: Crossing Boundaries in North American History,* ed. Martha Hodes (New York: New York University Press, 1999), 148.

8. Yellin, *Harriet Jacobs,* 157.

9. Joanne M. Braxton, *Black Women Writing Autobiography: A Tradition within a Tradition* (Philadelphia: Temple University Press, 1989), 19.

10. Ibid.

11. Ibid., 21.

12. Ibid., 24.

13. Ibid., 22.

14. Mary Prince, *History of Mary Prince, a West Indian Slave, Related by Herself. With a Supplement by the Editor, To Which is Added, The Narrative of Asa-Asa, A Captured African* (London: F. Westley & A. H. Davis, 1831), reprinted in *The Classic Slave Narratives,* ed. Henry Louis Gates Jr. (Markham, Ontario: Mentor, 1987), 194 (hereafter cited parenthetically).

15. The notion of withholding the body is cited by Sidonie Smith, who borrows it from Mary Ann Caws, "Ladies Shot and Painted: Female Embodiment in Surrealist Art," in *The Female Body in Western Culture: Contemporary Perspectives,* ed. Susan Rubin Suleiman (Cambridge, Mass.: Harvard University Press, 1986), 284–85.

16. Carleton Mabee, *Sojourner Truth: Slave, Prophet, Legend* (New York: New York University Press, 1993), 1–4; Erlene Stetson and Linda David, *Glorying in Tribulation: The Lifework of Sojourner Truth* (East Lansing: Michigan State University Press, 1994), 30.

17. Ibid., 4–6; 248 n. 22.

18. *Saginaw Daily Courier,* June 14, 1871, quoted ibid., 13.

19. Mabee, *Sojourner Truth,* 12–13; *Narrative of Sojourner Truth,* ed. Margaret Washington (1850; New York: Vintage, 1993), xv (hereafter cited parenthetically).

20. Though Isabella and Thomas were to be freed in 1827, their children were still obligated to serve their owners until they reached their twenties (Mabee, *Sojourner Truth,* 14). Before Isabella escapes, she takes the time to spin about one hundred pounds of wool for her master. And when she finally leaves, she purposely does not go very far so that her master will not have a difficult time finding her (*Truth* 26, 27, 29). If a slave is capable of showing such unusual consideration when escaping, then it is not inconceivable that she would also consider her master's economic interests as well when deciding how many children to take.

21. Mabee, *Sojourner Truth,* 14; *Narrative of Sojourner Truth: A Bondswoman of Olden Time, With a History of Her Labors and Correspondence Drawn from her "Book of Life"* (1878; New York: Oxford University Press, 1991), 194.

22. *Rochester Evening Press,* April 17, 1871; *Salem (Ohio) Anti-Slavery Bugle,* November 8, 1856, quoted in Mabee, *Sojourner Truth,* 15.

23. Braxton, *Black Women Writing Autobiography,* 74.

24. Margaret Washington clarifies the correct spelling of the Gidney family name, as opposed to the narrative's spelling of "Gedney" (see *Truth* 113 n. 10).

25. Jean M. Humez, "Reading *The Narrative of Sojourner Truth* as a Collaborative Text," *Frontiers: A Journal of Women's Studies* 16, no. 1 (1996): 29, 30, 35, 36; Nell Irvin Painter, *Sojourner Truth: A Life, a Symbol* (New York: Norton, 1996), 106.

26. Humez, "Reading *The Narrative,*" 43–44.

27. Nell Irvin Painter believes that the cruelty that Truth displays toward her children derives from the abuse that Truth suffered as a child from her owners: "Like many other people who had been beaten as children, she would later reenact her torment with her own children and beat them into silence when they cried out from hunger" (Painter, *Sojourner Truth,* 15).

28. *Narrative of Sojourner Truth and "Book of Life,"* 164.

29. Humez, "Reading *The Narrative*," 44.

30. *Narrative of Sojourner Truth and "Book of Life,"* 139.

31. Nell Painter also interprets Truth's actions as infantilizing the men (see Painter, *Sojourner Truth,* 140).

32. The white women who are called upon to examine Truth's breast in order to ascertain her sexual identity are angered and mortified by this suggestion. Harryette Mullen believes that the man who proposed this action, a doctor, who himself could have performed the examination, purposely enlisted the help of the white women present in a calculated move designed

> as much to warn the women in the audience against the hazards of public speaking as to mock and humiliate the speaker. The clear message is that a public platform is no place for a real woman. Sojourner Truth, with her bold gesture, subverted an attempt by white men to make white "ladies" and a black woman humiliate each other while putting each other in her "proper" place. Her shameless gesture denies social propriety its oppressive power to define, limit, or regulate her behavior, and might be seen as a pointed comment on the conventions of femininity as well as a brazenly heroic response to her male hecklers.

See Mullen's "'Indelicate Subjects': African-American Women's Subjugated Subjectivity," *Sub/versions* (Winter 1991): 3.

33. Painter, *Sojourner Truth,* 16.

34. Washington, introduction to *Narrative,* xxxii. See also Mullen's "Indelicate Subjects."

35. Washington, introduction to *Narrative,* xxxi; Humez, "Reading *The Narrative*," 37, 51 n. 23.

36. Humez, "Reading *The Narrative*," 38.

37. *Narrative of Sojourner Truth and "Book of Life,"* 139. Of the relationship between the voice, body, and maternity of black women, Mullen states: "The materiality in which slave women are embedded necessitates that the voice of the black women be supplemented by a display of her female body, stripped of the ideological trappings that modestly draped the body of the white woman, yet contextualized by the slave woman's experience as a mother" (Mullen,"Indelicate Subjects," 3).

38. *Narrative of Sojourner Truth and "Book of Life,"* 138.

39. "Calculated theatricality": Glenn Hendler, *Public Sentiments: Structures of Feeling in Nineteenth-Century American Literature* (Chapel Hill: University of North Carolina Press, 2001), 210.

40. Painter, *Sojourner Truth,* 140.

41. See chapter 4 for my discussion of Jackson's adoption of a nonthreatening maternal demeanor to disarm three ministers who want her dead.

42. Braxton, *Black Women Writing Autobiography,* 31.

43. I agree with Joycelyn Moody, however, that several of Foote's direct addresses to her readers throughout her narrative could be interpreted as sermons, such as chapter 29 ("Love Not the World") and the endings of several earlier chapters (Joycelyn Moody, *Sentimental Confessions: Spiritual Narratives of Nineteenth-Century African American Women* [Athens: University of Georgia Press, 2001], 135, 141, 151).

44. Micah 4:13: "Arise and thresh, O daughter of Zion, for I will make your horn iron and your hoofs bronze; you shall beat in pieces many peoples, and shall devote their gain to the Lord, their wealth to the Lord of the whole earth" (Revised Standard Version).

45. Joel 2:28, 29: "And it shall come to pass afterward, that I will pour out my spirit on all flesh; your sons and your daughters shall prophesy, your old men shall dream dreams, and your young men shall see visions. Even upon the menservants and maidservants in those days, I will pour out my spirit" (Revised Standard Version).

46. Jackson titles the section of her narrative that describes the dissolution of her marriage as "My Release from Bondage" (147).

47. Thanks to Ken McClane, professor of English at Cornell University, for suggesting this interpretation.

48. "To go around" (note from Alonzo Hollister's anthology of Jackson's rough-draft writings, 17, quoted in Jackson, *Gifts of Power,* ed. Humez, 86 n. 27).

49. "A skeleton—or meager person" (ibid.)

50. I borrow the term "visionary literacy" from Harryette Mullen, professor of English at the University of California at Los Angeles. She defines visionary literacy as "a spiritual practice in which divine inspiration, associated with Judeo-Christian biblical tradition, is syncretically merged with African traditions of spirit possession." She asserts that in addition to a "tradition of secular literacy," which is evident in the narratives of ex-slaves, an "alternative tradition of visionary literacy may be traced to narratives and journals of spiritual awakening and religious conversion written by freeborn and emancipated Africans and African-Americans in the 18th and 19th centuries" (see Harryette Mullen, "African Signs and Spirit Writing," *Callaloo* 19, no. 3 (1996): 673.

51. "Editorial tyranny": Jackson, *Gifts of Power,* ed. Humez, 19. After Jackson's conversion and sanctification, she has a strong desire to read the Bible, but she explains that she is the only one of all her siblings who received no education. Her household duties and work as a seamstress left her no time for schooling, so she approaches her brother to give her some reading lessons. This he promises to do, but his fatigue at the end of each day causes him to renege on this promise. Jackson enlists Joseph's help in writing letters for her. On one particular occasion, she dictates a letter and asks him to read it back to her. But to her dismay, she discovers he has actually reworded her letter: "'Thee has put in more than I told thee.' This he done several times. I then said, 'I don't want thee to *word* my letter. I only want thee to *write* it" (Jackson 107; Jackson's emphasis). Joseph's frustrated response to his sister's request and the manner in which he has written the letter wounds Jackson's feelings. She soon hears a voice saying, "'Be faithful, and the time shall come when you can write" (Jackson 107). One day as she is sewing, she again hears a voice assuring her that she will learn to read. She lays down her sewing, picks up her Bible, prays, and begins to read. Both husband and brother are incredulous when she first informs them, but she soon convinces them of her miraculously acquired skill. Jackson seems particularly eager to demonstrate her new gift for her brother, declaring, "I will write thee a letter" (Jackson 108). And this is exactly what she does.

CHAPTER SIX

Epigraph: Pauli Murray, *Pauli Murray: The Autobiography of a Black Activist, Feminist, Lawyer, Priest, and Poet* (Knoxville: University of Tennessee Press, 1987), 426–27 (hereafter cited parenthetically). This autobiography was formerly entitled *Song in a Weary Throat: An American Pilgrimage.*

1. Eleanor Holmes Norton, introduction to *Pauli Murray*, ix.

2. Ibid., xii.

3. My sources for this biographical sketch are: Pauli Murray, *Autobiography;* Darlene Clark Hine, Elsa Barkley Brown, and Rosalyn Terborg-Penn, eds., *Black Women in America: An Historical Encyclopedia,* vol. 2 (Brooklyn: Carlson, 1993), 825–26; and Bettye Collier-Thomas, *Daughters of Thunder: Black Women Preachers and Their Sermons, 1850–1979* (San Francisco: Jossey-Bass, 1998), 223.

4. In his annual congressional address delivered in January 1941, President Franklin D. Roosevelt articulated a postwar vision of "'a world founded upon four essential human freedoms'–freedom of speech, freedom of religion, freedom from want, and freedom from fear" (see Daniel J. Boorstin and Brooks Mather Kelley, *A History of the United States* [Lexington, Mass.: Ginn, 1986], 550).

5. Jean Humez, "Pauli Murray's Histories of Loyalty and Revolt," *Black American Literature Forum* 24, no. 2 (1990): 330–31.

6. Angelo Costanzo, *Surprizing Narrative: Olaudah Equiano and the Beginnings of Black Autobiography* (New York: Greenwood Press, 1987), 49–50; William L. Andrews, ed., *Sisters of the Spirit: Three Black Women's Autobiographies of the Nineteenth Century* (Bloomington: Indiana University Press, 1986), 10–11.

7. This is the former title of Murray's autobiography.

8. Humez, "Pauli Murray's Histories," 317.

9. Murray was also present at the death of her aunt Pauline in 1955, which was an early step in laying the groundwork for her ministry. Regarding the significance of this occasion, Murray reflects, "It was . . . a life-changing experience for me, although I was too baffled at the time to recognize its significance. In my first confrontation as an adult with the ultimate crisis of human existence, I was thrust into a role of such awesome spiritual depth that eighteen years later I looked back upon it as a sign clearly pointing me toward the ordained ministry" (Murray 302).

10. Humez, "Pauli Murray's Histories," 330.

11. Collier-Thomas, *Daughters of Thunder,* 223.

12. Anthony B. Pinn, "Religion and 'America's Problem Child': Notes on Pauli Murray's Theological Development," *Journal of Feminist Studies in Religion* 15, no. 1 (1999): 28.

13. Caroline F. Ware, epilogue to Murray, *Pauli Murray,* 436.

14. Collier-Thomas, *Daughters of Thunder,* 223.

15. Norton, introduction to Murray, *Pauli Murray,* xii.

16. Ibid., ix.

17. Doreen Marie Drury, "'Experimentation on the Male Side': Race, Class, Gender, and Sexuality in Pauli Murray's Quest for Love and Identity, 1910–1960" (Ph.D. diss., Boston College, 2000), 2. On the "politics of respectability" espoused by African Americans during the late nineteenth and early twentieth centuries, see Evelyn Brooks Higginbotham, *Righteous Discontent: The Women's Movement in the Black Baptist Church, 1880–1920* (Cambridge, Mass.: Harvard University Press, 1993), 185–229.

18. Drury, "Experimentation on the Male Side," 106.

19. As mentioned, Murray's father was institutionalized at Crownsville State Hospital in Maryland, where he was murdered in 1923. Murray's eldest sister, Grace, was committed to this

same psychiatric hospital in 1941 and diagnosed with paranoid schizophrenia. In addition, Murray's older brother, William Jr., spent three years in a psychiatric hospital in Washington, D.C, from which he was released in 1938 (see Murray, *Pauli Murray,* 55–56; Drury, "Experimentation on the Male Side," 21–22, 106, 182, 243).

20. Drury, "Experimentation on the Male Side," 106.

21. Ibid., 101, 205, 209.

22. Ibid., 102, 103, 120.

23. Ibid., 149.

24. Ibid., 212.

25. "Gender-ambivalent": ibid., 63.

26. Ibid., 102, 103, 109, 177, 274, 275.

27. Ware, epilogue to Murray, *Pauli Murray,* 436.

28. I am using Collier-Thomas's *Daughters of Thunder* as the source for Murray's sermons.

29. Collier-Thomas, *Daughters of Thunder,* 225.

30. Murray, "Women Seeking Admission," in Collier-Thomas, *Daughters of Thunder,* 241.

31. Ibid., 243.

32. Ibid.

33. Ibid., 241.

34. Collier-Thomas, *Daughters of Thunder,* 230–32.

35. Gustavo Gutiérrez, *A Theology of Liberation: History, Politics and Salvation* (Maryknoll, N.Y.: Orbis, 1973), ix, quoted in Murray, "Salvation and Liberation," in Collier-Thomas, *Daughters of Thunder,* 265. The words in brackets in this passage are Collier-Thomas's.

36. Rosemary Radford Ruether, *Liberation Theology: Human Hope Confronts Christian History and American Power* (New York: Paulist, 1972), 9, quoted in Murray, "Salvation and Liberation," in Collier-Thomas, *Daughters of Thunder,* 265.

37. Ibid.

38. Ibid., 267–68.

39. Letty M. Russell, *Human Liberation in a Feminist Perspective—A Theology* (Philadelphia: Westminster, 1974), quoted in Murray, "Salvation and Liberation," in Collier-Thomas, *Daughters of Thunder,* 267.

40. Gutiérrez, *A Theology of Liberation,* 177, quoted in Murray, "Salvation and Liberation," in Collier-Thomas, *Daughters of Thunder,* 267.

CODA

1. Marilyn Richardson, foreword to William L. Andrews, ed., *Sisters of the Spirit: Three Black Women's Autobiographies of the Nineteenth Century* (Bloomington: Indiana University Press, 1986), viii.

2. "Religious social activism": ibid.

3. See Lee 40.

4. C. Eric Lincoln and Lawrence H. Mamiya, *The Black Church in the African American Experience* (Durham, N.C.: Duke University Press, 1999), 281–85.

5. Joanne M. Braxton, *Black Women Writing Autobiography: A Tradition within a Tradition* (Philadelphia: Temple University Press, 1989), 73–74.

6. In *Narrative of Sojourner and "Book of Life"* (*Narrative of Sojourner Truth: A Bondswoman of Olden Time, With a History of Her Labors and Correspondence Drawn from her "Book of Life"* [1878; New York: Oxford UP, 1991]), the feminist abolitionist Frances Gage relates her version of a speech given by Truth at a women's rights convention in Akron, Ohio, in 1851. According to Gage, during this speech, Truth defended women's rights in part through an allusion to Eve's actions in the biblical book of Genesis: "if de fust woman God ever made was strong enough to turn the world upside down, all 'lone, dese togedder . . . ought to be able to turn it back and get it right side up again, and now dey is asking to do it, de men better let em" (135).

BIBLIOGRAPHY

Allen, Richard, and Jacob Tapisco. *The Doctrines and Discipline of the African Methodist Episcopal Church*. Philadelphia: Allen & Tapisco, 1817.

The American Heritage College Dictionary. 3rd ed. Boston: Houghton Mifflin, 1993.

Anderson, Benedict. *Imagined Communities: Reflections on the Origin and Spread of Nationalism*. London: Verso, 1991.

Andrews, William L., ed. *Sisters of the Spirit: Three Black Women's Autobiographies of the Nineteenth Century*. Bloomington: Indiana UP, 1986.

——. *To Tell a Free Story: The First Century of Afro-American Autobiography, 1760–1865*. Urbana: U of Illinois P, 1986.

Andrews, William L., Frances Smith Foster, and Trudier Harris. *The Oxford Companion to African American Literature*. New York: Oxford UP, 1997.

Anzaldúa, Gloria. *Borderlands/La Frontera: The New Mestiza*. San Francisco: Spinsters/ Aunt Lute, 1987.

Bednarowski, Mary Farrell. "Outside the Mainstream: Women's Religion and Women Religious Leaders in Nineteenth-Century America." *Journal of the American Academy of Religion* 48.2 (1980): 207–31.

Bernard, Jacqueline. *Journey toward Freedom: The Story of Sojourner Truth*. New York: Dell, 1967.

Block, Sharon. "Lines of Color, Sex and Service: Comparative Sexual Coercion in Early America." *Sex, Love, Race: Crossing Boundaries in North American History*. Ed. Martha Hodes. New York: New York UP, 1999. 141–63.

Boorstin, Daniel J., and Brooks Mather Kelley. *A History of the United States*. Lexington, MA: Ginn, 1986.

Boylan, Anne M. "Benevolence and Antislavery Activity among African American Women in New York and Boston, 1820–1840." *The Abolitionist Sisterhood: Women's Political Culture in Antebellum America*. Eds. Jean Fagan Yellin and John C. Van Horne. Ithaca, NY: Cornell UP, 1994. 119–37.

Brasher, Lawrence J. *The Sanctified South: John Lakin Brasher and the Holiness Movement*. Urbana: U of Illinois P, 1994.

Braude, Ann. *Radical Spirits: Spiritualism and Women's Rights in Nineteenth-Century America*. 2nd ed. Bloomington: Indiana UP, 2001.

Braxton, Joanne M. *Black Women Writing Autobiography: A Tradition within a Tradition.* Philadelphia: Temple UP, 1989.

Brekus, Catherine A. *Strangers & Pilgrims: Female Preaching in America, 1740–1845.* Chapel Hill: U of North Carolina P, 1998.

Brereton, Virginia Lieson. *From Sin to Salvation: Stories of Women's Conversions, 1800 to the Present* (Bloomington: Indiana UP, 1991).

Brown, Elsa Barkley. "Negotiating and Transforming the Public Sphere: African American Political Life in the Transition from Slavery to Freedom." *Public Culture: Bulletin of the Project for Transnational Cultural Studies* 7 (1994): 107–46.

Bruce, Dickson D., Jr. *And They All Sang Hallelujah: Plain Folk Camp Meeting Religion.* Knoxville: U of Tennessee P, 1974.

Burns, Deborah E. *Shaker Cities of Peace, Love, and Union: A History of the Hancock Bishopric* Hanover, NH: UP of New England, 1993.

Campbell, Ted A. *Methodist Doctrine: The Essentials.* Nashville: Abingdon, 1999.

Carby, Hazel V. *Reconstructing Womanhood: The Emergence of the Afro-American Woman Novelist.* New York: Oxford UP, 1987.

Collier-Thomas, Bettye. *Daughters of Thunder: Black Women Preachers and Their Sermons, 1850–1979.* San Francisco: Jossey-Bass, 1998.

Collins, Patricia Hill. *Black Feminist Thought: Knowledge, Consciousness, and the Politics of Empowerment.* New York: Routledge, 1991.

Cone, James H., and Gayraud S. Wilmore, eds. *Black Theology: A Documentary History.* Vol. 1: 1966–1979. 2nd ed. Maryknoll, NY: Orbis, 1993.

Connor, Kimberly Rae. *Conversions and Visions in the Writings of African-American Women.* Knoxville: U of Tennessee P, 1994.

Costanzo, Angelo. *Surprising Narrative: Olaudah Equiano and the Beginnings of Black Autobiography.* New York: Greenwood, 1987.

Cott, Nancy F., ed. *History of Women in the United States: Historical Articles on Women's Lives and Activities.* Vol. 13 (Religion). Munich: K. G. Saur, 1993.

Davies, Carole Boyce. *Black Women, Writing and Identity: Migrations of the Subject.* London: Routledge, 1994.

Davis, Cyprian. *The History of Black Catholics in the United States.* New York: Crossroad, 1990.

Dieter, Melvin E. *The Holiness Revival of the Nineteenth Century.* Metuchen, NJ: Scarecrow, 1980.

——. "The Wesleyan Perspective." *Five Views on Sanctification.* Ed. Stanly N. Gundry. Grand Rapids, MI: Zondervan, 1987. 11–55.

——, ed. *The Nineteenth-Century Holiness Movement.* Vol. 4. Kansas City, MO: Beacon Hill P of Kansas City, 1998.

Dodson, Jualynne. "Nineteenth-Century A.M.E. Preaching Women: Cutting Edge of Women's Inclusion in Church Polity." *Women in New Worlds.* Eds. Hilah F. Thomas and Rosemary Skinner Keller. Nashville: Abingdon, 1981. 276–89.

Dougherty, Mary Agnes. "The Social Gospel According to Phoebe: Methodist Deaconesses in the Metropolis, 1885–1918." *Perspectives on American Methodism: Interpretive Essays.* Eds. Russell E. Richey, Kenneth E. Rowe, and Jean Miller Schmidt. Nashville: Kingswood/Abingdon, 1993. 356–68.

Douglass-Chin, Richard J. *Preacher Woman Sings the Blues: The Autobiographies of Nineteenth-Century African American Evangelists.* Columbia: U of Missouri P, 2001.

Drury, Doreen Marie. "'Experimentation on the Male Side': Race, Class, Gender, and Sexuality in Pauli Murray's Quest for Love and Identity, 1910–1960." Diss. Boston College, 2000.

Du Bois, W.E.B. *The Souls of Black Folk.* Fisk Diamond Jubilee ed. Nashville: Fisk UP, 1979.

Duclow, Geraldine. "The Shaker Family of Philadelphia." *Shaker Messenger* 13.3 (1991): 5–7.

Elaw, Zilpha. *Memoirs of the Life, Religious Experience, Ministerial Travels and Labours of Mrs. Zilpha Elaw, An American Female of Colour; Together with Some Account of the Great Religious Revivals in America [Written by Herself].* London, 1846. Rpt. in *Sisters of the Spirit: Three Black Women's Autobiographies of the Nineteenth Century.* Ed. William L. Andrews. Bloomington: Indiana UP, 1986. 49–160.

Ellison, Ralph. *Shadow and Act.* New York: Random House, 1964.

Ewens, Mary. "The Leadership of Nuns in Immigrant Catholicism." *Women and Religion in America.* Vol. 1: The Nineteenth Century. Eds. Rosemary Radford Ruether and Rosemary Skinner Keller. San Francisco: Harper & Row, 1981. 101–49.

Fleischner, Jennifer. *Mastering Slavery: Memory, Family, and Identity in Women's Slave Narratives.* New York: New York UP, 1996.

Flexner, Eleanor, and Ellen Fitzpatrick. *Century of Struggle: The American Woman's Rights Movement in the United States.* Enlarged ed. Cambridge, MA: Belknap-Harvard UP, 1996.

Foote, Julia A. J. *A Brand Plucked from the Fire: An Autobiographical Sketch by Mrs. Julia A. J. Foote.* Cleveland: W. F. Schneider, 1879. Rpt. in *Sisters of the Spirit: Three Black Women's Autobiographies of the Nineteenth Century.* Ed. William L. Andrews. Bloomington: Indiana UP, 1986. 161–234.

Foster, Frances Smith. *Witnessing Slavery: The Development of Ante-bellum Slave Narratives.* 2nd ed. Madison: U of Wisconsin P, 1994.

——. "Harper, Frances Ellen Watkins (1825–1911)." *Black Women in America: An Historical Encyclopedia.* Vol. 1. Eds. Darlene Clark Hine, Elsa Barkley Brown, and Rosalyn Terborg-Penn. Brooklyn: Carlson, 1993. 532–37.

Gates, Henry Louis, Jr., ed. *The Classic Slave Narratives.* Markham, Ontario: Mentor-Penguin, 1987.

Gilkes, Cheryl Townsend. *If It Wasn't for the Women: Black Women's Experience and Womanist Culture in Church and Community.* Maryknoll, NY: Orbis, 2001.

Ginzberg, Lori D. *Women and the Work of Benevolence: Morality, Politics, and Class in the Nineteenth-Century United States.* New Haven, CT: Yale UP, 1990.

"Grace." *The American Heritage College Dictionary.* 3rd ed. Boston: Houghton Mifflin, 1993.

Gramsci, Antonio. *Selections from the Prison Notebooks of Antonio Gramsci.* New York: International, 1971.

Grant, Jacqueline. "Womanist Theology: Black Women's Experiences as a Source for Doing Theology, with Special Reference to Christology." *Journal of the Interdenominational Theological Center* 13 (1986): 195–212.

——. "Black Theology and the Black Woman." *Black Theology: A Documentary History.* Vol. 1: 1966–1979. Eds. James H. Cone and Gayraud Wilmore. Maryknoll, NY: Orbis, 1993.

Greer, George Dixon. "A Psychological Study of Sanctification as a *Second* Work of Divine Grace." Diss. Drew University, 1936.

Gundry, Stanley N., ed. *Five Views on Sanctification.* Grand Rapids, MI: Zondervan, 1987.

Gutiérrez, Gustavo. *A Theology of Liberation: History, Politics and Salvation.* Maryknoll, NY: Orbis, 1973.

Hansen, Debra Gold. "The Boston Female Anti-Slavery Society and the Limits of Gender Politics." *The Abolitionist Sisterhood: Women's Political Culture in Antebellum America.* Eds. Jean Fagan Yellin and John C. Van Horne. Ithaca, NY: Cornell UP, 1994. 45–65.

Hardesty, Nancy A., and Adrienne Israel. "Amanda Berry Smith: A 'Downright, Outright Christian.'" *Spirituality and Social Responsibility: Vocational Vision of Women in the United Methodist Tradition.* Ed. Rosemary Skinner Keller. Nashville: Abingdon, 1993. 61 79.

Hardesty, Nancy, Lucille Sider Dayton, and Donald W. Dayton. "Women in the Holiness Movement: Feminism in the Evangelical Tradition." *Women of Spirit: Female Leadership in the Jewish and Christian Traditions.* Eds. Rosemary Ruether and Eleanor McLaughlin. New York: Simon & Schuster, 1979. 225–54.

Harley, Sharon. "Northern Black Female Workers: Jacksonian Era." *The Afro-American Woman: Struggles and Images.* Eds. Sharon Harley and Rosalyn Terborg-Penn. Port Washington, NY: Kennikat, 1978. 5–16.

——. "When Your Work Is Not Who You Are: The Development of a Working-Class Consciousness among Afro-American Women." *"We Specialize in the Wholly Impossible": A Reader in Black Women's History.* Eds. Darlene Clark Hine, Wilma King, and Linda Reed. Brooklyn: Carlson, 1995. 25–37.

Harley, Sharon, and Rosalyn Terborg-Penn, eds. *The Afro-American Woman: Struggles and Images.* Port Washington, NY: Kennikat, 1978.

Harris, Barbara J., and JoAnn K. McNamara, eds. *Women and the Structure of Society: Selected Research from the Fifth Berkshire Conference on the History of Women.* Durham, NC: Duke UP, 1984.

Hendler, Glenn. *Public Sentiments: Structures of Feeling in Nineteenth-Century American Literature*. Chapel Hill: U of North Carolina P, 2001.

Higginbotham, Evelyn Brooks. *Righteous Discontent: The Women's Movement in the Black Baptist Church, 1880–1920* Cambridge: Harvard UP, 1993.

Hine, Darlene Clark. *Hine Sight: Black Women and the Reconstruction of American History*. Brooklyn: Carlson, 1994.

Hine, Darlene Clark, Elsa Barkley Brown, and Rosalyn Terborg-Penn, eds. *Black Women in America: An Historical Encyclopedia*. Vols. 1, 2. Brooklyn: Carlson, 1993.

Hine, Darlene Clark, Wilma King, and Linda Reed, eds. *"We Specialize in the Wholly Impossible": A Reader in Black Women's History*. Brooklyn: Carlson, 1995.

Hodes, Martha, ed. *Sex, Love, Race: Crossing Boundaries on North American History*. New York: New York University Press, 1999.

The Holy Bible. Revised Standard Version. Dallas: Melton, 1971.

hooks, bell. *Black Looks: Race and Representation*. Boston: South End, 1992.

Houchins, Susan, ed. *Spiritual Narratives*. New York: Oxford UP, 1988.

Humez, Jean. "My Spirit Eye: Some Functions of Spiritual and Visionary Experience in the Lives of Five Black Women Preachers, 1810–1880." *Women and the Structure of Society: Selected Research from the Fifth Berkshire Conference on the History of Women*. Eds. Barbara J. Harris and JoAnn K. McNamara. Durham, NC: Duke UP, 1984. 129–43.

——. "Pauli Murray's Histories of Loyalty and Revolt." *Black American Literature Forum* 24.2 (1990): 315–35.

——. "Jackson, Rebecca Cox (1795–1871)." *Black Women in America: An Historical Encyclopedia*. Vol. 1. Eds. Darlene Clark Hine, Elsa Barkley Brown, and Rosalyn Terborg-Penn. Brooklyn: Carlson, 1993. 626–27.

——, ed. *Mother's First-Born Daughters: Early Shaker Writings on Women and Religion*. Bloomington: Indiana UP, 1993.

——. "In Search of Harriet Tubman's Spiritual Autobiography." *This Far by Faith: Readings in African-American Women's Religious Biography*. Ed. Judith Weisenfeld and Richard Newman. New York: Routledge, 1996. 239–61.

——. "Reading the Narrative of Sojourner Truth as a Collaborative Text." *Frontiers: A Journal of Women's Studies*. 16.1 (1996): 29–52.

Hunter, Tera. *To 'Joy My Freedom: Southern Black Women's Lives and Labors after the Civil War*. Cambridge, MA: Harvard UP, 1997.

Hurston, Zora Neale. *Their Eyes Were Watching God*. New York: Harper & Row, 1998.

Israel, Adrienne M. *Amanda Berry Smith: From Washerwoman to Evangelist*. Studies in Evangelism. No. 16. Lanham, MD: Scarecrow, 1998.

Jackson, Rebecca. *Gifts of Power: The Writings of Rebecca Jackson, Black Visionary, Shaker Eldress*. Ed. Jean McMahon Humez. Amherst: U of Massachusetts P, 1981.

Jacobs, Harriet A. *Incidents in the Life of a Slave Girl, Written by Herself*. Boston, 1861. Ed. Jean Fagan Yellin. Cambridge: Harvard UP, 1987.

Jones, Charles Edwin. *Perfectionist Persuasion: The Holiness Movement and American Methodism, 1867–1936.* Metuchen, NJ: Scarecrow, 1974.

Keller, Rosemary Skinner. "Creating a Sphere for Women: The Methodist Episcopal
Church, 1869–1906." *Perspectives on American Methodism: Interpretive Essays.* Eds.
Russell E. Richey, Kenneth E. Rowe, and Jean Miller Schmidt. Nashville: King-
swood/Abingdon, 1993. 332–42.

——, ed. *Spirituality and Social Responsibility: Vocational Vision of Women in the United Methodist Tradition.* Nashville: Abingdon, 1993.

Kienzle, Beverly Mayne, and Pamela J. Walker, eds. *Women Preachers and Prophets
through Two Millennia of Christianity.* Berkeley: U of California P, 1998.

Lapansky, Emma Jones. "The World the Agitators Made: The Counterculture of Agi-
tation in Urban Philadelphia." *The Abolitionist Sisterhood: Women's Political Culture in
Antebellum America.* Eds. Jean Fagan Yellin and John C. Van Horne. Ithaca, NY:
Cornell UP, 1994. 91–99.

Lee, Jarena. *The Life and Religious Experience of Jarena Lee, A Coloured Lady, Giving An
Account of Her Call to Preach the Gospel. Revised and Corrected from the Original Manuscript, Written by Herself.* Philadelphia, 1836. Rpt. in *Sisters of the Spirit: Three Black
Women's Autobiographies of the Nineteenth Century.* Ed. William L. Andrews. Bloomington: Indiana UP, 1986. 25–48.

——. *Religious Experience and Journal of Mrs. Jarena Lee, Giving an Account of her Call to
Preach.* Philadelphia, 1849. Rpt. in *Spiritual Narratives.* Ed. Susan Houchins. New
York: Oxford UP, 1988.

Lincoln, C. Eric, and Lawrence H. Mamiya. *The Black Church in the African American
Experience.* Durham, NC: Duke UP, 1990.

Lindström, Harald. *Wesley and Sanctification.* Wilmore, KY: Asbury, 1981.

Litwack, Leon F. *North of Slavery: The Negro in the Free States, 1790–1860.* Chicago: U
of Chicago P, 1961.

Lobody, Diane H. "'That Language Might Be Given Me': Women's Experience
in Early Methodism." *Perspectives on American Methodism: Interpretive Essays.* Eds.
Russell E. Richey, Kenneth E. Rowe, and Jean Miller Schmidt. Nashville: King-
swood/Abingdon, 1993. 127–44.

Loewenberg, James, and Ruth Bogin, eds. *Black Women in Nineteenth-Century American
Life: Their Words, Their Thoughts, Their Feelings.* University Park: Pennsylvania
State UP, 1976.

Mabee, Carleton. *Sojourner Truth: Slave, Prophet, Legend.* New York: New York UP,
1993.

"Manger." *The American Heritage College Dictionary.* 3rd ed. Boston: Houghton Mifflin,
1993.

Mannard, Joseph G. "Maternity . . . of Spirit: Nuns and Domesticity in Antebellum
America." *History of Women in the United States: Historical Articles on Women's Lives*

and Activities. Vol. 13 (Religion). Ed. Nancy F. Cott. Munich: K. G. Saur,1993. 74–93.

McKay, Nellie Y. "Nineteenth-Century Black Women's Spiritual Autobiographies: Religious Faith and Self-Empowerment." *Perspectives on American Methodism: Interpretive Essays.* Eds. Russell E. Richey, Kenneth E. Rowe, and Jean Miller Schmidt. Nashville: Kingswood/Abingdon, 1993. 178–91.

Moody, Joycelyn. *Sentimental Confessions: Spiritual Narratives of Nineteenth-Century African American Women.* Athens: U of Georgia P, 2001.

Morrison, Toni. *Beloved.* New York: Plume, 1987.

——. *Jazz.* New York: Plume, 1992.

——. *Playing in the Dark: Whiteness and the Literary Imagination.* Cambridge, MA: Harvard UP, 1992.

Mullen, Harryette. Class lecture. Slave Narratives and the Production of Afro-American Literature. Cornell University, Ithaca, New York. Fall 1990.

——. "'Indelicate Subjects': African-American Women's Subjugated Subjectivity." *Sub/versions.* Winter 1991: 1–7.

——. "African Signs and Spirit Writing." *Callaloo* 19.3 (1996): 670–89.

Murray, Pauli. *Pauli Murray: The Autobiography of a Black Activist, Feminist, Lawyer, Priest, and Poet.* Knoxville: U of Tennessee P, 1987.

——. "Black Theology and Feminist Theology: A Comparative View." *Black Theology: A Documentary History.* Vol. 1: 1966–1979. Eds. James H. Cone and Gayraud Wilmore. Maryknoll, N.Y.: Orbis, 1993. 304–22.

——. "Salvation and Liberation." Sermon. Unitarian Society of Germantown, Philadelphia. 1 Apr. 1979. *Daughters of Thunder: Black Women Preachers and Their Sermons, 1850–1979.* Ed. Bettye Collier-Thomas. San Francisco, Jossey-Bass, 1998. 263–69.

——. "Women Seeking Admission to Holy Orders—As Crucifers Carrying the Cross." "Inaugural" Sermon. Emmanuel Church, Boston. 3 Mar. 1974. *Daughters of Thunder: Black Women Preachers and Their Sermons, 1850–1979.* Ed. Bettye Collier-Thomas. San Francisco, Jossey-Bass, 1998. 240–44.

Narrative of Sojourner Truth. Ed. Margaret Washington. 1850. New York: Vintage, 1993.

Narrative of Sojourner Truth; A Bondswoman of Olden Time, Emancipated, With a History of Her Labors and Correspondence Drawn from Her "Book of Life." 1878. New York: Oxford UP, 1991.

Nelson, Emmanuel S., ed. *African American Autobiographers: A Sourcebook.* Westport, CT: Greenwood, 2002.

Norton, Eleanor Holmes. Introduction. *Pauli Murray: The Autobiography of a Black Activist, Feminist, Lawyer, Priest, and Poet.* By Pauli Murray. Knoxville: U of Tennessee P, 1987. ix–xii.

Pagels, Elaine. *The Gnostic Gospels*. New York: Vintage, 1989.

Painter, Nell Irvine. *Sojourner Truth: A Life, A Symbol*. New York: W. W. Norton, 1996.

Peters, Pearlie. "Masking." *The Oxford Companion to African American Literature*. Eds. William L. Andrews, Frances Smith Foster, and Trudier Harris. New York: Oxford UP, 1997. 483.

Peterson, Linda H. "Gender and Autobiographical Form: The Case of the Spiritual Autobiography." *Studies in Autobiography*. Ed. James Olney. New York: Oxford UP, 1988. 211–22.

Pinn, Anthony B. "Religion and 'America's Problem Child': Notes on Pauli Murray's Theological Development." *Journal of Feminist Studies in Religion* 15.1 (1999): 21–39.

Prince, Mary. *History of Mary Prince, A West Indian Slave, Related by Herself. With a Supplement by the Editor, To Which is Added the Narrative of Asa-Asa, A Captured African*. London: Westley and Davis, 1831. Rpt. in *The Classic Slave Narratives*. Ed. Henry Louis Gates Jr. Markham, Ontario: Mentor-Penguin, 1987. 183–242.

Proctor-Smith, Marjorie. *Women in Shaker Community and Worship: A Feminist Analysis of the Uses of Religious Symbolism*. Studies in Women and Religion. Ser. 16. Lewiston, NY: Edwin Mellen P, 1985.

Rector, Theresa. "Black Nuns as Educators." *Journal of Negro Education* 51.3 (1982): 238–53.

Richardson, Marilyn. Foreword. *Sisters of the Spirit: Three Black Women's Autobiographies of the Nineteenth Century*. Ed. William L. Andrews. Bloomington: Indiana UP, 1986. viii–ix.

Richey, Russell E., Kenneth E. Rowe, and Jean Miller Schmidt, eds. *Perspectives on American Methodism: Interpretive Essays*. Nashville: Kingswood/Abingdon, 1993.

Roediger, David R. *The Wages of Whiteness: Race and the Making of the American Working Class*. London: Verso, 1991.

Rowe, Kenneth E., ed. "The Ordination of Women: Round One; Anna Oliver and the General Conference of 1880." *Perspectives on American Methodism: Interpretive Essays*. Eds. Russell E. Richey, Kenneth E. Rowe, and Jean Miller Schmidt. Nashville: Kingswood/Abingdon, 1993. 298–308.

Ruether, Rosemary Radford. *Liberation Theology: Human Hope Confronts Christian History and American Power*. New York: Paulist, 1972.

Ruether, Rosemary, and Eleanor McLaughlin, eds. *Women of Spirit: Female Leadership in the Jewish and Christian Traditions*. New York: Simon & Schuster, 1979.

Ruether, Rosemary Radford, and Rosemary Skinner Keller. *Women and Religion in America*. Vol. 1: The Nineteenth Century. San Francisco: Harper & Row, 1981.

Russell, Letty M. *Human Liberation in a Feminist Perspective—A Theology*. Philadelphia: Westminster, 1974.

Sample, Maxine. "Jarena Lee (1783-?)." *African American Autobiographers: A Sourcebook.* Ed. Emmanuel S. Nelson. Westport, CT: Greenwood, 2002. 230–35.

——. "Julia A. J. Foote (1823–1900)." *African American Autobiographers: A Sourcebook* Ed. Emmanuel S. Nelson. Westport, CT: Greenwood, 2002. 138–42.

Sasson, Sarah Diane. "The Shaker Personal Narrative: Studies in a Nineteenth-Century Autobiographical Tradition." Diss. U of North Carolina at Chapel Hill, 1980.

Shea, Daniel B. *Spiritual Autobiography in Early America.* Princeton, NJ: Princeton UP, 1968.

Smith, Amanda. *An Autobiography: The Story of the Lord's Dealings with Mrs. Amanda Smith the Colored Evangelist.* Chicago: Meyer, 1893. New York: Oxford UP, 1988.

Smith, Christian. *The Emergence of Liberation Theology: Radical Religion and Social Movement Theory.* Chicago: U of Chicago P, 1991.

Smith, Sidonie. *Subjectivity, Identity, and the Body.* Bloomington: Indiana UP, 1993.

Smith, Timothy L. *Revivalism and Social Reform in Mid-Nineteenth-Century America.* New York: Abingdon, 1957.

Smith-Rosenberg, Carroll. "The Female World of Love and Ritual: Relations between Women in Nineteenth-Century America." *Signs* 1.1 (1975): 1–29.

Soderlund, Jean R. "Priorities and Power: The Philadelphia Female Anti-Slavery Society." *The Abolitionist Sisterhood: Women's Political Culture in Antebellum America.* Eds. Jean Fagan Yellin and John C. Van Horne. Ithaca, NY: Cornell UP, 1994. 67–88.

Stein, Stephen J. *The Shaker Experience in America: A History of the United Society of Believers.* New Haven, CT: Yale UP, 1992.

Sterling, Dorothy, ed. *We Are Your Sisters: Black Women in the Nineteenth Century.* New York: W. W. Norton, 1984.

Stetson, Erlene, and Linda David. *Glorying in Tribulation: The Lifework of Sojourner Truth.* East Lansing, MI: Michigan State UP, 1994.

Stone, Bebb Wheeler, "Celebrating Embodied Care: Women and Economic Justice." *Reformed Faith and Economics.* Ed. Robert Stivers. Lanham, MD: UP of America, 1989.

Synan, Vinson. *The Holiness-Pentecostal Tradition: Charismatic Movements in the Twentieth Century.* Grand Rapids, MI: Eerdmans, 1997.

Tarbox, Gwen Athene. *The Clubwomen's Daughters: Collectivist Impulses in Progressive-Era Girls' Fiction.* New York: Garland, 2000.

Thomas, Hilah F., and Rosemary Skinner Keller, eds. *Women in New Worlds.* Nashville: Abingdon, 1981.

Tompkins, Jane. *Sensational Designs: The Cultural Work of American Fiction.* New York: Oxford UP, 1985.

Traylor, Eleanor W. "Naming the UnNamed: African American Criticism and African American Letters." *Black Books Bulletin: WordsWork* 16.1–2 (1993–94): 64–75.

Walker, Alice. *In Search of Our Mothers' Gardens*. San Diego: Harcourt, 1983.

Ware, Caroline F. Epilogue. *Pauli Murray: The Autobiography of a Black Activist, Feminist, Lawyer, Priest, and Poet*. By Pauli Murray. Knoxville: U of Tennessee P, 1987. 436–37.

Weisenfeld, Judith. *African American Women and Christian Activism: New York's Black YWCA, 1905–1945*. Cambridge: Harvard UP, 1997.

Weisenfeld, Judith, and Richard Newman, eds. *This Far by Faith: Readings in African-American Women's Religious Biography*. New York: Routledge, 1996.

Welter, Barbara. *Dimity Convictions: The American Woman in the Nineteenth Century*. Athens: Ohio UP, 1976.

West, Cornel. *Prophetic Fragments*. Grand Rapids, MI: Eerdmans, 1988.

White, Deborah Gray. *Ar'n't I a Woman?: Female Slaves in the Plantation South*. New York: W. W. Norton, 1999.

——. *Too Heavy A Load: Black Women in Defense of Themselves, 1894–1994*. New York: W. W. Norton, 1999.

Whitson, Robley Edward, ed. *The Shakers: Two Centuries of Spiritual Reflection*. New York: Paulist, 1983.

Williams, Richard E. *Called and Chosen: The Story of Mother Rebecca Jackson and the Philadelphia Shakers*. ATLA Monograph Ser. 17. Metuchen, NJ: Scarecrow, 1981.

Wills, David W. "Womanhood and Domesticity in the A.M.E. Tradition: The Influence of Daniel Alexander Payne." *Black Apostles at Home and Abroad: Afro-Americans and the Christian Mission from the Revolution to Reconstruction*. Eds. David W. Wills and Richard Newman. Boston: G. K. Hall, 1982. 133–46.

Wills, David W., and Richard Newman, eds. *Black Apostles at Home and Abroad: Afro-Americans and the Christian Mission from the Revolution to Reconstruction*. Boston: G. K. Hall, 1982.

Women's Devotional Bible 2. New International Version. Grand Rapids, MI: Zondervan, 1995.

Yee, Shirley J. *Black Women Abolitionists: A Study in Activism, 1828–1860*. Knoxville: U of Tennessee P, 1992.

Yellin, Jean Fagan. *Harriet Jacobs: A Life*. New York: Basic Civitas, 2004.

Yellin, Jean Fagan, and John C. Van Horne, eds. *The Abolitionist Sisterhood: Women's Political Culture in Antebellum America*. Ithaca, NY: Cornell UP, 1994.

INDEX

Abolitionism, 23–27, 43, 138, 161, 194–95*n*28
Abraham and Isaac, 202*n*58
Adam and Eve, 70–71, 90, 103, 214*n*6
Africa, 16, 62, 145–46
African Americans. *See* Black women; Blacks; Radical spiritual motherhood
African Methodist Episcopal (AME) Church: Board of Stewardesses within congregations of, 36–37; criticisms of materialism against, 35; and Daughters of Zion, 36; deaconesses in, 37; educational standards of ministers of, 60; and Jackson, 16, 134, 207*n*31; and Lee, 11–12, 35–36, 59; licensed female evangelists in, 37; and ordination of women, 34–35; praying bands of, 96–98; Smith's call in, 98–99; Smith's membership in, 16; spiritual songs of, 202*n*63; and women's preaching, 11, 34–37, 59, 60. *See also* Methodist Episcopal Church
African Methodist Episcopal Zion (AMEZ) Church, 14, 15, 37–38, 78
Africanism, 133
Alcohol abuse, 45. *See also* Temperance movement
Allen, Rev. Richard, 11–12, 35–36, 52, 108, 109, 111
Altar theology/terminology, 42
AME Church. *See* African Methodist Episcopal (AME) Church
AMEZ Church. *See* African Methodist Episcopal Zion (AMEZ) Church
Anderson, Benedict, 205*n*1
Andrews, William, 57, 108, 202*n*56, 204*nn*39–40, 205*n*, 205*n*2
Anthony, Susan B., 26, 195*n*41
Anzaldúa, Gloria, 56

Association of the Holy Slavery of the Mother of God, 64, 200*n*26
Audience-oriented subjectivity, 52–54. *See also* Subjectivity
Augustine, St., 5
Autobiography. *See* Spiritual autobiography
Ayers, Mary Ann, 141

Balas, Marie Madeleine, 40
Bambara, Toni Cade, 3
Baptists, 49, 119–20, 124–25
Barlow, Irene "Renee," 178–82
Bates, Paulina, 72, 139–41, 207–8*n*58
Bednarowski, Mary Farrell, 135, 206*n*29
Beman, Rev. Jehiel C., 14, 78
Benedict the Moor, Saint, 64
Benevolence and mutual aid, 21–23, 26
Berry, Miriam, 15, 79–80
Berry, Samuel, 15
Bethune, Mary McCleod, 189
Bible. *See specific books of the Bible*
Bible readings, 43
Biological motherhood: compatibility of spirituality and, 67–68; in context of slavery, 155; enslaved women seen as breeders, 49, 148, 155, 162; radical spiritual motherhood versus, 4, 50–51, 75–88; rejection of, by Catholic nuns, 38–39, 58; of Sojourner Truth, 153–55, 209*n*27
Black church, 29, 59–60, 78, 97, 195–96*nn*49–50, 202*n*56, 204*n*30. *See also specific denominations*
Black theology, 8, 9
Black women: and abolitionism, 23–25; benevolent and mutual aid societies of, 21–23; black church's role for, 29; as Catholic nuns,

225

Eades, H. L., 201–2*n*48

Education: of AME ministers, 60; of black children, 13, 40, 41, 64; and black women's clubs, 29; and Catholic nuns, 40; of freedpeople, 27; of radical spiritual mothers, 61; of slaves, 40, 41

Elaw, Joseph, 12–13

Elaw, Zilpha: and AME Church, 36; authority of, as spiritual leader, 127–29; and benevolent work, 22; biographical sketch on, 12–13; "breaking up housekeeping" by, 13, 54, 81; and calling to preach, 121–22, 128; and camp meetings, 13, 58, 81–82, 124–29; and celibacy, 162; and communities of faith, 117–29, 178; conversion of, 12; daughter of, 12, 63, 76, 81–83, 119, 120–21, 122, 162, 169; and daughter's conversion, 81–82; domestic labor by, 60; domestic ministry by, 46, 58, 122–23; in England, 13, 82, 117, 118, 120; fears and identity crisis of, in southern states, 128–29; female messengers to, 119–20; finances of, 63; and God's providential care, 63, 163; health problems of, 119–21; home of, during itinerant preaching career, 121; itinerant preaching career of, 13, 56, 82, 117–29, 162–63; Lee's collaborative preaching with, 13, 118; marriage of and husband's lack of support for, 12–13, 63, 122; and Methodist Episcopal Church, 12–13, 118; and Methodist women's group in Salem, Mass., 118–19, 127; and moment of sanctification, 13, 125, 127; mother of, 162; negative treatment of, 57–58; out-of-body experience of, 127; and outraged motherhood, 162–63; preaching by, 13, 36, 53, 118; and Quakers, 12; and radical spiritual motherhood generally, 1–2; and relationship between biological and radical spiritual motherhood, 81–83; and Salem, Mass., ecumenical prayer meetings, 119; and sanctification, 13, 48, 58, 125; and school for black children, 13, 64; and sister Hannah's illness and death, 120, 121–22, 180, 205*n*10; in slave states, 56, 118, 128–29, 162–63; spiritual autobiography by, 36; on variations in worship services, 123–24; vision of, 12

Emancipation Proclamation, 27

Emancipatory narratives: Fleischner on, 191*n*2; Humez on "mediated" or "facilitated" narratives, 155–56; by Harriet Jacobs, 2, 146–48, 151, 160, 161, 163, 166, 167, 208*n*6; portrayals of women in slavery by male and female writers of, 66–67; as preferred term, 191*n*2; by Mary Prince, 2, 149–52, 161; and radical spiritual motherhood, 2; and secular literacy, 211*n*50; Traylor on, 191*n*2; of Sojourner Truth, 2, 153–62, 209*n*20. *See also specific enslaved black women*

Embodied subjectivity, 54–55, 152. *See also* Subjectivity

Employment: of black men, 17, 18, 19, 20, 60; of black women, 17–18, 20–21, 49, 60–61, 202*n*55; of immigrants, 19, 20; as washerwomen, 17–18, 61, 81, 92; of white women, 20

England: Elaw in, 13, 82, 117, 118, 120; prohibition against women preaching in, 99; Smith in, 16, 63, 99–100

Enslaved black women. *See* Emancipatory narratives; Slaves; *and specific slaves*

Entire sanctification. *See* Sanctification

Ephesians, Letter to, 92–93, 119

Episcopal Church, 3, 176–77, 181–88

Episcopal Women's Caucus, 176

Evans, Rachel, 36

Eve's temptation, 70–71, 90, 103, 214*n*6

Exodus, Book of, 204*n*40

Female body. *See* Body; Sexuality

Female homosocial networks, 137–38

Feminism, 29, 174–78, 182. *See also* Sexism; Women's rights activism

Fifteenth Amendment, 27

Finneyites, 43

Fisher, Anna, 143

Fitzpatrick, Ellen, 195*n*41

Fleischner, Jennifer, 191*n*2

Flexner, Eleanor, 195*n*41

Fontier, Soeur Ste-Marthe, 40

Foote, George, 14

Foote, Julia A. J.: and African Methodist Church, 14; biographical sketch on, 13–15; and calling to preach, 101–3; conversion of, 100; and cult of true womanhood, 105; death